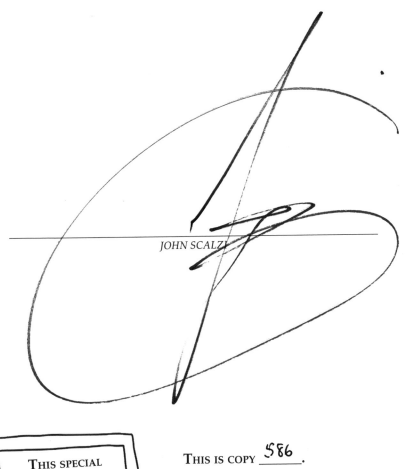

JOHN SCALZI

THIS SPECIAL
SIGNED EDITION IS
LIMITED TO
1000 NUMBERED
COPIES.

THIS IS COPY _586_.

DON'T LIVE FOR YOUR OBITUARY

DON'T LIVE FOR YOUR OBITUARY

ADVICE, COMMENTARY AND PERSONAL OBSERVATIONS ON WRITING, 2008–2017

JOHN SCALZI

SUBTERRANEAN PRESS 2017

First Edition

ISBN
978-1-59606-858-2

Subterranean Press
PO Box 190106
Burton, MI 48519

subterraneanpress.com

DEDICATION

To Paul Sabourin, Greg "Storm" DiCostanzo, Jonathan Coulton and William Beckett, all of whom wrote songs for my books.

Also to Angela and Aubrey Webber, who wrote a song about how not popular I am. To be fair, I asked for it.

Hey, Look, It's One of Those Introduction Thingies

Oh, hello! I didn't see you there. I'm John Scalzi, and you might know me from such novels as *Old Man's War* and *Redshirts*, the latter of which won the Hugo Award, and from my blog Whatever, which I've been writing for coming on twenty years now. Yes, it's a long time. Yes, I know blogs are sort of passé now. Don't worry, I'm on Twitter too. See? Still hip to what the kids are doing. I know that's important for everyone.

(And yes, if you're reading this in an era where Twitter has disappeared into the dusty recesses of digital memory, go ahead and have your knowing chuckle. Your direct-brain communication medium will be old someday too! You read it here first!)

The point is, I'm a working writer. And as one of those folks, I write frequently about writing and the writing life, most prominently on that blog of mine. I have been known to give advice, comment on the various writing controversies of the day, muse on the then-current state of publishing and even occasionally opine about whatever damn foolishness other writers and media figures are doing. Some of it (the advice) might be useful. The rest of it has varying utility but might be interesting as a sketch of a certain moment in time in the world of writing and publishing, and also in *my* life as a working, public writer.

That moment in time, in this case, is the period between January 2008 and June 2017—most of a decade. During that moment, the US had three presidents (one in my opinion pretty good, the other two...not so much); the publishing industry, along with many others, nearly cratered as part of the worldwide recession; self-publishing rose as a viable means for writers to build a career; social media became both a blessing and a curse; and the trolls that had been lurking on the sidelines of, well, everything, made a hard drive into the mainstream.

In my own career, I went from a newbie fiction writer who made most of his writing income from other means (corporate consulting, non-fiction books, general freelancing), to a best-selling, award-winning full-time novelist—although that path wasn't always a straight shot upward; there was three-year gap in there between novels—from 2008 to 2011—because my primary publisher and I had what I would now call a philosophical disagreement over my worth. We eventually figured it out. Now everything's fine, and I can say that I am in a very fortunate position as writer: One who knows he can sell novels, and that there will be an audience for them, and doesn't have to do anything else to pay the bills. It's great. I hope it lasts.

So, this book is part memoir about a decade in my writing life, part observation of the business of writing and publishing over that same period of time, and part advice for writers, both those coming up and currently making a go of it. It's a little bit of each, which I suppose means that if you're coming to this book only for one of those, you might be disappointed. As I was compiling the book, one of the questions I did have was who this book might be for—who its audience is.

The best answer I can give is that the book is for anyone who is interested in *all* of it—all of the aspects of the writing life, as they are told from the point of view of someone who is in the middle bit of his career, the part where the first books have been published and the consequences of that, good and bad, are unfolding from there. To be clear, my point of view, and my career, as a writer is not a universal one—I've been lucky in many many ways, and I know it—but it's definitely not *unexamined*. In the decade this book covers, I've written a lot on the subject of writing, and on the subject of being a writer. It's not an exhaustive book (I had to keep it within a certain word count), but it covers a lot of ground. I hope you're the audience it's for, or, at least, might be willing to read enough of it to see if you are.

A note about the organization of this book. I've broken it up into five large chapters, covering (respectively) advice, publishing and the online world, other writers and publishing personalities, controversies and hot takes, and finally my career in particular. I will note that these chapters are both general and leaky; that is to say that in each chapter you'll find pieces that could probably have found a place in other chapters—a piece in "advice" chapter might have publishing commentary, a snarky comment on a controversy, or a discussion on something a particular author (or I) did. Or all of them at the same time. Lots of judgment calls were made in putting the book together.

The chapters are mostly arranged alphabetically by entry title. I say "mostly" because in each chapter I've moved some pieces out of alphabetical order for effect (i.e., some pieces I wanted first or last in a chapter) or because one piece follows directly after another thematically and chronologically and separating them would be confusing. With the exception of those I just noted, the pieces in this book are not arranged chronologically; they will jump around in time.

Most of the pieces originally ran on Whatever, my blog. I have done a little light editing of them for the book to add context when on the blog there might have been a link to another article, either on my site or elsewhere, or to fix an occasional error. Most of the pieces stand on their own, but in places where I think it's useful or necessary (or there's something else I want to call out), I'll add a little info bit at the top of the entry.

One final disclaimer: As noted, this is all written by me, and much of it is about me (and my career), and in all cases these are my takes on things. Be aware—I'm sure you are, but I feel compelled to say it anyway—that I'm not infallible, and not all of my takes are pure gold, and that indeed, in the course of a decade, there are even things about which I might have adjusted or entirely changed my thoughts. And sometimes, depending on your own opinions and experiences, I might come across as a jerk. Hey, it happens.

My point is: This is me, writing about the writing life and world, over a decade. This is my experience. I hope you like it—and you should see it as just one take of the writing life and world, over a decade. Find others, too. You may be surprised at how different the takes are. And those takes won't be wrong. Just different.

There, I think we've done enough for one introduction. Let's get to the actual book, shall we?

—John Scalzi
June 20, 2017

GOLDEN NUGGETS OF WRITERLY WISDOM, OR, THIS IS WHERE I OFFER UP SOME WRITING ADVICE, TAKE IT OR DON'T

UNASKED-FOR ADVICE TO NEW WRITERS ABOUT MONEY

Feb

11

2008

(Note: One of my personal bugaboos about writing advice is that there's relatively little of it involving the business of writing, i.e., what to do with the money one makes, and how to design one's life in order to be able to build a writing career without starving or having the bills pile up. This piece was designed as some practical "tough love" for writers about money, and across a decade, most of the advice here still stands. I still use it as a basis for talks I give to writers about the practical aspects of the writing life.

One minor and possibly obnoxious note: My yearly writing income has, uh, gone up since 2008. For which, I am the first to say, I am thankful.)

I made $164,000 last year from my writing. I've averaged more than $100,000 in writing income for the last ten years, which means, for those of you who don't want to bother with the math, that I've made more than a million dollars from my writing in the last decade. In 2000, I wrote a book on finance, *The Rough Guide to Money Online*. For several years I wrote personal finance newsletters for America Online. When I do corporate consulting, it's very often been for financial services companies like Oppenheimer Funds, US Trust and Warburg Pincus. I mention this to you so that you know that when I offer you, the new, aspiring and dewy-eyed writer, the following entirely unsolicited advice about money, I'm not talking entirely out of my ass.

Why am I offering this entirely unsolicited advice about money to new writers? Because it very often appears to me that regardless of how smart and clever and interesting and fun my fellow writers are on every other imaginable subject, when it comes to money—and specifically their *own* money—writers have as much sense as chimps on crack. It's not just writers—all creative people seem to have the "incredibly stupid with money" gene set for *maximum expression*—but since most of creative people I know are writers, they're the nexus of money stupidity I have the most experience with. It makes me sad and also embarrasses the crap out of me; people as smart as writers are ought to *know better*.

The following advice is not complete; there's lots I won't be covering here. Some it is repeated from things I've written before but are so far down in the archives I know you'll never find them. Some of this advice may not apply to you; some of it may apply to you but you may be too delusional or arrogant to acknowledge it, or you may decide you don't like my tone and ignore it all because of that. Most of it is applicable to writers who are not new, too, but I don't know how many of them are interested in taking advice from *me*. This is US-centered although may be generally applicable elsewhere. It's meant for writers but may have application to you in other fields; decide for yourself.

I do not guarantee this advice will make you a more successful writer or a better human being. Follow this advice at your own peril. That said, know that it's generally worked for me. That's why I'm sharing it with you.

One more thing: This is long.

1. You're a writer. Prepare to be broke.

Writers make crap. Why do they make crap? For many reasons, beginning with forces outside their control (publishers pay as little as humanly possible; lots of would-be writers willing to work for pennies, keeping the pay rates low) and working up to forces entirely *within* their control (writers playing with their Xbox 360s instead of writing; willingness to be to paid stupid low rates for their work). Most salaried writers in the US are lucky if they get above $50,000 a year; most freelance writers in the United States (which includes novelists, screenwriters, etc) could make more money being assistant manager at the local Wal-Mart. It's not a joke.

(But, you say to me, *you're* a freelance writer and you've made at least $100,000 a year for the last decade. Yes I have. And I'm an *outlier*; I'm over there to the right of the writing income bell curve. I'm there for many reasons, luck, skill and business sense being the big three, and all three interact with each other. Skill and business sense you can work on; luck happens, or doesn't. There are lots of writers I know who have two out of the three. Many of them make less than I do. It's not necessarily fair. Funny how that works.)

(Also, and not coincidentally, *before* those last ten years were the seven in which I was making rather quite a bit *less*. Oh, my, yes. That income didn't come from nowhere; I did my time in the salt mines, trust me.)

It's *possible* to make a good amount of money as a writer. Most writers *don't*. You should assume, strictly for business purposes, that you won't, or at the very least, won't for a very long time. It's not all about you, it's also about the market. Don't get defensive. The median personal income in the US in 2005 was $28,500. You have a lot of company in the bottom half.

More to the point, coming to peace with the fact that writing is likely *not* to make you a lot of money means that you can realistically look at that money going forward, which will put you in a better financial position than someone who just blunders along assuming that any minute now people are going to start tossing money at them for their lovely, lovely writing. These people become bitter and intolerable soon enough. You don't want to be one of them.

Noting all the above, we come to point two:

2. Don't quit your day job.

Lots of wanna-be writers wax rhapsodic about how great it would be to ditch the day job and just spend all their time clickety-clack typing away. These folks are idiots. Look, people: someone is paying you money and giving you benefits, both of which can support your writing career, and all *you* have to do is show up, do work that an unsupervised monkey could do, and *pretend to care*. What a scam! You're sticking it to The *Man*, dude, because you're taking that paycheck and turning it into *art*. And you know how The Man hates that. You're supposed to be buying a big-screen TV with that paycheck! Instead, you're subverting the dominant paradigm better than an entire battalion of college socialists. Well done, you. Well done, *indeed*.

People who aren't full-time writers tend to have a hazy, romanticized view of the full-time writing life, in which writers wake up, clock four-to-six hours of writing *truth*, and then knock off for the rest of the day to be drunk and brilliant with all the rest of their writer friends. They tend to gloss over the little things like all the time you spend worrying about where the next writing gig is coming from, or all the e-mails and phone calls to publishers reminding them that, hey, they've owed you a check for nine months now, or (due to the previous) deciding which bill you can allow to go to a second or third notice, or the constant pressure to produce something you can sell, because you've heard of this crazy idea called "eating," and you think you might like to give it a whirl. The full-time writing life isn't about writing full-time; it's about a full-time quest to *get paid* for your writing, both in selling the work, and then (alas) in collecting what you are owed. It's not romantic; it's a pain in the ass.

Think of all the writers whose work you love. The vast majority of them have day jobs, or *had* them for a significant portion of their working lives, usually until it became quite clear that they were shooting themselves in the foot, economically speaking, by not writing full-time (this happens *rarely*). But even then, their having had a day job was a good thing, because it meant that they actually developed some life experience, not the least of which was consorting with real live human beings who *weren't* writers. Yes, they exist. Try the grocery store; they hang out there and *buy* things.

Yes, having a day job takes time away from your ability to write. So does watching TV or playing video games or sucking on your toes or posting angry screeds on the Internet. Unlike any of those things, however, a day job *gives you money*, which is something you as a writer will generally find hard to come by. Your day job is a friend to your writing career (not to mention to your family, your mortgage, and to your eventual retirement). Don't be in a rush to give it up. Instead, prioritize everything else you do, and see where you can find writing time in that.

3. Marry (or otherwise shack up with) someone sensible with money, who has a real job.

Hear me now, and note well what I say to you, because I am dead serious here: The single smartest thing I *ever* did for my writing career was to marry my wife. And this is why:

a) She is incredibly good with money by training and temperament and handles the domestic finances for us, leaving me free to focus on *making* money through my writing;

b) She has a real job with benefits, which gives us a month-to-month income (i.e., a secure economic baseline), shields us from the classic American financial disaster of the medical emergency, and has allowed me to take chances with my writing career I might not have been able to otherwise.

Also, you know. It's nice to have someone to listen to me whine, to cheer me on, and generally to go through life with. But *economically*, which is what we're concerned with here, a fiscally responsible spouse with a solid bennies-laden job is a pearl beyond price for writers.

Let me note *strongly* here that one thing I'm *not* saying here is that this sensible, fiscally-responsible spouse should expect to have to support you for years and years while you fiddle away on your Great American Novel (which is code for "playing Halo from 9:30 to 4:30"). Letting your spouse support you while you tinker pointlessly makes you no better than all those heavy metal bassists who spend entire careers sponging off a series of girlfriends. You *better* be working, and contributing to the household income. For us, that meant using a fair amount of my writing time doing consulting work (not romantic writing but pays well) as well as writing books. It also meant being the at-home parent, which saved us a bundle on daycare (which kept our costs down, which counts as "contributing").

Or to put it another way: Your spouse is giving you a gift by giving you security and flexibility. Make sure you're making it worth their while, too. And make sure they know *you* know how much they're doing for you. Don't be a heavy metal bassist.

Let me also note that this is the one piece of advice that I suspect writers will have the least control over. It's hard enough getting people to like you *anyway*; finding one who is fiscally responsible *and* willing to pitch in for you while you develop your writing career is a tall order. What I'm saying is that if such a person comes along, grab them with both hands, make snarly territorial noises at all the other writers hovering nearby, and then try *really hard* not to screw up the relationship. In addition to being likely to make you happy as a human, this person will also likely be an excellent economic complement as well. It's nice when that happens.

4. Your income is half of what you think it is.

When you work for someone, the employer withholds your income and Social Security taxes for the IRS, pays part of your Social Security, automatically deducts for your 401(k) and health insurance, and (if you're not an idjit) also kicks in a bit for the 401(k). When you're a freelance writer, *none* of this happens. The problem is, lots of writers forget that and spend everything they get when they get it, so when taxes come due (which is quarterly, because per the earlier notation, the government quite sensibly doesn't trust freelancers to pay their taxes in one lump sum) lots of writers go "oh, *crap*" and have to suck change out of sofas and the few remaining pay phones to square the debt. This is also why many writers never get around to funding IRAs or other retirement vehicles, and spend their lives hoping they don't slip or catch cold or get hit by a taxi, because they have no health insurance.

Simple solution: Every time you get a check, divide it in two. One half is yours to pay for bills, rent and groceries, and if there's anything left over, to play with. The other half, which you deposit into an interest-bearing account of some sort, goes to federal, state and local taxes and your Social Security taxes, and anything that's left over goes to fund your IRA (do the Roth IRA, it'll pay off in the end) and, if you're not lucky enough to have either number two or three above, your health insurance (have a day job or a spouse with bennies? Save it anyway. Be one of the wacky single-digit percent of Americans who actually save something in the bank. Also, and more usefully, that money you're saving becomes a "buffer" for the times when you have bills but no income on the way. The buffer is your friend. Love the buffer. *Fund* the buffer).

Yes, it sucks to take half of your money and never see it again. But you know what else sucks? Owing the IRS a huge chunk of money sucks. Hospitals playing musical chairs with you because they don't want your uninsured ass cluttering up their emergency room sucks. Not ever being able to stop working because you didn't plan for it sucks. All of these things, in fact, suck *worse*. So suck it up and put that half of the check aside.

Related to this and extremely important: *The money you have in hand is all the money you have.* For the purposes of budgeting, do not allow yourself to think "oh, well, such-and-such publisher owes me this, and then I should get royalties for that, so that's more money coming in..." That's a really fine way to spend money you don't have and maybe aren't going to get.

Is the money in your hands? Then it's yours (half of it, anyway). Is it not in your hands? Then it doesn't exist.

5. Pay off your credit cards NOW and then use them like cash later.

If you're anything like the average American, and economically speaking you probably are, at some point or another in your life you bought into the idea that the credit limit on your credit card was actually money you could spend—and should spend! On an iPod! And a big tv! And on pizza! In Italy!—and now you have close to $10,000 in consumer debt at 19% APR which you are making monthly minimum payments on, which means that you'll still be paying off that debt when you're 70. Congratulations, average economic American! You *rock*.

Okay: Remember when I told you to put aside half of your income for taxes, and then if there was anything left, to invest it an IRA and otherwise save it? Well, if you have more than a token amount of credit card debt, forget about saving it and apply it to your credit card payment instead. Why? Because it makes absolutely *no* sense to save or invest money if the return rate for that investment is less than the annual percentage rate of your credit card debt. Net, you'll lose money (especially if you're investing from scratch). You need to buy down that credit card debt as quickly as you sensibly can. It is your number one debt priority. Once you've paid down your debt you can begin saving and investing. But pay that debt *first*.

So, now it is some indeterminate amount of time later and you've paid off your credit card debt. Do you tear up all your credit cards and swear never to use them again? No, because as sensible as it would seem to be, there is some benefit to using credit cards. For example, I use a card for all my business-related purchases because at the end of the year I get an annual statement, which makes it a hell of a lot easier for me (or, actually, my accountant) to do my taxes. And like it or not, regular (and responsible) activity on credit cards is useful for your credit rating.

No, what you do is you get rid of all your credit cards but one, and when you use it, you only put on it what you can pay off at the end of the month—you don't carry a balance, since carrying a balance is the root of all credit card evil. You treat it as cash, and if you don't have the cash to pay off what you're charging, you don't buy it. Simple. Personally, I use American Express because it is technically a charge card, not a credit card—i.e., it *has* to paid off at the end of the month, and Amex looks askance at you if you try to carry anything over. This helps keep me from overspending, and as mentioned earlier also helps me keep track of my business-related purchases.

Just remember that credit cards are not your friends; their entire purpose, from the point of view of the bank that gives them to you, is to make you a consistent and eternal source of income, forever and ever, amen. If you want to be in economic thrall to a bank until the very moment you *die*, that's your business, but it's a pretty dumb way to go about things. Especially if you're a writer, who doesn't necessarily have a solid month-to-month income anyway.

Related to this *very* strongly:

6. Don't have the cash for it? You can't have it.

To reiterate, the reason that Americans are as generally economically screwed as they are at this moment in time is because they bought into the fundamentally *insane* idea that buying tons of shiny crap they didn't need on a high-interest installment plan made any sort of *rational* sense at all. And as completely idiotic as it is for the average American, it makes even *less* sense for a writer, who often doesn't know when or even *if* they're going to paid again. Committing to a non-essential monthly cost when you don't have to is *stupid*. You need somewhere to live, so a monthly rent or mortgage payment makes sense. You don't need a monthly charge for two years to pay for that 42-inch 1080p TV. Use your brain.

But you *want* that 42-inch 1080p TV! I understand; I want it too. What you do is *save* for it. When you save for something, it's like you're making a payment on it, except that you don't have an evil credit card company charging you 19% for the privilege. I realize it's condescending to put it that way, but, look: If people actually *knew* this, they wouldn't have thousands in credit card debt, now, would they? And yes, it's true that while you're saving for that HDTV (or whatever), you don't *have* it, and we as a nation are no longer used to the idea of not having what we want now now now now *now*. Well, *get* used to it, you insolvent jackass. Otherwise some bank owns your ass well into the next life. Really, that's all I have to say about that.

And in the meantime, there's always the local sports bar. Pay your $3 for a beer and watch the game on *their* massive HDTV. That's why they put the HDTV there in the first place. And while you're packing away the money to buy the 42-inch 1080p widescreen TV, there's likely to be a bonus, in that the cost of that TV is likely to come down a bit, because that's what happens with so many consumer goods over time. It's like getting cash back on your purchase.

The other advantage of having to save for things, incidentally, is it makes you ask yourself if you *really* need it (or, at least, want it so much that you're willing to part with your money for it). You are likely to be surprised at how many things it turns out you don't really need if you have to wait to get them, and can actually *see* the mass o' cash you're laying out for 'em. And that's all to the good for you.

7. When you do buy something, buy the best you can afford—and then run it into the ground.

I am not now, nor have I ever been, an advocate for cheap crap. Cheap crap sucks; it's badly made, it breaks, and then you have to go buy a replacement, so effectively the cost of whatever cheap piece of crap you bought is twice what you originally paid for it (or more, since having learned your lesson, you didn't buy cheap crap the second time).

I am an advocate for *thrift*, however, and in my life, being "thrifty" means that you buy well, and then you use what you buy until it no longer has value. You buy it for the long haul. This was something that came naturally to people of my grandparents' generation (the Great Depression kind of drummed it into them) but these days, when the marketing folks at Apple strive to make you feel a wave of intense, personal *shame* that you didn't pony up for the Mac Air the very *instant* it was released, this is a virtue we've lost track of. And it's true enough that if every single American thought like this, the economy would collapse even faster than it is doing at the moment. But you know what? Let the rest of America worry about that. We're here to worry about *you*.

I practice what I preach, here. In 1991, when I was out of college and starting my first job, I bought the best car I could afford: an '89 Ford Escort, Pony edition (i.e., even more underpowered than the average Escort!). I paid $4800 for it and I drove it for 12 years until it could barely chug into the dealership to meet its replacement (not an Escort). In 1997, we bought Krissy a Suzuki Sidekick; she still has it 150,000 miles later. Going back to 1991, I bought a stereo system for $400; I used it until just this last Christmas, when it finally gave up the ghost as it spun a holiday CD. The TV I bought for myself in 1991 still chugs away in my bedroom; we're likely to replace it when the switchover to digital happens next year, but then again, we might not (it's hooked up to Dish Network, which will scale down the signal to 480p). Hell, our answering machine is seven years old; I think it may use a *tape*.

Point is, we're not afraid of spending money, but we don't spend money *just* to spend money; we look for something that we can live with for a long time. That usually requires spending a bit more upfront, in order to save a lot more on the back end. As long as you combine this with point six, and buy with money you've already saved, this shouldn't be a problem.

It *does* require, as writer Charles Stross would put it, the ability to make a saving throw against *the shiny*; i.e., internalizing the idea that you don't need every new thing just because it's nice and pretty and can do one thing that thing *you* have like it can't do. This is a tough one for me, I admit. I do so love *the shiny*, and sometimes I give in when I shouldn't (as long as I have the money for it). But most of the time, I buy well, and buy to last—and then use it until it begs me to let it die. And then I use it for a year after that! Grandpa would be proud.

8. Unless you have a truly compelling reason to be there, get the hell out of New York/LA/San Francisco.

Because they're friggin' expensive, that's why. Let me explain: Just for giggles, I went to Apartments.com and looked for apartments in Manhattan that were renting for what I pay monthly on my mortgage for my four bedroom, 2800 square foot house on a plot of land that is, quite literally, the size of a New York City block ($1750, if you must know, so I looked at the $1700–$1800 range). I found two, and one was a studio. From $0 to $1800, there are thirteen apartments available. On the *entire island* of Manhattan. Where there are a million people. I *love* that, man.

Admittedly, mine is an extreme example; I don't think very many writers want to live where I live, which, as I like to say, is so far away from *everything* that the nearest McDonald's is eleven miles away. At the same time, between the bucolic splendor of the Scalzi Compound and the insanity that is the Manhattan real estate market is rather a lot of America, most of it quite tolerable to live in, and almost all of it vastly cheaper than the cities of NYC/LA/SF.

But, I hear you cry, I *need* to live in New York/LA/San Francisco because that's where all the *work* is. To which I say: *Meh.* I will tell you a story. From 1996 through early 2001, I lived outside Washington DC, which was a great place for writing work, because I had a lot of clients in the area for consulting work, and I could fly up to New York quickly for meetings and whatnot. But then my wife decided that we needed to move to Ohio so our daughter could be closer to my wife's family. I agreed, but I warned her that the move was likely to compromise my ability to get work. She understood and we moved. And two weeks after I moved, all my clients called and said, more or less "so, you're moved in now? You can get back to work now?" and started sending me work. *Nothing had changed.*

Now, maybe that's a testament to how *awesome* I am, but all ego aside, I think it's rather *more* to the point that thanks to the miracle of the Internet and such, it just doesn't matter where people are. Look, we live in an era where people working in adjoining cubicles IM each other rather than exercise their vocal cords. Leaving aside the interesting pathology of this fact, IMing someone half a continent away feels no different than IMing someone ten feet away. Distance hardly mattered when I was doing my consulting work, and now that I'm mostly writing books, it matters even less.

Don't get me wrong: I love LA, and San Francisco, and New York. They are some of my favorite places. I'm always excited to have an excuse to visit. But we're talking about money here. Your money—of which you will have little enough as it is—will go further almost every other place in the United States than these three cities. Your living space will be cheaper and more expansive. You will have more money for bills and to draw down debt. You will have more money to save. It will cost you less to do just about everything. People don't realize this when they are in thrall to NYC/LA/SF, but once they leave, as if people coming out of hypnotism, they shake their heads and wonder what they were thinking.

Think about it this way: once you're hugely successful, you can always go back. And now that the housing bubble is popping, it might even be cheaper then! Go, recession, go! But until then, find someplace nice that you like and feel you can do productive work in, and try living there instead.

9. Know the entire writing market and place value on your own work.

A few years ago I was at a science fiction convention, on a panel about making money as a writer, and one of the panelists said something I found absolutely appalling, which was: "I will write anything for three cents a word." This was followed up by something I found even *more* appalling, which was that most of the other panelists were nodding in agreement.

I was appalled not by the fellow's work ethic, which I heartily endorse (I, too, will write pretty much anything, although not for that quoted rate), but by the fact that he and most of the other folks on the panel seemed to think three cents a word was somehow an acceptable rate. It's really *not*; in a word, it is (yes) appalling. The problem was, this very talented writer, and the others on the panel, had largely confined themselves to the science fiction writing markets (and other related markets), in which the *major* outlets pay the grand sum of six to nine cents a word, and in which three cents a word is considered a "pro" rate.

Well, not to be an ass about this, but *this* pro doesn't consider it a pro rate; this pro won't even roll out of *bed* for less than twenty cents a word. Anything below that rate and it becomes distinctly not worth my time; if I do it, it's because it has some other value for me other than money (i.e., mostly because I find it amusing or interesting in some way). I can have this snooty attitude not because I'm *so damn good*, but because I know that out in the real world, I can get 20 cents a word (and usually more—20 cents a word is the lower bound for me) writing other sorts of things for other markets, and so can many other writers with anything approaching a competent work record. To be sure, this can often mean doing writing that's not typically described as "fun"—things like marketing pieces or Web site FAQ text or technical writing. But this sort of writing can pay well, expand your repertoire of work experience and (paradoxically) allow you the wherewithal to take on the sort of stuff that doesn't pay well but is fun to do or is otherwise interesting to you.

There is nothing wrong with writing as a sideline and not worrying overly much about payment. But, if writing is something you want to do full-time, it needs to be something you *can* do full-time; that means finding ways to make it pay and be worth the time and energy you put in it. Part of that is understanding the entire universe of writing opportunities available to you, not just the ones that appeal to you (a *Writer's Market* is a good place to start). Part of it is understanding that getting that writing gig that is dead boring but pays off the electric bill is in its way as valuable as selling that short story, or humor piece, or music review, all of which will pay crap but which you enjoy.

Be willing and ready to write anything—but make sure that you're making the attempt to make *more* than three cents a word off it. Because I will tell you this: If you only value your work to that amount, that's the amount you're going to find yourself getting paid. Over and over again.

This brings us to our final point today:

10. Writing is a business. Act like it.

Every writer who writes for pay is running a small business. You have to create product, track inventory, bid on work, negotiate contracts, pay creditors, make sure you get paid and deal with taxes. Work has to be done on time and to specification. Your business reputation will help you get work—or will make sure you don't get any more. This is your job. This is your business.

If you don't mind your own business then others will do it for you—and make no mistake that you *will* lose out, not because the people you are working with are evil or shifty, but simply because they are approaching their end like it is a business and will naturally take anything you leave on the table. That's business. That's how business works.

Lots of writers miss this, or ignore it, or try to pretend that it's different than this. Lots of writers assume or just want to believe that the only thing they have to do is *write,* and the rest of the stuff will take care of itself. It won't, and it doesn't. This is why so many writers find themselves in financial trouble: they don't have enough money because they valued their work too cheaply, or they weren't wise with the money they received, or they lost track of the money they were owed.

If you can't or won't approach writing as a business, then think about doing something else with your time. Stick with the day job as your main source of income and think about writing as a hobby or side gig. *There is nothing wrong with this.* Some of the best writers did their work "on the side"—as recreation away from their primary profession. Writing part-time does *not* lessen the work; the work is its own thing.

But if you *are* going to try to write as a serious profession, primary or otherwise, treat it seriously. As a writer, you're going to make little enough as is; why give any away through negligence or lack of focus? That's just *silly*. But it really is up to you. This is your work, your *money*, and your business. Respect the first two by paying attention to the third.

Done now.

Don't Live For Your Obituary

Via Nick Mamatas I see a mediation, on writer Colin Wilson, who passed away in the last week. It begins:

> How dismayed the late Colin Wilson would have been if, through some of the occult powers in which he believed, he had been able to read his own obituaries.
>
> The man whose first book The Outsider caused him to be lionised in 1956 by the literary greats of the day has been remembered in several blogs for his later novel Space Vampires, which inspired a famously trashy Hollywood film. In the broadsheets, the life of a self-proclaimed genius has been given the faintly amused treatment favoured by obituarists when dealing with a life of eccentricity or failed promise.
>
> Yet there is sort of heroism in the way that Wilson, having been abandoned by those who once praised him, remained loyal to his own talent, living a life of writing, reading and thinking—probably in that order.

The article, which you might be able to tell from the excerpt, is playing both ends of the game with regard to Wilson (which is why Nick pointed it out, I suspect—to mock it). Wilson would be dismayed, but on the other hand he did what he wanted, but on the other *other* hand here's a checklist of things to avoid if you want your obits to be properly reverential.

And, I don't know. One, I think if Mr. Wilson is still sentient after his death, he's got other, more interesting things to think about than his obits; I suspect at that point worrying about your obits would be like worrying about the end-of-year assessment of your kindergarten teacher once you were out of college ("Nice kid. Hopefully will figure out paste is not for eating.").

Two, if Mr. Wilson had any sense at all—or any ego, which by all indications he certainly did—then he recognized (before he passed on, obviously) that to the extent he and his work will be remembered at all, obituaries, transient news stories that they are, are insignificant. He'll be remembered for the work, and the status of the work in the context of history is not settled at the time of the obituary.

Salient example: Gaze, if you will, on the *New York Times* obituary for Philip K. Dick, on March 3, 1982. It is four graphs long (the final two graphs being two and one sentences long, respectively)—which for a science fiction writer is pretty damn good, when it comes to obits in America's Paper of Record, but which, shall we say, does not really suggest that Dick's notability would long survive him. Now, look at the voluminous record of writing about Dick in the NYT post-obit—an index of five pages of thumbsuckers. Pre-death, I find one note about Dick in the index, and it's one of those Arts & Leisure preview bits.

So, yes. The obit was not the final word, because the work continues—or at least, *can*. In Dick's case, the majority of his fame has come after his death, alas for him. He (nor any of us) would not know that from the four paragraphs in the NYT on 3/3/82.

I noted it before and will like do so again: As a creative person (or, really, any other sort of person), you have absolutely no control how history will know you, if indeed they know you at all. For most creative people, to the extent they are remembered at *all*, they will be remembered for one thing, because the culture at large only has so much space for any of us. You won't get to choose which one thing for which you are remembered. If, for Wilson, the one thing he's remembered for is *Space Vampires* rather than *The Outsider*, then that is still one *more* thing for which he is remembered than the billions of us who go to our graves and are swallowed up by them. So well done him.

But even then, the culture's memory is not infinite. Wilson's work, one way or another, is not likely to survive the vicious cultural culling that happens over the course of time; it's unlikely to be remembered by anyone but academics in a hundred years, or even them long after that (nor, to be clear, will mine, or the unfathomably large majority of works being created today). The good news is the judgment of the obits will have passed from this world long before then. And in any event the sun is going to swell up into a red giant in five billion years and likely swallow up the planet, so that'll be the end of all of it.

(Obit for the sun: "A long, pedestrian life followed by a brief illness; survived by Jupiter, three other planets and numerous moons and comets. In lieu of flowers, please donate to the Orphaned Trans-Neptunian Objects Fund.")

I don't know Mr. Wilson to any degree—I am one of those who knew him best for creating the source material for *Life Force*, which was a *terrible* movie—but my wish for him was that he lived the sort of life where he didn't actually *care* what his obits said, and instead enjoyed his life and left work that had the possibility of speaking for itself, over time. If you're a creative (or indeed any other) person, let me suggest you don't worry about your obits either. As well as you can, live the life you want to live and make the work you want to make. After you're gone, it'll all be sorted out or not. You won't be around to worry about it. Focus on the parts you're around for.

HOW TO BUILD A NEW YORK TIMES BESTSELLER (OR MAYBE NOT)

Jun

21

2012

(Note: The week my novel Redshirts came out in 2012, it hit the NYT Hardcover bestseller list.)

A question from the gallery:

Now that Redshirts *has become a* New York Times *bestseller, to what do you attribute its success? Anything that could be replicated by the rest of us?*

To answer the second part first: Maybe. To answer the first part second, there are several factors which I think came into play, which I will lay out below. But be sure to stick around for the end, because I will have a point to make there.

So, here's how I think we—and by we I mean me and a whole bunch of other people at Tor Books and beyond—made a NYT best seller:

1. I wrote seven other largely successful science fiction novels first, two of which (*The Last Colony* and *Fuzzy Nation*) were NYT best sellers in their own right, albeit on the paper's extended list. Which is to say *Redshirts* didn't pop up out of nowhere. I'm in my seventh year of being a published novelist, I've published regularly, stayed (and built an audience) in a single genre and—this is important—I've been fortunate that all the novels I've published so far have generally been critical and commercial successes, meaning that so far at least I've not had to spend time rebuilding a fiction career that's had a setback. All of which contributes to a certain amount of personal momentum going into *Redshirts* out of the gate.

2. I wrote a commercially accessible book. Independent of the quality of the book itself, the concept of the book is accessible and easy to understand, both to devotees of the genre and—again, this is important—to those outside of it. I can explain the book to anyone in a sentence ("The crew of a starship realize they're doomed if they go on away missions and try to change their fate") and almost everyone who has not lived under a rock for the past 40 years knows enough about televised science fiction that the possibilities for the book open up in their head.

In her LiveJournal review of *Redshirts*, spec fic writer and fan Marissa Lingen (whose opinion I respect quite a bit) was puzzled why, in 2012, I would essay the concept of red shirts, because it's not exactly a new idea out there in the world. The answer to her question, however, is implicit in the question itself. The idea of "red shirts" has been out there in the world for long enough to reach a level of cultural critical mass, which made it a good time to write a novel about it—which is a thing that hadn't been done yet. Jokes, skits, short stories and subplots about them? Yes. A novel where they are out front? Not really. And as it happens a novel is a fine format to dig into the concept more than one might be able to do in a short story, skit or subplot, which is a distinct advantage in this case.

3. I wrote a book that didn't suck. A commercially success-ful book does not necessarily have to be well-written, but it doesn't hurt things if it is. *Redshirts* is well-written—or, perhaps more accurately, it's written in a manner which is easy for most literate humans to read, with efficient prose and a light, speedy style that rewards swallowing the book in big gulps rather than sipping it slowly. Even more simply put, it's designed to be fun to read, and to read fast. These are fine qualities for a novel to have when one is hoping for commercial success.

4. I had the support of my publishers and they executed flawlessly in production and promotion. The book was given a fantastically accessible look by Tor Art Director Irene Gallo and cover designer Peter Lutjen. My publicist Alexis Saarela wrangled strategically advantageous interviews and appearances leading up to the arrival of the book and plotted a month-long book tour to help push the book and to get me in front of readers and booksellers. Tor's marketing folks and bookstore representatives were canny in building excitement for the book prior to release. My editor Patrick Nielsen Hayden rode herd over all of it and helped tweak strategy and kept me in the loop (which is actually important). On the audiobook side, Steve Feldberg at Audible helped put together an audio package that that included Wil Wheaton reading the book—a perfect match for the material, both in terms of Wil's acting history and also his affinity for the material.

Having publisher support is a huge deal. As with anything else, it's not determinative regarding success—anything can succeed or fail—but it increases the options available to you and the number of potential paths you have for success. In my case, this publisher support follows on points one through three: I have a good track record and I gave them a book that was marketable. But after that it's about what they do on their end, and in this case, they nailed it, and are continuing to do so.

5. We released a large chunk of the book early and for free (and promoted it). Releasing the prologue and the first four chapters of *Redshirts* on Tor.com and then through electronic retailers gave fans a sneak preview to get them excited about the book and also helped to give readers who were not familiar with my writing (or not sure a book about red shirts would be to their liking) enough of a taste that they could decide whether to commit to buying the whole thing. This helped drive presales, which were a significant portion of the first week sales, particularly electronically. I also and anecdotally believe that offering that first chunk of the book probably trimmed back the desire to illegally post the book online; we made it easy for people to read enough to know whether they wanted to support the book or not that posting the whole thing was in many ways superfluous.

6. We released the eBook DRM free (and when retailers slapped DRM on it inadvertently at first, made it easy for people to get the DRM-free versions we promised them). I suspect there is a significant number of people who bought *Redshirts* to help make the point that trusting one's readers and letting them *own* their electronic versions of the book was the right thing to do, or for whom the DRM-free status of the eBook was the thing that tipped them from maybe getting the book to definitely getting it. I like it when people make statements like this, and hope they keep doing it for all my Tor releases in the future.

7. Jonathan Coulton wrote a kick-ass theme song. Jonathan Coulton's audience and mine overlap heavily but are not completely congruent, so having him write a theme song and having that out there for his fans to pick up on helped the more curious ones to check out the book (and vice-versa). Likewise, for my fans, it gave them an awesome earworm a week ahead of the release, which I think had a positive effect on sales.

8. The book came out just ahead of Father's Day. Given the number of books I signed that featured the inscription "Happy Father's Day," I think that *Redshirts* was a popular gift for this particular holiday, and that probably had an impact on first week sales.

Finally,

9. I have a big online presence and that allows me to let lots of people know about my upcoming work. We've talked about this before, right? Right.

And now that you've stuck through all the reasons that I think allowed *Redshirts* to hit the best seller list, here's that caveat I warned you about:

10. This is not the only path, or a guaranteed path, to the NYT list (or to writing success in general). All these things worked for me this particular time. There are lots of writers who have written more books than I—and have admirably successful careers—who have never hit the NYT list. There are lots of people who write accessible, readable books who don't hit the list. Lots of books have strong publisher support and don't make the list. And so on. Likewise, there are books that come out of of nowhere, writers with their first books, books that are terribly and/or challengingly written, which hit the list. There are no guarantees about anything.

Keep in mind that the NYT lists are not just about raw sales: the *New York Times* uses its own secret sauce of sampling and algorithms to build its rankings, and beyond that rankings are influenced by other relative factors. It's why, for example, *Redshirts* dropped off the Hardcover Fiction list in its second week despite selling as many books in its second week as *Fuzzy Nation* (which made the extended list) did in its first week. Mysterious are the ways of the NYT best seller lists.

Also keep in mind that a book can be successful and never chart on a bestseller list. *Old Man's War* is my best-selling book but it didn't get anywhere near the NYT list in any format. All it does is sell, week after week, year after year. Likewise, prior to *Old Man's War*, my most successful book was *Book of the Dumb*, which sold over 100,000 copies, many through Costco and Sam's Club, which at the time the book was released didn't have their sales sent into BookScan. From the point of view of bestseller lists, it was as if those books were never sold. I still got paid for them, however. Which is nice.

Ultimately, I think the secret of *any* success, writing-wise, is just to write the book that you want to write. I didn't write *Redshirts* in a calculated attempt to scale a list; I wrote it because I thought I would have fun writing it and maybe people would have fun reading it. I did, and for the most part it seems people do. In that regard it's a successful book. Everything else, including the NYT list, is frosting on the cake.

How Many Books
You Should
Write In a Year

<table>
<tr><td>Sep</td></tr>
<tr><td>17</td></tr>
<tr><td>2015</td></tr>
</table>

Folks have pointed me toward a particular Huffington Post piece, begging self-published authors not to write four books a year, because the author (Lorraine Devon Wilke) maintains that no mere human can write four books a year and have them be any good. This has apparently earned her the wrath of a number of people, including writer Larry Correia, whose position is that a) the premise of the article is crap, and b) authors should get paid, and if four books a year gets you paid, then rock on with your bad self. I suspect people may be wanting to have me comment on the piece so I can take punches at either or both Wilke or Correia, and are waiting, popcorn at ready.

If so, you may be disappointed. With regard to Correia's piece, Larry and I disagree on a number of issues unrelated to writing craft, but we align fairly well here, and to the extent that I'm accurately condensing his points here, we don't really disagree. One, there are a lot of writers who write fast and well, for whom four books a year of readable, enjoyable prose is not a stretch. And, you know. If you *can* do that, and you *want* to do that, and you see an economic benefit to it, then why *not* do it?

Two, there really isn't a huge correlation between time writing and quality of the finished work. Yes, as Wilke notes, *The Goldfinch* took Donna Tartt eleven years to write, and she got a Pulitzer for it, but so what? *A Clockwork Orange*, by Anthony Burgess, was famously written in three weeks and is generally considered to be one of the great novels of the 20th Century. We can have an argument to which novel of the two is better, but that's not the point, and anyway no matter what the two are within hailing distance of each other. The point is, again, there's not a huge correlation between time writing and quality of finished work, particularly when one is cherry-picking one's examples.

How much time does it take to write a novel? As long as it takes. I wrote *Redshirts* in five weeks; it took me most of a year to write *The End of All Things*. Which is better? It's a subjective call. On average it takes me three to four months of daily work to write a novel. Would my novels be *better* if I took two years each on them? Maybe, but I kind of doubt it. I write the speed I write because that's the speed I write. If I inherently wrote faster, then they would take less time. If I inherently wrote slower, then they would take more. I suspect the inherent quality of the work would remain about equal, because I am the writer I am.

Also, you know. What a "novel" or "book" is, is a very fungible thing. The term "novel" encompasses a book like *The Goldfinch*, which is almost 300,000 words, and *Redshirts*, which was 55,000 words, not counting the codas. The more-or-less official lower length of a novel is 40,000 words; at the other extreme, Alan Moore's novel *Jerusalem*, slated for publication next year, is a million words long. I don't recommend trying to write four *Jerusalems* in a year. But on the other hand, four 40,000 word stories? That's *entirely doable* for a very large number of writers.

Moreover, with specific reference to self-pubbed folks, they have a considerable amount of flexibility toward the length of their books. All of my novels are contracted to be around 100,000 words, because that makes for a nice-sized book on the bookstore shelf (this is one reason, among others, why I added the codas to *Redshirts*). I have some flexibility there, but add up the total word count for all my published novels to date, and you get very close to 100k as an average word count number. Self-pubbed books can be considerably shorter, and many are. So again, four books of competent, readable prose is not a stretch in that case.

The economic argument for writing that much in a year is pretty simple: If you do, you give yourself more sales opportunities; there are more targets with which to draw in new readers and to keep continuing readers happy. Wilke might argue that these all aren't Pulitzer-quality works, but even if they aren't: So what? Not everything readable has to be in serious contention for the Pulitzer. It's okay to eat a cheeseburger; it's okay to read the literary equivalent of a cheeseburger. Believe it or not, some people will read both *The Goldfinch* and a literary cheese-burger! Because people are like that.

With all that said, I suspect that at least part of what Wilke was aiming at was that one shouldn't feel *compelled* to write four books a year, just because a self-pubbed author (or any other type of author, for that matter) read something somewhere that said four books a year was what every self-pubbed author should or *must* do to make money. And you know what? If that's actually part of Wilke's argument, then she's correct.

She's correct for a couple of reasons. One, and most simply: Not everyone can write four books worth reading in a year, regardless of length. Because here's a thing: There's more to a book than word count. There's also what you *do* with the words, not to mention general plotting and organization and, moving away from the purely "creative" aspect, production and distribution, the latter aspects of which self-pubbed authors have to attend to directly (other authors get the benefit of a publisher to deal with a lot of that). Some people have a lot of bandwidth for this sort of stuff; other people don't.

If you're one of the people who don't, then aiming for four books in a year, every year, isn't going to be beneficial for you. You'll end up drained and fatigued, and writing/producing inferior work, and it will be obvious. You'll be punished for it, in the sense that people will stop paying you for your work. If you're writing four books worth of crap, well. People will eat cheeseburgers, but very few people will eat crap. Don't serve up crap.

What is actually important for writers to do, all of them, regardless of publishing method, is to find their pace for how they write, and what they write. One writer can happily crank out four books a year, in which case, good for them. Another writer will take years to write a book they're happy with. In which case, good for them, too. These two writers should not try to write at each others' pace; they'll both be unhappy.

Nor is it 100% certain that the "four books a year" writer will make more money than the "one book every few years" writer. Andy Weir, as far as I know, has only one book, but that one book is *The Martian*, so it's a reasonable guess he's making more than almost every "four books a year" author. The four books a year author has more shots on goal, but if your one shot hits the bullseye, then it doesn't matter. Yes, I did just mix metaphors there. Deal with it. Point is: money is possible at every speed.

Which bring me to my next point: be aware that there's more than one recipe to making money as a writer. I write a novel in three to four months on average, and I have a backlog of story ideas, so it's a pretty safe bet that I *could* write three or even four novels a year. I don't. Why? Well, because I do other things with my time that make money, and also, make me happy. One novel a year, more or less, plus my other activities, has done very well for me. Other writers publish more and are happy; others publish less and are also perfectly happy. There's not a right path for everyone. There is, however, likely a best path for you.

(Nor is it a given that every writer should have as their hard goal for writing "making money." It's a fine goal—I'm all for it!—and if indeed you want to write as your primary means of income then clearly you have to factor that into your workflow. But not every writer wants to, or should. You can be a writer, and be a *professional* writer, and do other things too. It's allowed. And indeed, in many circumstances it can offer you more flexibility for your writing than being a full-time writer allows. Just to put that out there.)

So how many books should you write in a year? As many as you like, and as many as you can do, within your ability, for the sort of writing you want to do. What you need to do is to discover what your own capabilities are, and then work within them. Write the books you would want to read, and buy. If you can do four of those a year, great. If you do one of those every eleven years, that's good too. Most writers, I suspect, will fall in between those two data points. That'll work.

In Which I Harangue Creative Types to Update Their Wills and Estates

Today my wife and I went into our lawyer's office and updated our everything, including wills, living wills, donor registries and so on. Why did we do this? Because at this point in our life we have a fair number of assets, and given my recent deal, it's likely we'll have more in the future. Moreover, as a creative person, I have a considerable amount of intellectual property, which will need to be attended to if something should happen to me. If Krissy and I didn't specify what was to become of all of that, it would be up to the state to deal with it. No offense to the state, but I don't know it all that well. So Krissy and I have made sure that our own wishes for everything are in legal documents and up to date. Now there is no confusion about our wishes.

I frequently harangue writers and other creative types about financial issues, so allow me to do it again here: Creative folks, you *must* do some estate planning. You have assets. You have intellectual property. You (probably) have family or friends that you might want to have benefit from your work after you're gone—and you might have some people (which may even include family) that you might not want to have a say in what happens to your work when you are dead. If you die—and you *will* die, one day!—and you have not left direction toward the disposition of your intellectual and real property, then someone else will make those choices for you. As a result, some of the people you would want to benefit might get nothing. Some you don't want to get anything could get a lot. And in the meantime, it's all going to be stuck in probate, which is fun for exactly no one.

No, it doesn't matter if you're young. Young people die all the time, and creatives are famously prone to bad habits that increase their risks (including, in the US, not carrying health insurance). No, it doesn't matter that you're not famous or that your work doesn't have wide circulation. There are tons of artists who became far more famous (and rich!) after their death than before it. In my field, a fine example of this is Philip K. Dick, who struggled financially in life and has become a multi-millionaire in death as his stories have been turned into successful films.

And yes, it does matter to your legacy if you don't give direction for what happens to your work after you die. Academic James Boyle notes that something like 95% of all copyrighted material since 1900 is "orphaned"—that is to say, material for which there is no clear owner (either an estate or designated individual), and so cannot be legally reproduced. If you want your work to be legally available after you die, the best thing you can do is leave clear instruction as to what or whom owns the rights (including, if you so desire, giving the work a Creative Commons license until it makes it into the public domain a ridiculously long time after you are dead).

Beyond that, I know personally writers who have died and whose families have decided to withdraw all of that writer's work from the public sphere, forbidding reproduction or republication. In the particular case I'm thinking of, it's almost impossible that this choice is what the writer would have wanted. But the writer never said in life what they wanted to have happen to the work, and therefore in death no longer has a say.

This is important stuff, people. I can't stress this enough. And yes, it costs money, and yes, it takes time, and yes, you might think it doesn't matter. But it's worth the time and money, and if you believe your choices about your work matter while you're alive, there's no reason that they shouldn't matter after you are gone. And if you have people you love and care about, whom you wish to see benefit from what you've created, then it's smart—and *kind*—to make a document that makes your wishes clear and spares them the pain, aggravation and expense of having to deal with your lack of planning while you were alive.

So: The Scalzi Estate is now updated and planned for. Is yours? If the answer is "no," ask yourself why not. And ask yourself if there is anyone in the world for whom a little bit of planning on your part would make their lives easier if and when you go. And then, go take care of this stuff. It matters.

Mastering One's Own Domain, and No, This Is Not a Seinfeld Reference

I was asked by an aspiring writer whether at this point it's still worth it as a writer to own one's own domain, i.e., in the age of everyone being on Facebook, setting up one's online shingle elsewhere is like opening a business on a dusty street a mile away from Main Street.

My thought on this: Hey, remember when everyone was on America Online? And then everyone was on Friendster? And then everyone was on MySpace? And now everyone's on Facebook? Yeah, you'll notice a pattern here, perhaps.

Yes, but Facebook is *huge*, you say, with unspeakably large numbers of users worldwide and a valuation of $70 billion.

Wow, I say, just like America Online was *huge*, with an unspeakably large number of users online and a valuation of over $100 billion.

Yes, but everyone knows that AOL was wildly over-valued, you say.

Really, I say. And then I let that just hang there as long as it needs to until you get my point.

Popular sites come and go. One day MySpace is so popular that Weird Al snarks about it on a Top Ten hit, the next it's being sold for parts for a sliver of its previous valuation. Friendster topped off at over 100 million users; now it's got less than 10 million, most of them in Asia, and the Onion smacks them around. AOL, well. AOL, man. And don't even make me haul out GeoCities or Angelfire, the latter of which, incredibly, is still around in some strange form, along with Lycos, which bought them in the 90s. Knowing that Angelfire and Lycos still exist in some form is like hearing that somewhere out there Matthew Perry and

Lisa Kudrow are still putting on new "episodes" of *Friends* for anniversary parties and bar mitzvahs.

So, let's go back to 1998. You're a new writer and you want to establish a permanent residency online. Which would be wiser: Having your own site at your own domain, or putting up a site at GeoCities?

It's 2001, same drill: Which is wiser: Having your own domain, or creating a site on AOL servers?

2003: Your own domain, or a Friendster page?

2007: Your own domain, or a MySpace page?

(Hindsight is a useful thing.)

And now it's 2011 and the choice is one's own domain or a page on Facebook. Guess which I think you should do.

Which is not to say I don't think you *shouldn't* have a Facebook page. You should, if you like, just like I had a MySpace page, and a Friendster page and even a Web site on AOL's servers (no GeoCities page, alas). There's nothing wrong with having an outpost where people are, wherever they are. But if you're going to be online, it's best to have a site that isn't at the whims of stock evaluation, or a corporate merger, or an ambitious executive's "content strategy," or whatever. Ultimately, your online home should be something you control, and something you can point the people at Facebook (or MySpace, or Friendster, etc) to.

Having one's own domain isn't always simple and has its own share of headaches (as you will find if you ever have the need to change your ISP), but at the end of the day what it has is stability. I've had Scalzi. com since March of 1998, which has been enough time for at least four generations of online social networking sites. They come and go; my site remains. And it will remain when the hip kids roll their eyes at whatever pathetic dinosaurs still remain on Facebook (hint: that's already happening). Online, that's as good as permanence gets.

PIZZA AND PARTICLES: AN OBSERVATION ON WRITING

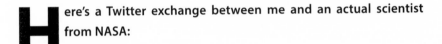

Feb
7
2016

(Note: This entry includes spoilers for my book Redshirts, *so if you haven't read it and want some elements to be a surprise, go ahead and stop reading now.)*

Here's a Twitter exchange between me and an actual scientist from NASA:

NASA Scientist: Really enjoyed Redshirts! Q: What happened to the atoms from the pizza they ate in 2012 after 6 days?

Me (in reply): I could tell you but I would need an easel and a particle accelerator

Me (to everyone else on Twitter): Super proud of this bullshit answer to a question I didn't actually think about. TO A NASA SCIENTIST, EVEN.

Now, you may ask, why would this matter? Because as a plot point in the book, time travelers had about six days to get back to their own time before they began to disintegrate—the atoms of their bodies from the future also existed in the past they're visiting, and the atoms (eventually) can't be two places at the same time and would choose to "exist" in the positions where they were in the current frame of reference.

Which is fine as long as you don't mix atom eras. But when the characters ate pizza, they were commingling atoms from the book's 2012 with their own atoms several centuries later—and what happens to those atoms from the pizza when the characters return to their own time? Because the atoms gained from the pizza would simultaneously be present elsewhere, and, as already noted, the atoms default to where they were supposed to be in their then-current frame of reference. Right?

As you can see from the tweet above I avoided the answer by giving a completely bullshit response (and then bragging about it). I'm delighted to say I was immediately called on it by another NASA scientist, and I responded appropriately, i.e., by running away. I'm the Brave Sir Robin of science, I am.

But it *is* actually an interesting question, both for itself and for what it says about my writing process. So now let me try to answer it more fully, because why not.

First, here are the some of the options for what happened to the pizza atoms:

1. After six days they were pooed out and that was the end of it (so to speak). This is a glib answer, and immediately brings up other questions like: So, people from the future don't absorb atoms from the past at all? Wouldn't they get hungry? Or thirsty, because presumably it would work the same for liquids? How would they respire? Wouldn't it be the case in this scenario that everyone from the future would be dead in five minutes from lack of oxygen? These are all reasonable questions, and if correct would have made for a shorter and rather more tragic book, so let's assume this scenario is not in fact the correct one.

2. After six days the atoms do what they do and revert to their then current locations. What does this mean for each individual? I suspect in the long term not too much. One, a fair number of the atoms will no longer be in the body anyway; they'll have left through excretion, both through the alimentary canal and respiration. As for the rest, some of them would still be in the body as waste product (i.e., in the process of being expelled but not yet), while the ones that were in the body would be roughly evenly distributed so their sudden disappearance would... *probably*...not be substantially noticed or cause great disruption to body systems. But it's certainly possible (depending on how much you eat and/or the positions of these atoms in one's body) there might be side effects. In this scenario, time travel carries risk analogous to exposure to high radiation levels: Probably fine in small doses, but the more you do it, the more problems potentially crop up. This scenario is logical, given the rules of the particular universe in the book.

3. But wait! At the very end it was revealed there was yet another layer of reality, maybe, and also, maybe, a prime mover of the story independent of the story itself, an *author*, if you will, who probably could, at their whim, decide that the pizza atoms would just stay where they were, or at least not cause any damage as they left because the author had promised the readers that everyone in the book lived happily ever, so he wouldn't, like, have them die stupidly from vaporizing atoms, what kind of bullshit is *that*. This scenario is not outside the realm of possibility, given the rules of the particular universe in the book, but it *is* kind of slapdash and lazy. *Or is it?* (Yes.) (Maybe.)

So what's the actual answer? The *actual* answer is as the writer I didn't give the pizza atom scenario any thought whatsoever—it just didn't come up at all while I was writing—so when this fellow asked the question, I had no idea what the actual answer was, aside from "I don't know, I didn't think about it at the time, or really ever, until just now."

Why *didn't* I think of it? For one thing it wasn't directly material to story at hand, either immediately or long term, so as a plotting consideration it wouldn't have been anything I would have spent time on. For another thing I was writing quickly and even if I had thought about it at the time, my answer would have likely been "it doesn't matter to the story, keep going."

For a third thing, and this is the most relevant thing, I think, writing fiction isn't necessarily about so thoroughly developing your world that you as an author have an immediate answer for every possible consequence of the development of your universe. What you are often going for is *sufficiency*—that the world is logical enough to play in for the purposes of your story—and *direction*—moving people along in the story quickly enough that they don't have time *or the interest* to question your worldbuilding or story-telling choices, at least until the story is done and you've bundled them back out into the real world, waving and smiling.

This doesn't mean you settle for bad or sloppy worldbuilding, on the idea that you'll just move readers along quickly enough that they don't see the seams. No, you still attempt to make the universe you're creating *sound*. If you set up rules for the universe, you have to follow them as a writer. What it means, however, is that once you've made up the rules for the universe, you don't necessarily have to have an answer for every single question that might come up later. If you've built the universe soundly, when previously unanswered questions come up, you can create plausible answers based on the rules of the world you've built. Or, more likely, *others* can, in fan forums and blog posts and Twitter streams, while you sit back and every once in a while say "This is a very interesting theory you have! It might even be true!"

The point is that authors are often an interesting combination of god and tour guide: We create worlds, but then only let readers see the parts of the worlds that suit our own needs—that tell the story we want to tell. What *that* means is sometimes there are parts to our world that we haven't seen either, that we only see when or if a reader gets away from us and asks a question we didn't think to ask ourselves. Sometimes, that question is about pizza.

A Portrait of the Artist as an Asshole

(Note: The genesis of this piece was an artist friend of mine writing a piece where he looked at himself critically, saw an asshole in the mirror, and made a vow to work on himself. I applauded the effort, and used it as a springboard to discuss assholes in creative fields in general.)

So, I'd like to address the topic of creative people being assholes.

1. Some creative people are assholes. This is for whatever value of "asshole" you use, because what makes someone an asshole is a somewhat subjective thing—like pornography, we tend to know it when we see it. Some creative people are assholes because "creative people" is a subset of "people," and some people are just assholes, independent of their chosen line of work. There are asshole cops, asshole lawyers, asshole doctors, asshole grocery checkout people, asshole presidents, asshole postal workers, asshole baristas, etc.

Additionally, everyone's occasionally an asshole, because people are fallible. If you have a reputation as an asshole, it's probably because you're often visibly an asshole to others and/or when your being an asshole is pointed out to you, you tend to see it as a feature rather than a bug. Be that as it may, everyone's an asshole once in a while, and has the potential to be an asshole more often than that. Trying not to be an asshole all the time is usually a good thing to work toward.

Finally, some people will think you're an asshole no matter who you are or what you do. Sometimes they may be right! But other times you may have done nothing other than exist. Honestly, just about the only person in the entire world I have never heard of someone speaking ill toward is Fred Rogers, and I'm sure there's someone out there who thinks even *he* was kind of an asshole (please note that if you actually believe Mr. Rogers was an asshole, you're almost certainly an asshole yourself and should seek help for that).

That some creative people are assholes should not be news. However:

2. Most creative people who are assholes are assholes independent of their creative drive. It's correlation, not causation. There are the rare individuals who find specifically within their assholishness a deep and abiding wellspring of creativity, because creativity is a mysterious thing. Their numbers are fewer than you would think. For most creative folks, the foundation of their creativity lies elsewhere than in the impulse to attack or belittle or to jump on other people.

Now, there are times when someone will use creativity to amplify their assholishness, because creativity is their tool, or weapon, against other people, and besides it's often enjoyable, at least in the short term, to take a punch at someone. This is especially the case if that creative person, like any number of creative people, has a cheering section out there in the ether. But using creativity as a tool for being an asshole is different from one's creativity being forged out of that particular aspect of one's make up. Most people who are creative are still creative when they are not actively being assholes to someone else.

3. Art does not justify being an asshole to others. The first of those is a thing one creates or does. The second of those is who one is to others. Again, these are largely entirely separate things. One can create gorgeous things, but if one is also an asshole, it's fair for people to say "that dude's an asshole, and I don't care how well he creates, I'm not going to support his work." There will be people who don't care (or care, but not enough to stop consuming the work), and that's fine,

too. But at the end of the day the artist has to live with themself, and may want other people to live with them, too. In which case curbing the impulse to be an asshole might be a thing they want to consider. Very few people will tolerate living with an asshole for long.

But censorship! I hear some of you cry. If you can't be an asshole, you limit your options as a creator. Well, no:

4. Creating challenging/controversial art is (usually) separate from being an asshole to people. Which is to say that an artist and creator should have the right to question, to provoke and to upend assumptions in their work, and to follow the muse wherever the muse goes. When the work gets out there, the rest of the world has their say. How the creator responds to the criticism is a largely separate thing.

And yeah, it can be tricky, which is a really polite euphemism for it. Also, yes: sometimes a creator cluelessly blunders into a controversy they did not intend and has no idea how to respond to when it happens, and as a result makes a few asshole moves. Welcome to the modern world, where such things occur. It's time to recognize that is part of the landscape.

Criticism is often really hard for creative folks to take—and can be especially so when the criticism is about something the creator wasn't expecting (or may not have even known about prior to the criticism). If you don't know the landscape of a particular field or line of criticism, it can also seem unfair. All of this raises the chance of the creator flubbing the response.

Does this mean creators should muzzle themselves? No. They should do the work they want to do. It does mean they should be aware of the world into which their work is released. They should be prepared for criticism, and should be aware the criticism may not be what they expect. That criticism may or may not have an influence on their future work, as the case may be.

(Mind you, sometimes creators *do* make something specifically to antagonize others—they know what they're getting into with that.)

5. A creator's audience is not always their friend, when it comes to the asshole thing. I'm not gonna lie—it's *fun* to have a cheering section, i.e., a group of fans who enjoy you as a public personality as much as they admire you as a creator, and who enjoy your adventures and pump their fists wildly as you go into battle against... well, whomever it is you're going into battle against, for whatever reason you go into battle. They can be relied on to have your back, to tell you it's the *other* guy who is the asshole, and to say and do all the things that let you rationalize being a jerk to someone else, or a whole group of someone else's, or whatever.

The thing creators have to remember is that to a very real extent they are *fictional characters* to their fans—and that what fans want (the product they like, they way they like it, served up by someone who they often see as being just like them, only more interesting/exciting/successful/etc) isn't always going to conform to what they actually *need* in their lives. Additionally, fans will construct narratives to justify whatever behavior a creator dishes up...as long as the end result is more of what they want. Enabling! It's a *thing*.

In the real world, however, and being an asshole can have ramifications in one's career and in the day-to-day personal life of the creator. A fan can make the argument that decades from now, no one will care whether you were an asshole or not. The thing is *creators live today*, and today being an asshole can make a big difference in your creative life. It can restrict opportunities. It can keep people from working with you or buying what you create. It can make people who care about you move away from you, because you are intolerable to be with.

Creators are actual live people. The lives they lead matter, both to them, and ultimately to the sort of work they will create, by which they will presumably be judged.

(Also, you know what? Decades from now, maybe they *will* care that you were an asshole. We have no control over how posterity perceives us; it's always in flux. And at the end of the day, if you leave a long paper and/or electronic trail of your being a complete asshole to people, then there's a *pretty good chance* that's going down on your permanent record.)

THE PROS & CONS
OF BOOK TOURING

May
26
2011

(Note: written while I was on tour for my book Fuzzy Nation*)*

I've been on tour since May 10, and away from home (meaning, not going back home after an appearance but instead living out of a hotel) for two straight weeks. I will continue to be doing so until Sunday—assuming I'm able to get home without delay by taking a Memorial Day Weekend flight, which to my knowledge I have never once been able to do. When everything wraps up I will have been on tour for three weeks, which for a normal human is a long time to be away from home, and this particular instance if nowhere else, I happen to be a fairly normal human.

While I have been about on tour, folks have asked if I like touring, or if I'm having fun, or if I miss being home—or more generally, what it's like to be on a book tour for an extended period of time. So to answer these questions, I've made a little list of the pluses and minuses of being on a long book tour.

To begin, let's start with the pluses:

1. An opportunity to promote your book. This is of course the whole point of the tour, and it's not an insignificant point. Lots of books get released every week, even in just science fiction and fantasy, and you have to work hard to differentiate yours from every other book and get people excited about it. Showing up in physical form in a place your readers can find you is one of the ways to do that.

In my case at least there's some evidence that touring helped punt the book up and through that ineffable goalpost known as the New York Times Bestseller List—not wholly through the number of people showing up to the events but also through the second-order stuff like media covering the event and people talking about the tour and so on. It's that second-order awareness raising that makes a difference in the long run and justifies a tour, even if the numbers of readers showing up at any particular spot varies significantly.

2. A chance to meet fans. I'm under the impression that it's exciting for fans to meet authors, but it works the other way, too— it's *very neat indeed* to show up at a bookstore and see dozens of people (or more!) waiting to see you and meet you and being excited about your work. Writing is a process usually done alone and staring into a computer, and most writers are not so well known that they are stopped on the street by the adoring masses. A tour is a nice way to be assured that indeed, all of our hard work and hair-pulling angst in writing a novel does not result in the book falling down a dark hole; people really do read it, and like it, and show up to let us know about it. I assume other writers are grateful about that; I know I am.

3. An opportunity to road-test material. In my case, when I'm on the road, I try not to read from the book I'm touring, since presumably people either have already read it, or will be reading it once I sign their book. Instead, I present material from upcoming works, and that serves two purposes: One, it gives me an idea of how that particular piece is working with people who are core fans of my writing; two, it both rewards people for showing up to my reading (they get an exclusive sneak peak!) and if they like it, at least, gives them something to be excited about for the future.

4. See friends and other places. I live in rural Ohio and most of my friends live a significant distance away, so a book tour gives me a chance to get out of my little hometown for a bit and at most stops to spend some time with friends who I would not otherwise easily see. At nearly every stop on the tour there were at least a couple of friends I had not seen in a while and was happy to be able to spend at least a little time with. Also, occasionally on tour you have an opportunity to meet with people you have always wanted to meet, but managed not to up until that point. That's fun too.

5. Most everything is paid for by someone else. Hotels, airfare, dinners? Paid for by the publisher or expensible. That's fairly awesome.

So those are upside happy things. Now here are the disadvantages:

1. Discombobulation. What day is it? Where am I? What's on my schedule that I have to do this time? There's an actual rest of the world outside my tour? After a couple of days it really does become a blur, because usually at each stop one is heavily scheduled. It's not just the event—there's meeting with booksellers, signing stock, being driven about, doing interviews and other work on the road, and so on...and doing that all while constantly moving.

When I did my first tour for a novel, I was told I'd have a media escort at each stop, and I thought, why on earth would I need one of those? By the second stop I knew: Because you're doing so much, and usually in a place where you don't know where anything is, that you really do need someone to guide you around and sometimes do the simple things, like, you know, make sure you *eat* and make it to the airport for your next flight.

2. Performance mode. This isn't an actual minus, but it's taxing, which is why I put it in this category. When I do an event, I am essentially doing a live and generally high-energy performance: I do a significant chunk of reading, which I try to deliver in something other than a pedantic monotone, because that would suck; then I do a fairly extensive Q&A session, which obliges me both to think on my feet and to be entertaining while doing so, and then I do a signing session, which is an hour or more of making sure that everyone who gets a book signed feels they get at least a moment where it's just them and me talking. When all is said and done it's two or three hours of being *on*.

As fun as that is for me—and it is fun, a *lot* of fun—it's also very tiring. When I'm done with what I call my "Performing Monkey Mode" at the end of every tour event, I'm usually wiped out. Friends with whom I go to dinner after an event usually notice it—I am quiet(er) and appear a little withdrawn and tired, and slightly dazed. And you do that every day for a couple of weeks.

3. Time pressure. So, the good thing about touring is that you get to see friends. The bad thing about touring is that you often don't get to see them as much as you like, and the fact is, you're working, and you have to fit your friends around that work. So often that means that someone you'd really like to spend an hour or two with you end up being able to spend maybe fifteen minutes with, or even just a couple of minutes in the signing line. And while I expect most of those folks know you're busy and working and don't hold it against you, it's still not the best circumstance. And of course sometimes there are people you want to see, but then your schedules just don't match up. So you're in a town of one of your friends and what you end up doing is waving at their house as you fly out.

4. Isolation. You see friends, you see fans, you meet people on your tour. But you're still out of your usual circumstances and you are usually flying solo and you are generally only in any one place for a short period of time, and you travel around a whole lot. So you end up spending a lot of time alone, and not just alone but alone away from familiar places and people. Which leads to being (for me) a little isolated and out of sorts. I tell people that my usual limit for being away from my wife, child and pets is about three days, and after that I start being cranky and moody. So now I'm on day fourteen of that, with a few more days to go. I'm pretty sure I'm not letting my existential yearning for home show much—and to be clear I'm still enjoying myself quite a bit and am looking forward to the last few days on the road—but it's there. I am very much ready to be home and not having to go anywhere or do anything other than be with my family.

So there are the ups and downs of the life of the touring author, at least when the touring author is named John Scalzi. Other authors may tell slightly different tales. But I think in general we'd all say: these tours are a lot of fun, we have a wonderful time when we're on them, and when they're done, it's nice to be home.

A Useful Moment
From a Mentor

May

19

2015

(Warning for those who need it: discussion of rape scenes in storytelling)

So, many years ago, when I was still a very young writer, I made the acquaintance of Pamela Wallace, and she and I became friends. At the time I was a film critic, and she was a screenwriter—and not just a screenwriter, but one who had won an Oscar, for her work on *Witness*. She also wrote novels, which were at the time something I was thinking about doing at some point. So she and I talked a lot about movies and stories and the writing life. She was a very cool mentor for a young writer to have.

One day I was over at her house and I was talking to her about a story idea I had; I can't specifically remember what the story idea was, but I vaguely recall it being some sort *Silence of the Lambs*-esque thriller, in which an investigator and a serial killer matched wits, you know, as they do. And at some point, I dragged the investigator's wife into the story, because, as I was, like, twenty-four years old and didn't know a whole hell of a lot, I thought it would be an interesting character note for the investigator, and a good plot development for the book, for the serial killer to basically rape and torture the wife—

—at which point Pamela immediately went from interested to disgusted, threw up her hands, and had them make motions that I immediately interpreted as *oh God Oh God this horrible idea of yours get it off me right now.*

Aaaaand that was really the last time I ever considered rape as an interesting character note or plot device. Because, I don't know. If you're a twenty-four-year-old wannabe fiction writer and an Oscar-winning storyteller is *physically repelled* by your casual insertion of rape and violence against women in your story, mightn't that be a sign of something? That maybe you should pay attention to? Perhaps?

Now, as I got older and became a more accomplished storyteller (and human), there turned out to be many other reasons for me to decide not to put those sorts of scenes willy-nilly into my books aside from "dude, you just disgusted your successful writer friend with your plot twist." But I'm not going to lie and pretend that this very significant clue, dropped by my friend, did not in fact make a long-lasting impression.

Which continues to this day. I've written eleven novels now, most with lots of action, adventure, peril and danger to characters of several genders, and lots of tough scenes that show loss and violence (see: most of *The Ghost Brigades*). No rape scenes. They weren't necessary for the narrative—and more concretely, as narratives to stories don't just magically happen but are the result of the author's intention, I chose not to make circumstances in my novels where they *would* be necessary.

Sadly, not every young male novice storyteller has a woman friend who is also an Oscar winner to set him straight on the errors of his shallow narrative ways. Would that they did! So for everyone else I would just say that while you *can* put these sorts of scenes into your work, maybe before you do, you should ask yourself *why*. Ask yourself what actual value they will bring to your work. Ask yourself if you are entirely sure about that value.

And while you're asking yourself that, keep my friend Pamela's reaction to my proposed rape scene in your head. She's not alone in that reaction these scenes, nor was she wrong to have it. Neither are other people.

WRITING AND BABIES

Apr

2

2009

(Note: For those of you who don't know, my daughter's name is Athena. She's in college now. Time flies.)

Jess Nevins asks:

How did you manage to be a productive writer in the first two years of your child's life?

Which is to say: what was your work schedule like? How did you manage to produce coherent text when you were exhausted from getting up every three hours to feed the baby? How did you manage to be productive and not let your wife feel like she was having to do everything herself?

(Why, yes, I have selfish reasons for asking).

Heh. I'm sure you do.

I had no problem at all with writing when Athena was an infant and toddler, to tell you the truth, and in fact I found it much easier to write when she was that age than I did when she was older. Here's some of what I did:

1. I was a night owl back then, and Krissy got up reasonably early, so we'd divide feeding responsibilities according to our own sleep schedules. I'd handle the 10 p.m., 1 a.m. and the occasional 3:30-ish feedings (from a formula bottle, to be clear), while Krissy slept. Then she'd handle the morning feeding before she went off to work and that would take care of Athena until 9 a.m. or so. So I would get a reasonable amount of sleep.

2. I was the stay at home parent, so you would think that would cut into the time I had to write. But it didn't really. Infants when they're young tend to sleep quite a lot, so for me it was reasonably easy to get work done while Athena napped (I would make business phone calls while she was asleep, for example). I'd do shorter work during the day, and then as I was also on the night owl schedule, I would do a lot of longer writing at night when everyone else in the house was asleep and I'd have stretches of time to work. You have to be able to be both flexible and disciplined to do this, but it worked for me.

3. One thing I did which seemed to help was that I put Athena's playpen into my office with me, and made sure she had lots of stuff to keep her amused. That way she was generally fairly content because I was in the same room as her, and she had things to keep her occupied. As she got older we moved from a playpen to a larger, gated area of the office, and then to a toddler gate at the office door. And of course lots and lots of toys.

4. I did make sure that I took breaks during the day to focus attention on Athena, which served two purposes: One, it was good for her to have directed play and two, it was good for me to step away from my computer every once in a while and give my brain and my typing fingers a break. A little of this could go a long way for both me and Athena.

5. When she was edging into toddlerhood, I bought a new computer, set my older computer on a kid-height desk, and then bought a bunch of toddler software. It was sort of astounding how quickly she took to it, and how it would keep her occupied. One has to be sure the kid doesn't get completely swallowed into it, of course, but it was fun for her and it helped me get work done.

In all, the first two years went pretty smoothly, in terms of work, and I can tell you when it became harder to get work done: Once Athena started talking (in complete sentences rather than words), because then she wanted to have lots and lots of conversations, and started making real—albeit totally adorable—impositions on my work day that she hadn't before. She still does, although now she's at school half the day, so I have time for longer work. Even so, on balance, I was more productive during those first couple of years than I was in the years immediately after.

Now, I did have a couple of good breaks in there: Being stay-at-home and not having to conform to a set schedule gave me more flexibility than most people have, and oddly enough I found that when I was doing corporate work a lot of my clients were more than happy to work around my baby-tending schedule, I think partially because stay-at-home dads were still something of a novelty when Athena was a baby. We could go off on why it is that me caring for a baby was seen as a positive by corporate America (or the part I consulted for) while it would have been seen as a liability if a woman were doing it, but that's a whole other slice of thing that would take lots of time to work through. Unfair or not, it really wasn't a problem for me. And of course, it was huge that there was another parent in the household and that both of us were willing to work out a schedule that had each of us taking a lead role while the other had time to rest and depressurize.

I think ultimately for writing when one has a baby around the secrets are: Be flexible in your writing schedule, and make sure you do, in fact, get enough sleep. Both take a little scheduling and patience, but both are worth it, if you want to get that writing done.

Writing: Find the Time or Don't

Sep

16

2010

Over the last couple of months I've gotten a fair number of letters from aspiring writers who want to write but find themselves plagued by the vicissitudes of the day, i.e., they've got jobs, and they're tiring, and when they come home they just want to collapse in front of the TV/spend time with family/blow up anthills in the backyard/ whatever. And so they want to know two things: One, how I keep inspired to write; two, how one manages to find the time and/or will to write when the rest of life is so draining. I've addressed these before, but at this point the archives are vast, so I'll go ahead and address them again.

The answer to the first of these is simple and unsatisfying: I keep inspired to write because if I don't then the mortgage company will be inspired to foreclose on my house. And I'd prefer not to have that happen. This answer is simple because it's true—hey, this is my job, I don't have another—and it's unsatisfying because writers, and I suppose particularly authors of fiction, are assumed to have some other, more esoteric inspiration. And, you know. Maybe other authors do. But to the extent that I have to be inspired to write at all on a day-to-day basis (and I really don't; you don't keep a daily blog for twelve years, for example, if you're the sort of person who has to wait for inspiration to get your fingers going across a keyboard), the desire to make money for myself and my family works well enough. Another day, another dollar, etc.

Now, bear in mind here I'm establishing a difference between inspiration for writing on a daily, continuing basis, and inspiration for specific pieces of work; those inspirations aren't necessarily related to getting paid, and can come from any place. But even then, I find the two inspirational motivations work in a complementary fashion. I am inspired to write a particular story or idea in a fanciful way, and then the practical inspiration of getting paid gets my ass in a chair to write the thing. It's a congenial, if somewhat unromantic, way of doing things.

As to the second of these, my basic response here is, Well, look. Either you want to write or you don't, and *thinking* that you want to write really doesn't mean anything. There are lots of things I think I'd *like* to do, and yet if I don't actually make the time and effort to do them, they don't get done. This is why I don't have an acting career, or am a musician—because as much as I'd *like* those, I somehow stubbornly don't actually do the things I need to do in order to achieve them. So I guess in really fundamental way I *don't* want them, otherwise I'd make the time. *C'est la vie.*

(This sort of skips over the question of whether I'd be *good* at either acting or music, but that's neither here nor there. By not trying, I'm not even achieving failure.)

So: Do you want to write or don't you? If your answer is "yes, but," then here's a small editing tip: what you're doing is using six letters and two words to say "no." And that's *fine.* Just don't kid yourself as to what "yes, but" means.

If your answer is "yes," then the question is simply when and how you find the time to do it. If you spend your free time after work watching TV, turn off the TV and write. If you prefer to spend time with your family when you get home, write a bit after the kids are in bed and before you turn in yourself. If your work makes you too tired to think straight when you get home, wake up early and write a little in the morning before you head off. If you can't do that (I'm not a morning person myself) then you have your weekend—weekends being what I used when I wrote *Agent to the Stars.*

And if you can't manage that, then what you're saying is that you were *lying* when you said your answer is "yes." Because if you really wanted to write, you would find a way to make the time, and you would find a way to actually write. Cory Doctorow says that no matter what, he tries for 250 words a day (that's a third of what I've written in this entry to this point), and if you write just 250 words a day—the equivalent to a single, double-spaced page of text—then in a year you have 90,000 words. That's the length of a novel. Off of 250 words a day. Which you could do. On the goddamned *bus*. If you really wanted.

This is why at this point in time I have really very little patience for people who say they want to write but then come up with all sorts of excuses as to why they don't have the time. You know what, today is the day my friend Jay Lake goes into surgery to remove a huge chunk of his liver. After which he goes into chemo. For the third time in two years. Between chemo and everything else, he still does work for his day job. And when I last saw him, he was telling me about the novel he was just finishing up. Let me repeat that for you: Jay Lake has been fighting cancer and has had poison running through his system for two years, still does work for his day job and has written novels. So will you please just shut the fuck up about how hard it is for you to find the time and inspiration to write, and just do it or not.

And to repeat: It's *okay* if you don't. There's nothing wrong with deciding that when it really comes down to it, you want to do things other than writing. It's even okay to start writing, work at it a while, and decide it's not for you. Being a writer isn't some grand, mystical state of being, it just means you put words together to amuse people, most of all yourself. There's no more shame in not being a writer than there is in not being a painter, or a botanist, or a real estate agent—all of which are things I, personally, quite easily do not regret not being.

But if you want to be a writer, than *be* a writer, for god's sake. It's not that hard, and it doesn't require that much effort on a day to day basis. Find the time or make the time. Sit down, shut up and put your words together. Work at it and keep working at it. And if you need inspiration, think of yourself on your deathbed saying "well, at least I watched a lot of TV." If saying such a thing as your life ebbs away fills you with existential horror, well, then. I think you know what to do.

WRITER, PROFESSIONAL, GOOD

Jan

28

2012

ere are three questions I was recently asked about writing. I'm going to condense the questions, because when they were asked, they meandered across several paragraphs; they boil down to three sentences, which are:

When may you call yourself a writer? When may you call yourself a professional writer? When may you say you are a good writer?

These are three separate but related questions. Let's start with the most fundamental.

When may you call yourself a writer?

I tend to be very small-c catholic on this question and say that if you write at all, you can consider yourself a writer. This annoys people who think that tweeting about your lunch or posting on Facebook that your cat horked up a hairball does not rise to the level of *true writing*, but, look, writing is an act of setting down in words the things about which you have a concern. If you are literate and you can manage to create meaning from the written word, you are, on a very basic level, a writer, even if what you're writing is "I've gone to the store for milk. Be back soon."

But for the sake of argument, let's tighten this up a bit. Let's say that just being able to write a meaningful sentence doesn't make you a writer, any more than being able to lie with a straight face makes you an actor, or doodling in a boring meeting makes you an artist. So where does the line exist, over which one may say "I'm a writer"?

In this scenario, the line manifests with intent. Does the person sending out an e-mail about where everyone is meeting for after-work drinks *intend* to write? Other than in the most practical and mechanical sense, no. E-mailing everyone is simply the easiest way to get the information to the largest number of people involved, with the best chance those people will get the information. If it were easier and more practical to send a group voice mail, that would be what would happen.

A writer, on the other hand, chooses written words, and chooses them not just for mechanical and practical reasons, but for (or also for) esthetic and artistic purposes. Writers *want* to write, rather than *have* to write. In presenting an idea, the medium they intend for it to be in is the written word.

This is still a bar too low for some people, but screw them, those guys are snobs. I say that if you *want* to write, and then you *do* write, then you are writer.

However, it doesn't make you a *good* writer. I'll give you an example, using a different creative field. I recently got a ukulele, and I enjoy playing it, and I actively make music with it. I am a musician. But I'm not a *good* musician, because right now my chording is merely adequate and my strumming is marginal. I'm no Jake Shimabukuro, nor am I likely ever to be. But that's fine because I don't play ukulele to be the best ukulele player ever; I play it because I enjoy it and it's fun.

Likewise, people may call themselves "writers" even if they recognize they are not very good at it at the moment, or if they suspect they may never be, but just enjoy it anyway. The act of writing—of putting ideas into the medium of the written word—is sufficient. You write? You meant to do that? What you've written is intelligible to other humans? Congratulations, you're a writer.

When may you call yourself a professional writer?

Are you writing with the intent to be paid? *Are* you being paid? Is writing consistently one of the ways in which you make your living over time? If the answers to each of these is "yes," then you can probably get away with calling yourself a "professional writer."

Note that writing, in general, is not a profession in the same manner as being a medical doctor is a profession. You don't have to go to school to be a writer (I didn't), you don't need to have a degree or a certification in the subject to practice it (I don't), you don't have to be licensed to do it (at least not in the US) and there are few if any laws that govern its practice. Now, you can go to school for writing, get degrees in the field and even join associations or unions of writers, who may have their own definitions of what constitutes a professional level of achievement (see, as an example, the membership requirements for the Science Fiction and Fantasy Writers of America, of which I am currently president). But those are choices, not requirements. If you write science fiction and fantasy, you *should* belong to SFWA (thus ends my plug). But if you *don't*, it's not as if the police will come to the door and arrest you for fraud.

"Professional" in this sense means that you are in the stream of commerce—which is to say, you offer your writing (or your talents as a writer) for sale, and your writing and/or talents are being used and compensated for by others. In my own opinion, for saying that you're a professional writer, it helps to be able to show that you've been able to make money at writing over time. Getting paid for *any* writing is not a bad thing, mind you. If you get paid for it, whatever the circumstance, then good for you. But let me give you an example from my own experience. When I was in college, I took third place in a student writing competition for a short story, for which I received $250. I got paid for that writing. Did it make me a professional writer of fiction? Not really, since I didn't then write another piece of fiction for sale for another decade.

I sold a science fiction short to *Strange Horizons* in 2001, but it too was something of a one-off, more of an experiment to see if I *could* sell a short story than an entrance into the field as a profession. I date my professional entry into the world of fiction with my sale of *Old Man's War* to Tor in 2002, because among other things it was part of a two-book deal, i.e., I'd be getting paid for my fiction work over time. Even then, it wasn't until *Old Man's War* was published in 2005 that I felt comfortable saying I was a professional fiction writer. Now, that's just me (and note that since I could call myself a pro writer for other reasons, having patience on that part was not difficult for me). Some folks really really really want to call themselves a pro writer the first time they get a check. I'm not going to go out of my way to crap on them for it if they do.

It's important to note that "professional" is not the same thing as "good," although in my opinion it does correlate pretty well with "competent"; it's hard to make money from writing if you can't actually write. But it's entirely possible to be a professional, published writer and be only competent. This is because, as I noted long ago, publishing is about what is competent rather than what is "good;" "good" is a value judgement, where "competent" is a standard that's as objective as we can get when we talk about language. Even in the realm of self-publishing, financially successful writing has to be competent at least.

Which brings us to the third question:

When may you call yourself a good writer?

When you are in control of your instrument. In the case of fiction in particular, this means having the ability to make your reader have the emotional response you intended for them to have, when you set down to write. To put it another way, when a competent writer tells you a story, you know what happened. When a good writer tells you a story, you feel it happen to you.

(When a great writer tells you a story, you feel your life change because of it. But let's not worry about that one now.)

Caveat: there is no bright line between "competent" and "good." Some writers can be good in some aspects of writing and merely competent in others. Other writers are competent today and good tomorrow, and vice versa. Good writers can have bad days; competent writers can have really good days, and then later be unable to repeat the performance at will. Writers often can't tell when what they're writing is good or just competent (or worse). This is one reason why so many of us are completely neurotic.

And here's something that *really* sucks—being a good writer doesn't necessarily mean that any particular thing you've written will get published, because being published is contingent on several things, some of which are not about the writing. I've noted here before that when I guest-edited *Subterranean Magazine*, I had to reject about half the stories

I really wanted to buy because I only had so much space and money. I had to pick and choose. The stories I rejected were *good*, and it killed me to have to let them go.

For all of that, a good writer is good at writing more often than not; the baseline skill is established and it's at a high level. How a writer becomes good is pretty much like how anyone becomes good at anything: Practice, practice, practice. Talent plays into it but I think talent is overrated and overprivileged, and there are lots of writers with raw talent who never pan out because they expect that raw talent should be all they have to bring to the game. Surprise! It's not. Lots of good writers are good simply because they've learned their craft and they've honed their skill.

I am a good writer, but I was a published writer before I was a good writer. The dividing line for me happened in 1997, after I spent a year as an editor for a humor magazine that ran on AOL. Before then I was a competent writer who assumed he was good because he was arrogant; after I had been an editor and spent time dealing with other people's writing I was able to see the flaws and problems in mine, and it made a difference. I think being a published writer before one is a good writer is not unusual. Lots of competent writers learn to be good writers on the job. It's part of that whole "practice, practice, practice" thing.

My advice to anyone who wants to be a good writer is simple: Stop thinking about being a good writer and start thinking about being a *better* writer. Work on the things you know you want to improve on. Stop thinking that you're going to cross some line and then suddenly you'll be a good writer. It doesn't work that way, and even good writers still have things to work on (trust me on this).

You'll know when you're a good writer when your craft is good enough that you don't worry about whether you *can* do what you want to do with your writing, and instead you wonder about *how* you're going to do it. You probably won't notice the first time this happens. When you do notice it, it probably won't be a big deal. You'll be more focused on the writing.

WORLDBUILDING, BRIEFLY

Aug

21

2009

(Note: The context here is that I wrote a humorous piece on bad design in the Star Wars universe—there is a lot of it—and the piece went viral. To keep the Star Wars fans at bay, I also wrote a piece about bad design in the Star Trek universe as well. Yes, there's a lot of it there, too.)

All the recent discussion of design in the *Star Wars* **universe has led to a fair question of how deeply someone designing a universe and the things in it has to go to make the thing plausible enough for its task—which, in my opinion, is to keep the audience engaged all the way through the work without once saying, "now, wait just a** *minute...***"**

Other worldbuilders will have to answer this one when talking about their own works, but as for me, in general, I try to build my worlds at least two questions deep—that is, you make your creations robust enough to stand up to a general question and then a more specific followup question. Thus:

Reader: Why did you give your genetically engineered soldiers cat's eyes in *Old Man's War?*

Me: Well, relating specifically to pupils, it allows better filtering for the range of visible light the soldiers work in across different planets and environments.

Reader: Okay, but why not just engineer eyeballs to make smaller *round* pupils?

Me: The scientists in the OMW universe find it easier to work with pre-existing genetic code than develop new code, so they do that whenever possible.

And for about 90% of your readers, that's going to be sufficient rationale. For about 10% of your readers, it won't be, but at some point, and simply as a practical matter, you realize that some folks aren't going to be happy with your worldbuilding no matter how far you drill down, and that you can just sort of accept that as the cost of doing business in a geek-rich field like science fiction. To a very real extent, what you're aiming for is sufficiency, not completeness.

(Mind you, that's if you're creating the way most people do, which is to have the world come out of the story, not the other way around. Tolkien, as an example and if memory serves, did it the other way around, which is that he built the world in detail first, and then told a story (two, actually) inside of it. You certainly *can* do it that way, and it is frankly awesome when pulled off well. But also it's sort of the long way around, and recommended primarily for nerdy, vaguely OCD people with secure day jobs and lots and lots of time to kill.)

I *think* by and large the OMW universe functions at the "two questions deep" level, although I suppose it does depend on *which* two questions someone asks. To be sure, I know of at least a couple of places where the universe is barely a single question deep, which was bad worldbuilding on my part, and the only thing to do about it at this point is not call attention to those specific places. Please move on, nothing to see here [insert Jedi handwave]. But overall, it's robust enough (and written well enough, which is a critical point) to get most people through each book without stopping to ask questions about the details therein.

Which is what I want, personally: If you get through the work before you start nitpicking, that qualifies as a victory condition for me.

THE FINE ART OF PUTTING YOUR BOOKS AND YOURSELF OUT THERE WITHOUT WANTING TO DRINK ACID, OR, LET'S TALK ABOUT PUBLISHING AND ONLINE PRESENCE

AIMING FOR
THE MARKET

Oct
6
2014

On his blog, author Steven Brust talks about why he doesn't like being asked for advice on publishing—the answer being that he has his own conflicted relationship to the business of publishing, the fact of which does not necessarily put him in the best of positions to counsel someone else with questions about the commerce side of things.

In the course of things Steven name drops me, noting "John Scalzi, if no one else, provides proof that consciously writing to a market is no hindrance to producing high-quality, entertaining work." Which is to say that I do something that Steven himself is not terribly comfortable with—essentially, calling my shots in terms of where I'm aiming for in the marketplace, and then swinging to get the ball (or book, in the case) where I called for it go.

Steven's not wrong. I have and do very consciously look at the marketplace when I'm thinking the books I write. *Old Man's War* is the first and most obvious example of this. I wrote it not just because I wanted to write a science fiction novel, but because I wanted to write a science fiction book I could sell—that it, something with enough obvious commercial appeal that a publisher could immediately see the value proposition in publishing the novel and getting it out in the book racks.

OMW, among all the other things it is (and isn't), is straightforward Heinleinian military science fiction—it's the science fiction equivalent of classic rock, in other words. It was designed to sell to a publisher, and was designed for that purpose so well that it sold to a publisher without me ever formally submitting it. It was, in other words, a very commercially *intentional* novel, and it lived up to its intention, for which I am grateful.

In novels and (most) shorter work since, I've continued to work in that commercially intentional mode, for several reasons. One, and most obviously, writing is what I do for a living, and I want to write books that sell not just to the people who are already fans (either of the genre or of me), but to other folks as well; the more, the better. Likewise, I think it makes sense to be actively looking at the market—not at what's hot now (if you can see it, you've generally already missed it) but where I think there's a potential to do interesting things for the future, where they will get noticed. Two, and happily for me, the style of writing in which I am most proficient—clear, transparent prose, snappy dialogue, plot jumping through hoops at a nice clip—is also one that is easy to sell. Three, I not only see the value of such writing, but as a reader I also enjoy it; I'm writing the work I would want to read, in other words.

I do think point three is significant. When I wrote *Old Man's War*, I was intentionally addressing what I saw as commercially viable science fiction sub-genre—military science fiction—but I also wrote it on my personal terms, with interplay between characters (including romance and affection), action that was vivid without being gratuitous (or without consequence), and a large portion of humor. I wrote to the market, but I put into the market something I thought was going to be worth reading *independent* of market positioning—or at least, worth reading to *me*.

This is where point four (which is really a sub-point of point three) comes into play: in many things, I have reasonably common tastes. I like a good three-minute pop song, I laugh at movies that aren't *good* but are good at what they intend to do, I eat a lot of candy and I enjoy a book that puts a value on entertaining me first, everything else as an add on. It's not the *entirety* of my tastes, to be sure. But it *is* a significant portion of my taste, and I don't feel at all apologetic about it. It helps my aim when it comes to writing things that sell.

(I do think it also was useful that I came to publishing fiction after a decade and a half of professional writing, including writing non-fiction books. It meant that I had a reasonably good understanding of the business end of writing and of freelance work, an unromantic view of writing as a day-to-day job, and that much of the desire for ego gratification that comes with publishing had already been dealt with. This helped with looking at fiction in a practical way from the get-go.)

Which is not to say that my aim is always good, or that people who do not do things as I do are destined to failure. Note that Steven Brust, whose relationship to the business side of publishing is different than mine, is nevertheless a *New York Times* bestselling author, and there are (I imagine) at least a few authors who write what they want to write, consider the market not at all, and just let other people figure that part out. And, you know what? Good for them. I couldn't do it. That would drive me crazy. I run the business side of my writing business in a way that I think makes sense for me: With an eye toward the market and commercial prospects. It's worked pretty well to date.

Amazon Tweaks Its Kindle Unlimited System. It Still Sucks For KDP Select Authors

Jun
21
2015

(Note: In addition to being a retail monolith, Amazon has a number of interests in publishing, including various print imprints, Audiobook publisher Audible (with whom I have a long-term contract), and a program called Kindle Unlimited, which lets readers access lots of writing (mostly self-published) for a monthly fee.

I'm not here to kvetch about the subscription service or self-publishing—both are fine—but one aspect of KU which is of note is that authors using the service get paid out of a "compensation pool" of money Amazon allots to the service. There's a finite amount of money allotted, so the authors compete with each other. This has interesting repercussions, and by "interesting," I mean "bad."

Amazon occasionally changes the formula for how authors get compensated for subscribers reading their work. That's the jumping off point to this piece.)

N ow that I've returned to the US and have parked myself in front of the computer again, people are asking me what I think of Amazon's plan to tweak the way its Kindle Unlimited system pays KDP Select authors. In the past, Amazon would designate a certain amount of cash as a payment pot, and all KDP Select authors participating in Kindle Unlimited would get a small bit of the pot if someone who downloaded their book read more than 10% of it. This predictably led to authors making short books in order to get to the 10% mark as quickly as possible, and equally predictably diluted the effectiveness of the tactic. It also made authors of longer works complain quite a lot, as they had to compete with bite-sized books for the same tiny bit of the pot.

As a result, Amazon is now tweaking its system so that instead of getting paid when one reaches that 10% marker, KDP select authors will get paid for each page read—a move that will, within the context of the KU system, at least, address the "small book vs. big book" disparity. The system will also define a standard "page" so fiddling with margins and type size won't fool it, and somehow track how much time you spend on each page, so just clicking through all the pages as quickly as possible won't do the trick (this makes me wonder what Amazon defines as a decent amount of time to read a page). The short version is: You get paid for what your readers read. If your readers don't read the whole book, you don't get paid for the whole book.

I have a lot of questions about how this will play out in theory—will an author get paid if you re-read a book? What about if you go back and re-read a page? Does that count? Doesn't this mean that authors of "Choose Your Own Adventure" books get really screwed? Not to mention any author who is writing anything other than a page-turning narrative?—but ultimately any objections or praise I might have for this new Amazon model is irrelevant, because of a simple fact:

Amazon is still making KDP Select authors compete against each other for a limited, Amazon-defined pot of money, and no matter how you slice it, that sucks for the authors.

Why? Because Amazon puts an arbitrary cap on the amount of money it's possible to earn—and not just a cap on what you, as an author, can earn, but what *every* author in the KDP Select system participating in Kindle Unlimited can make. Every KDP Select author participating in Kindle Unlimited can not, among all of them totaled up, make more than what Amazon decides to put into the pot. Why? Because that's the pot. That's how much Amazon wants to splash out this month. And the more pages are read in the month, the smaller any bit of the pie that you might get for your pages read becomes. It's a zero-sum game for every KDP Select author participating in Kindle Unlimited. Next month, who knows what the size of the pot will be? You don't—only

Amazon does. But whatever amount it is, it's an amount designed to benefit Amazon, not the individual authors.

This is a bad situation for the authors participating—bad enough that ultimately the minutiae of *how* the money is allocated is sort of aside the point, because the relevant point is: You will never make more for your work than Amazon wants you to make. And yes, *just* Amazon, as the work KDP Select authors put on Amazon are exclusive to Amazon.

I'm not one of those people who believes Amazon is glowy-red-eye evil—I remind people again that I've rather happily had a fruitful relationship with its Audible subsidiary for a number of years—but Amazon is looking out for Amazon first, and when it does, it's not an author's friend. There is no possible way in this or any other time-line that I would ever, as a writer, participate in the sort of scheme that Amazon runs with its KDP Select authors on Kindle Prime. I don't approve of putting a cap on my own earnings (particularly one I have no say on), and I don't approve of being in a situation where my success as an author comes by disadvantaging other authors, or vice versa. In the system in which I currently participate (i.e., the open market), there is no limit to the amount I can make, and no limit to what any other author can make. It's a great system! I support it, and so should you.

So, yeah: By page, or by percentage, KDP Select authors on Kindle Unlimited still can't make more than Amazon says they can. That sucks, and that's the long and short of it.

COVER ART

Mar
26
2008

Tor art director Irene Gallo, prompted by a blog post by Pyr publisher Lou Anders, talks a bit about cover art and what "works" and why when it comes to sf/f fantasy books, and notes a point that many people who gripe about covers miss:

> *...as much as I'd like it to be otherwise, I am not really hired for my personal preferences on cover art, but rather to get books past book buyers. If the books don't make it into the stores in the first place, readers can't buy them in the second place.*

Which is to say that cover art is explicitly commercial art; it's designed first to convince shopkeepers that this book will *move*, and second to convince readers in a glance what the book is about and that it's worth their time. In a book series there's a third dimension as well, which is maintaining a consistency in feel across a series. There's a reason that the cover to *Zoe's Tale* is by John Harris and features spaceships: Because every other cover in the OMW series is by John Harris and features spaceships. If there's a fifth book in the OMW universe, it is very likely to have a John Harris cover, and feature, yes, spaceships. The cover to Jay Lake's *Escapement* is by Stephan Martiniere and features an airship because the cover to the first book in the series...well, you get the idea.

Would people buy *Zoe's Tale* or *Escapement* without a cover consistent to their series? I like to think they would, but you might lose that sort of single-reflex, automatically-familiar snatch-and-grab motion that this pattern of familiarity (hopefully) engenders. Tor (and the book-sellers) want you to be able to recognize on OMW-series book across a crowded bookstore and home in on it like a heat-seeking missile. And for that matter, you know, so do *I*. So I'm glad I *like* my OMW series covers, and hope nothing bad ever happens to John Harris, as long as I'm writing in that universe.

What's interesting to me is *how* the cover dynamic changes, depending on the audience. For example, take the two covers for two different editions of *Old Man's War*: The paperback art, by John Harris, filled with spaceships, and Vincent Chong's art for the limited hardcover edition, which features a soldier in battle.

First, the Tor trade paperback edition. It's designed to speak to booksellers, as in "Look! John Harris spaceships! John Harris covers are on lots of successful science fiction books! Like *Ender's Game!* You sell a lot of *Ender's Game!* You'll sell a lot of this, too! And look! Sci Fi Channel says it's essential! Essential books *must* sell! And look! Here's a quote comparing the author to Heinlein, who, while dead, still sells! Lots! Sell! Sell! Sell!"

Note that I am *not* mocking Tor for doing this. We did, in fact, sell *tons* of the paperback of OMW, and the cover went a long way in selling to book to the booksellers. This cover did its job, and is a pretty cool cover at that. I'm deeply appreciative to Tor (and to John Harris, and Irene Gallo) for the work.

The second cover is the Subterranean Press limited hardcover edition of OMW. It's not aimed at booksellers, because most of Subterranean's business is direct to readers—and not just readers, but collectors, many if not most of whom have read the books they will now buy in this limited edition. This is what this cover says to them: "Hey, remember that time in *Old Man's War* where the human soldiers totally *squished* those inch high aliens with their *boots?* Yeah, that was *cool.*" It's still commercial art; it's just commercial in another direction, and to another audience. This cover did its job, too, and is also a cool cover. So thanks here to Bill Schafer and artist Vincent Chong.

One of the interesting questions that writers and publishers will face in the presumed ascendency of electronic books, whenever it will happen, is whether "cover art" will survive the translation into an electronic medium. My suspicion is that it will because of its function—it's advertising for the book. Whether it's packaged with the text, or part of a Web page promoting the work or whatever, it'll still be around, as long as it does the job of getting people to take a look at the text inside.

Dear Readers: Publishers Think of You as Customers I Swear

Dec
27
2011

(Note: I run a feature of my blog called "The Big Idea," in which authors write essays about their latest books. In the early part of the current decade, people would comment on these pieces, not about the book, but about the price of the eBook—a thing that authors published by traditional publishers have no control over. I decided it was a distraction, as well as uncool, to do this, so I announced I'd snip out comments about eBook prices. This got a reaction.)

A few days ago, Robin L., one of the bloggers of the Dear Author site, took exception, via Twitter, to my announcement that I would be deleting kvetching about eBook pricing on my Big Idea posts, that I consider such persistent ebook price kvetching as a symptom of a particular sort of entitlement, and that doing it at the author, who generally speaking has no control of the pricing and who is probably neurotic enough, is pretty mean. Robin L. believes differently, which is of course her right, just not here on my site, in a Big Idea comment thread.

However—and here we leave this issue of reader entitlement behind entirely—during our Twitter conversation on the matter, Robin L. made an assertion which I found frankly a bit silly, namely that publishers don't consider readers to be customers. I consider this a bit silly because, having worked with a number of publishers in a professional capacity for a dozen years now, in both non-fiction and fiction, at no time was it suggested to me, either by words or by how my books were sold, that my publishers *don't* consider readers to be their customers. To be certain, they are not the *only* customers; publishers work directly with retailers, who are often but not always the middlemen in the relationship with publishers and readers, and they also work with libraries and schools. But only a foolish publisher is not aware of and solicitous toward its relationship with the reader, who is, after all the ultimate consumer of the product. Indeed, many publishers, including ones I work with, like Subterranean Press, primarily sell via a direct relationship with readers, with mailing lists and other sales tools.

When I pointed this out, there was some backtracking, with the assertion that the publishers we're really talking about here were "the Big Six"—i.e., the major publishers in New York. Well, okay, but the assertion that these publishers don't have a direct relationship with readers isn't true either, since at least some of these publishers *do* have direct sales right off of their various Web sites.

But even if it *were* true, it only points out a flawed assumption, which is that a direct sales relationship is the only "customer relationship" that counts, which is on its face a really *interesting* assertion. A similar argument could be made about any company whose products are primarily sold through a retail middle man, from soda to jeans, and in each case it would be equally untrue. I wouldn't argue that Coca-Cola doesn't see retailers as important customers, in a manner very much like publishers see bookstores as important customers (and in much the same way, as both Coca-Cola and publishers use their own versions of "co-op" for product placement and the like), but anyone who suggests Coca-Cola isn't intensely aware of their ultimate consumers is being a bit foolish. In the same manner, publishers have their own marketing and publicity branches, whose entire purpose for existence is to address their customers: Retail, for one; libraries and schools, for another; and readers, for a third. In point of fact, publishers—even the big New York kinds (indeed, *especially* the big New York kinds)—spend a lot of time cultivating their relationships with readers to generate interest and enthusiasm for their products.

I said so; Robin L. responded with links to articles she felt bolstered her point, to which I pointed out that I wasn't entirely sure why she seemed to believe that article cites would be persuasive to me over my own personal experience. But, fair enough: Perhaps publishing seventeen books in a dozen years with six different US publishers ranging from Macmillan to NESFA Press and working intimately with each on matters of marketing and publicity—and, for that matter, dealing directly with editors, publishers and publicists for other authors on a nearly daily basis for four years now regarding the Big Idea feature—isn't, in fact, as persuasive as something you read somewhere on the Internet that you feel confirms every bad thing you think about publishers.

So I decided to ask someone who I figure is in a position to know better than I; namely, Patrick Nielsen Hayden, who in addition to being my editor at Tor, is also that publisher's Manager of Science Fiction, which means he spends a lot of time talking to other people in Macmillan about various publishing issues, including reader relations. The question I asked him specifically was: "Based on your own personal experience as an editor and in your involvement with major league publishing over the years, do major publishers see readers as customers? Or is major publishing customer focus solely on retailers?"

His response:

> *I think the observation that New York City trade publishers need to cultivate more and better relationships with their readers, as opposed to merely their retailers, has a lot of truth to it. So much truth, in fact, that for the past ten years or so pretty much everyone in New York City trade publishing has been repeating it, elaborating on it, and being inspired by it to engage in all kinds of initiatives. Whether it's major editors and publishers getting out into the net on blogs or Twitter or whatever, or Macmillan pouring immense amounts of staff time and money into stuff like Tor.com and Heroes & Heartbreakers, or similar projects like Del Rey's Suvudu, a lot of the reason is that everybody knows perfectly well that the world is changing, and nobody has any intention of just sitting around and becoming superannuated.*
>
> *Of course, there are thousands of people in New York trade publishing, and while some of them are brilliant, others are*

timeservers, and some of the brilliant people are brilliant-but-wrong, so lots of effort is wasted and we frequently manage to tie our own shoelaces together. This is how human enterprises work—lots of error. But you know something, the so-called Big Six didn't get to be the Big Six because they're run by nincompoops who pay no attention to the world.

Meanwhile, lots of self-publishers, small publishers, e-publishers, and so forth **also** repeat the observation to one another. For some (far from all!) of them, it seems to be something they tell each other to reinforce their shared belief that big publishers are Doomed Baby Doomed, that the dinosaurs will inevitably become extinct and leave the field to the small mammals, and therefore EVERYBODY WILL FINALLY WANT TO READ MY SELF-PUBLISHED BOOK. Good luck with that.

Another truism you hear all the time in trade publishing is that the genre publishers and imprints are way ahead of the pack when it comes to engaging directly with their readers; that's because so many of them have been going to SF cons and romance gatherings and Comic Con and so forth for years, decades. Some of us even came into trade publishing from SF fandom or the other-genre equivalents of SF fandom. We've been hanging out online, talking with and listening to our readers, since there was an "online," and we have the old Compuserve and Fidonet addresses to prove it. The predecessor of the original Tor Books web page was the Tor Books gopher server. So this is another of those truisms that's a truism because it's, hey, true.

Basically, from where I sit, it looks like trade publishing contains a heck of a lot of smart, savvy people working very hard to roll with a changing world, while in a few corners of the online world there's an odd subfandom of people devoted to the idea that we're all complete morons who will be dying out shortly and good riddance because we have NO CLUE ABOUT THE INTERWEBS FWOAR LOL. Okay then. Maybe it's true. We'll see.

(My prediction? Trade publishers will make some stoopid errors. Trade publishers will have some fabulous successes. A few small *scrappy e-publishers and self-publishers will be wildly successful. Lots will sink without a trace. People will be loudly wrong at one another on the internet. Readers will lay out money for stuff that gets their attention and seems likely to be worth their time.)*

Now, bear in mind I don't expect either my points or Patrick's observations to be at all persuasive to Robin L., roughly for the same reasons that someone who believes in astrology is going to be unconvinced by a planetary astronomer; i.e., what one believes one knows is often more persuasive than what those with direct knowledge and experience might say—because, of course, why *wouldn't* we say that. Our experience is a primary argument against believing what we say. If this is her worldview, then she's welcome to it, although I would recommend against others signing onto it without a little more digging. There's enough nonsense going around online about publishing these days.

Note well that this isn't to excuse publishers from falling down on customer relations or to avoid listening to readers with an open mind. That's something I *highly* encourage them to do, since it's readers who buy the books, read them and (hopefully) love them. Please, publishers, give the readers your ear and make it easy for them to find that ear, since among other things, it'll keep authors from having to deal with kvetches they can do nothing about.

But my own personal experience with publishers is that they are in fact rather very interested in what readers think, and think of them as their customers. I could be wrong. My experience says I'm not.

eBook Sales and Author Incomes and All That Jazz

Sep

23

2015

People are pointing me to this article in the *New York Times* about eBooks sales slipping and print sales stabilizing, and are wondering what I think of it. Well:

To begin, I think it's lovely that print sales and book stores are doing well; it was touch and go there for a while. I'm also not entirely surprised to find that many younger readers—the "digital natives"—like and often prefer physical books. That's certainly been the case with my daughter (who now, as it happens, works at the local bookstore). She's sucked into her phone as much as any person her age, or indeed, as much as most people alive, it seems. And yet, when she reads books, and she reads a lot of them, print is her preferred medium, and was even before the bookstore.

With that said, it's worth noting this bit in the article:

> It is also possible that a growing number of people are still buying and reading e-books, just not from traditional publishers. The declining e-book sales reported by publishers do not account for the millions of readers who have migrated to cheap and plentiful self-published e-books, which often cost less than a dollar.

Indeed, a couple of days before this particular article, my Twitter feed was alive with retweets of data showing that publishers' share of Amazon ebooks sales had decreased while indie sales had increased; since the data had come from a source that is unabashedly pro-indie (and less-than-subtly in my opinion anti-publishing), it also came with rhetoric implying that publishers were doomed, *doomed*, and so on.

So a couple of things here. First, if we are talking overall book sales, I do think we're missing a lot if we're not bringing indie sales into the discussion. There's a hell of a lot going on there and it's one of the most exciting places in publishing right now, "exciting" being used in many senses of the term. But no matter how you slice it, if you're lightly sliding over its existence, you're not accurately describing the current publishing market.

But, second, I don't think declining eBook sales from publishers means they're doomed, *doomed*, either. This is in part because (and this seems to be a point of some confusion) there's more to publishing than maximizing eBook sales numbers in the short term. Publishers, for example, might decide that it's in their long-term interest to stabilize and even grow the print market, and price both their eBooks and print books in a manner that advantages the latter over the former in the short term.

Why would they do that? For a number of reasons, including the fact that Amazon is still 65% of the eBook market in the US, and publishers, as business entities, are appropriately wary of a retailer which a) clearly has monopsonist ambitions and tendencies, b) has been happy to play hardball with publishers to get its way. Investing time in strengthening alternate retail paths makes sense in that case, especially if, as the article suggests, consumers are happy to receive the book in different formats for an advantageous price. If people fundamentally *don't care* if they read something in print or electronic format, as long as they get a price they like, that leaves publishers a lot of room to maneuver.

Which is not to say I think publishers are blind to the potential advantages of the digital space. Note well that publishers have not been idle addressing the digital-only market; numerous publishers now have digital-only (or "digital-first" with publish-on-demand print option) imprints, and several, including Tor, my primary fiction publisher, have started imprints devoted specifically to novellas, a format that is now emerging from a long commercial slumber thanks to digital formats. I think it's entirely possible that publishers have as their long-term strategy imprints and initiatives that primarily address particular media, with some imprints, books and authors primarily digital-facing and some primarily print-facing, depending on where their data tells them money is to be made with each book/author/ imprint/whatever.

The short version of all of the above is: I'm sure publishers are happy about print doing well, and I would be mildly surprised if publishers are too deeply concerned with the short-term dip in digital sales, especially if they are investing in positioning themselves for the long-term. Again I remind everyone that many if not most of these publishers have been around decades and have seen changes in the market as significant as the one we're going through today. They're tenacious bastards, publishing companies are.

While we're on the subject of publishing and writers, people have asked me what I thought about the Author's Guild survey that shows author incomes down substantially from what was reported in a 2009 survey, with full-time authors seeing a 30% decrease from $25k to $17.5K, and part-time authors reporting an even steeper drop. Added to that, a NPR piece noting the relatively meager sales of some of the books nominated for this year's Man Booker prize. Between the both of them, it's enough to make writers a little gloomy.

My first thought about the latter is to note there is not nor ever has there been a strong correlation between "literary excellence" and strong sales, nor when it comes to awards should there necessarily be. The Man Booker is a juried award, if I remember correctly, so awareness through sales isn't much of a factor in terms of what gets onto its long and short lists. So, no, it's not really surprising some of the finalists haven't sold that much prior to the announcement. They'll probably sell better *now*, however.

It's also not a huge surprise that most books don't sell that well. That, at least, is a consistent fact through time. The rise of self/indie publishing is kind of a wash on this, I suspect; it allows you to price a book very cheaply, but it also means the market is swamped and it's harder to stand out. It doesn't matter how low you price your book if no one ever sees it out there, etc.

But with respect to writer incomes dropping via the Author's Guild survey, this is one place where I wish we had better (which is to say more comprehensive and in some way independently verifiable) reporting from indie authors, because I suspect there's a lot of money not being reported out there, not only in terms of direct indie/self-publishing unit sales, but through other avenues like Kickstarters and Patreons, which I anecdotally see adding a non-trivial amount of income to writers' bottom lines. I suspect these are avenues that a lot of writers who are used to particular income paths are either not aware of, or exploiting—or perhaps *can't* exploit because their established audiences are used to paying in them in particular ways. I'd love to see the figures on who crowdfunds, in terms of age; my suspicion is that it skews younger.

Would this money I suspect is going missing substantially move the needle in terms of overall author incomes? I don't know. I suspect it might, but it's possible not as much as some people cheerleading indie/self-publishing would like to admit.

I've noted before that I think in general there are three kinds of authors: Dinosaurs, mammals and cockroaches, where the dinosaurs are authors tied to an existing publishing model and are threatened when it is diminished or goes away, mammals are the authors who rise to success with a new publishing model (but who then risk becoming dinosaurs at a later date), and cockroaches are the authors who survive regardless of era, because they adapt to how the market is, rather than how they want it to be. Right now, I think publishing might be top-heavy with dinosaurs, and we're seeing that reflected in that Author's Guild survey.

What we're missing—or at least what *I* haven't seen—is reliable data showing that the mammals—indie/self-publishing folks, in this case—are doing any better on average. If these writers *are* doing significantly better on average, then that would be huge. It's worth knowing.

How *Lock In* Is the #1 (and #20, and #107) Book in the US

Sep

8

2014

I f you've been following me here and on Twitter this week, then you know I've been delighted that *Lock In* has been doing very well in terms of sales: It hit the *New York Times* Hardcover Fiction best seller list and a few other lists as well. And in doing so, the list shows that the book is seemingly all over the charts.

For example, Bookscan, whose lists note sales at bookstores (well, *some* bookstores—the ones that report to Bookscan) reports *Lock In* as the #1 front list science fiction seller last week. The *New York Times* reports it as the #20 hardcover fiction book. The *USA Today* bestseller list, which I got sent to me today, ranked the book at #107—which seems a far cry from #20 or #1. So what's going on?

The answer is that all these lists report different things. Bookscan, as noted, reports bookstore point of sales, and the list in this case is confined to science fiction books (or even more specifically, books identified as science fiction), and to "front list"—books that are new to the market. Bookscan gets reports from many but not all bookstores, and focuses on print sales. So many sales won't get reported—sales from some indie stores, sales of electronic books and audiobook sales are not part of these reported numbers. The discrepancy is sometimes significant.

The *New York Times*, as I understand it, uses a combination of sales, sampling from specific bookstores and a few particular guidelines for each list it generates to create its rankings. So the Hardcover Fiction list focuses (generally) on new releases in (surprise!) hardcover fiction, not considering electronic or audio sales at all (NYT also has electronic only lists, as well as combined print/electronic lists, plus various fiction and non-fiction lists).

The *USA Today* list doesn't make any distinction between fiction and non-fiction or between older and newer books, or between print and ebook (although I think audio is still excluded); it simply puts them into one big pile and tells the ranking of everything that is selling that purports to be a book. On the *USA Today* list, *Lock In* competes with everything from *50 Shades of Grey* to *To Kill a Mockingbird* to Minecraft strategy guides.

So each of these lists tracks sales, but does it in a different way, using different metrics and lumping books in different piles. As a result, *Lock In* is legitimately the #1 book, and the #20 book, and the #107 book, in all of the United States. The #1 NYT hardcover fiction book last week, *The Long Way Home*, is #5 on the *USA Today* list. The #5 NYT hardcover fiction book (*The Broken Eye* by Brent Weeks—congratulations Brent!) is #26 on the *USA Today* list. And so on.

These variances may lead you to ask which is *really* the most accurate bestseller list, and the answer is: Well, based on what? Bookscan is based on pure sales—but only sales that Bookscan tracks. NYT chops up sales into categories and adds a few twists to the pure sales number, presumably to give a clearer picture of what's really moving among newer books. *USA Today* loads all books into the same pile but also does "analysis" based on sales. Again, each of these lists (and any other list you might name) are working off different numbers, and using different ground rules.

At the end of the day, what the best seller lists do is not exact. What they do, both individually and as a gestalt, is give you some idea of which books are the front of sales and front of mind, from week to week. I'm happy to say that what it means for me, no matter how you slice it, is that *Lock In* did pretty well for itself in its debut week. And that works for me.

KICKSTARTER IS COOL (AND PROBABLY NOT FOR ME)

Jan

11

2014

(Note: While I'm talking about Kickstarter here, I'll note that for me this applies to Patreon and other self-funding options for writers. Added to this is the fact that I now have a long-term contract with Tor Books that basically covers my expenses. This is nice for me, and I recognize I'm in a fortunate position.)

I am not infrequently asked whether or not I'll be running a Kickstarter campaign for some of the things that I want to do creatively, given that so many of my friends have done them and seem to have been reasonably successful at them, and because I think that in a general sense Kickstarters (and their various cognates via Indiegogo and other such funding sites) have been a very cool thing for a lot of creative folks. In many ways it would seem I'd be a prime candidate to do a Kickstarter.

I don't see one in my near future, however, save possibly one in which I have a cameo role at best, and for which I have no responsibility for planning or disbursement (for example, as I did with Paul & Storm, in which I chipped in a couple of extras if certain funding levels were met). The reasons for this have very little to do with the politics of self-funding—and there *are* politics of self-funding, which I find hugely irritating and enervating and kind of boring—and have mostly to do with my own circumstances and personal make-up. In no particular order, they are thus:

1. I'm already under contract for projects for the next couple of years. Which is to say, I'm busy and will continue to be so for a while, thank God.

2. The things I want to do that are not under contract I'm likely to get contracts (or similar business agreements) for. At this moment in time I am a reasonably safe bet for publishers, so many of them are willing to give me money for things, on terms I find largely congenial. This works for me, because:

3. I would prefer not to have to do everything. And most Kickstarters are a commitment to have to do everything. Some people want to have control over every step of the process, or at the very least are willing to put in the work. Good for them. I'm of the "I'd do all of it if I had no other choice, but if I have other choices I'd rather do that" school of thinking. Related to this:

4. Kickstarters are an immense commitment of time and energy, before, during and after. The initial planning, the advertising and marketing of the Kickstarter, the stretch goals and the planning for them, the fulfillment of said stretch goals in addition to the original products, so on and so forth. Jesus, I look at what some of my friends who do Kickstarters oblige themselves to in order to get their funding and *I get tired and want to cry.* Also:

5. I am aware of all the things I don't know about planning/budgeting/creating/marketing a finished product, and also aware that means there are all sorts of pitfalls that I won't see until I flail down into them. Again, some people have a taste for adventure and a willingness to put in the time and effort to learn all this stuff. Good for them. I'd much rather let other people who already have experience do that for me. And you may say here, well, you could hire those people! To which I say, well, yes. That's exactly what I do when I partner with a publisher.

All of which is to say:

6. By and large the advantages of doing a Kickstarter, for me, do not outweigh the disadvantages. The advantages are: People give you money! On your own terms! The disadvantages are:

Then you have to fulfill your promises! On the terms you set! Which may turn out not to be to your actual advantage, unless you are very smart *and* careful *and* lucky. I know myself well enough to know that the sort of person who is all three of those, in the context of a Kickstarter campaign, is unlikely to be me.

Again: The issue here is not the Kickstarter model, which I think is fine and which is perfectly congenial for some people. Some people really like the whole Kickstarter experience, and I think that's fantastic. It's just that *I* look at it and think *Oh God, so much work* and then hope that the world never gets to the point where it's the predominant model for funding creative work, because then I'm just going to sell blood plasma and live beneath an underpass.

So, yeah. I like Kickstarter (and other similar companies) in theory and as a new and vital avenue for works to be funded when they might not otherwise. I'm not sure it's for me—or at least, not right for me without a team of people behind me to do everything I don't want to/am not competent to do.

Fortunately for me, at the moment at least I can already work with teams of competent people willing to do the stuff I don't want to, called "publishers." I'm going to keep working that angle for a while, I think.

NEW WRITERS, EBOOK PUBLISHERS, AND THE POWER TO NEGOTIATE

Mar

10

2013

(Note: Early in 2013 Random House launched a trio of digital-only imprints, whose initial contracts for authors were, to put it bluntly, rapacious: No advances, foisting the cost of marketing/PR on to writers, making it difficult or even impossible to earn out, the whole bit. They were bad enough that the Science Fiction Writers of America, of which I was president at the time, threatened to "delist" Random House as a qualified market for the organization. This and a bunch of very bad press the contracts engendered helped to get Random House to walk back the contracts and offer better ones.

For all that, some people kvetched about me and others writing about these horrible contracts and warning people off them, and this piece is about that.

Incidentally, there was and continues to be arguments about whether advances for authors are entirely necessary; one of the agents at my own literary agent's house offered up a rebuttal. I'm still not convinced—or, more accurately, I wouldn't accept a "no-advance" deal as a standard practice, and don't think others should, either.)

In writing the pieces about Random House and its egregious, non-advance paying eBook imprints and how no writer ever should submit to them, or indeed work with any publisher that does not offer an advance, there are some folks in the comments and elsewhere on the Internet who are saying things along the lines of the following (paraphrased to condense points into a single statement):

That's easy for Scalzi to say because he has power now, but us newer authors have no power to negotiate. And the market is changing and there are lots of good eBook publishers who just happen not to pay an advance.

One word for all of the above: Bullshit.

First, for those you who think the "Hey, let's not pay you an advance but instead you can share in the backend!" model of publishing was first thought up in relation to electronic publishing:

AH HA HA HA HA HAH HA HA HA HA.

No.

This shit's been *around*, my friends. It's been around for *decades*, and writers groups and others who make it their business to warn aspiring authors about scams and pitfalls have been raising flags about it all that time. The idea that that because it's now attached to electronic publishing, that somehow makes it *different* (and, more to the point, *better*) is highly specious, to say the least.

Sprinkling the Internet on a bad business model does not magically make it a good business model. It merely means that the people who are pursuing a bad business model are hoping you are credulous enough to believe that being *electronic* is space-age zoomy and awesome and there is no possible way this brilliant business plan could ever fail. Or even worse, that *they* believe that being electronic means all these things, which means *they* are credulous. Which is not a very good thing to have as the basis of one's business model.

So why are so many eBook-only publishers attempting to run with the "no advances" business model? If I had to guess, I would say because many of these then-erstwhile publishers assumed that publishing electronically had a low financial threshold of entry (not true, if you're serious about it) and they fancied being publishers, so they started their businesses undercapitalized, and are now currently in the process of passing the consequences of that undercapitalization unto the authors they would like to work with. Alternately, as appears to be the case with Random House, they're looking for a way to pass as much of the initial cost of publishing onto the author as possible, and one of the best ways to bring down those initial costs is to avoid paying the author anything up front. Both of these are bad business models, although one is more maliciously so, and both are to be avoided. Just because someone has stupidly or maliciously planned their business, doesn't mean you're obliged to sign a contract with them.

But, these publishers and their defenders may say (and have said), *the publisher takes all the risk in producing a book!* Yeah? Hey, to publishers and their defenders who say that: Fuck you. Fuck you for asserting that the author has shouldered no risk, when she's invested the time, opportunity cost and material outlay required to create a manuscript. Fuck you for asserting the the author sees no risk to her own career from the choices that the publisher imposes on the publishing process that the author has no control of: everything from cover art (which, if horrible and/or out of step with the market, can sink a book) to the size and distribution of the initial print run, to the marketing plan the publisher has for retail.

Fuck you for lightly passing over the risk that the author has if the book fails—that any additional books in the contract might be cancelled or put out with the bare minimum of contractual obligation, that the author might not be able to sell another book to the publisher or other publishers because of a track record of poor sales—and for lightly passing over the fact the publisher mitigates its own risk of the failure of a single book by having an entire portfolio of releases. If one single book fails but the publisher's line holds up generally, then the risk the publisher encounters to its livelihood is minimal. The risk to the author, on the other hand, is substantially greater. Yes, to all of that, "fuck you," is probably the politest thing to say in response.

Tell me *again* how *all* the risk lies with the publisher in producing a book. I want to hear it again. And I expect you can imagine what I would say to that assertion, again.

Any publisher who would assert that the risk of publishing is all on them is one who simply does not understand publishing. I sure as hell wouldn't work with them. Especially one that has the gall to not pay advances and shift production costs to the author by arguing that doing so offers a more equitable apportionment of risk. It's certainly an *advantageous* apportionment of risk—to the publisher. But "advantageous" in this case is almost certainly not the same as "equitable."

On the subject of risk and investment—when a writer gets an advance from a publisher, it's the publisher signaling two things: One, it acknowledges the risk and investment the writer and only the writer *has made to that point* in creating a manuscript that the publisher sees as having commercial potential. Two, it's signalling how much risk and investment that the publisher *is willing to make* in the property.

Both of these are important. As regards the first, why work with people who don't acknowledge that the work you've done has value, even as they are trying to license the product of that work? Two, why work with people who have signaled they have no intention of making a material investment in the work? And if they wish to suggest that they *will* make that material investment—by way of editing, marketing, production, etc—again we come to the question of why everyone else is getting paid *ahead* of the writer.

(And as for "but, but—profit sharing!" my answer is, groovy: The advance is advanced against the expected profits (as opposed to against royalties, which is a separate thing entirely). Rule of thumb: If *anyone* gets paid, the writer gets paid. First. Because, once again: What the writer provides is *why* everyone else gets paid—and the writer has already done the work.)

Now, let's talk about me for a minute. Yes, I am in a position where I have some influence on how my contracts are negotiated, what's in them and what's not, up to and including how much of an advance I get. But here's the thing: Back when I was selling my very first novel? I was *also* in a position to have influence on how my contracts were negotiated, what was in them, up and including the advance.

Why? *Because I had something the publisher wanted.* Namely, the novel in question.

People: Unless the publisher you're talking to is a complete scam operation, devoted only to sucking money from you for "publishing services," then the reason that they are interested in your novel is because someone at the publisher looked at it and said, *hey, this is good. I can make money off of this.* Which means—surprise! Your work has value *to* the publisher. Which means you have leverage *with* the publisher.

Publishers are not grand mystical portals into a realm of fantastic living and eternal happiness. They are companies looking to make a profit so they can continue existing, staffed by people who are looking for manuscripts that will make their companies a profit, so the companies can continue existing and *they* don't have to work at Wal-Mart, stocking shelves. I've met my publisher and editor. They are lovely people and I like them a lot, and they've done pretty well for me. But then, I've done pretty well for *them*, too, and at the end of the day none of us is sporting the majestical look of destiny. We're just people, doing our respective jobs.

So when a publisher comes to you and says "We like your book, can we buy it?" *do not* treat them like they are magnanimously offering you a lifetime boon, which if you refuse will never pass your way again. Treat them like what they are: A company who wants to do business with you regarding one specific project. *Their* job is to try to get that project on the best terms that they can. *Your* job is to sell it on terms that are most advantageous to you.

You can do that even when you're starting out. I did. So have many other debut authors. Because they all had something the publisher wanted: The work.

But you will *not* be able to do that if you go into the negotiation assuming you have no leverage. Forget the *publisher* screwing you— you have screwed *yourself.* And if that's the case you can't blame the publisher for then taking you for every single thing they can. Because, remember, that's their job. They don't even need to be *evil* to do it; they just have to be willing to take every advantage *you let them have.* That's business. This is a business negotiation. They're going to assume you know what you're getting into. That's why they have contracts: So it's all down in black and white and you can't say you didn't know.

So, yeah. Damn *right* I negotiated terms from contract number one. And the fact I did put me in much better stead for the next contract, and the next one and all the ones after that. I had that power then—the same as any new or first time author.

What have we learned today?

1. Not offering advances is not a great new business model, it's a crappy old one;

2. Writers are not responsible for propping up crappy business models;

3. Don't believe anyone who tells you publishers carry all the risk of publication;

4. Even new writers have leverage with publishers;

5. If you don't respect yourself or your work, no one else will either.

Now go out there and sell to a publisher who deserves your work, and make them show just how much they deserve it.

THE PROBLEM WITH 1,000 TRUE FANS

<table>
<tr><td>Mar</td></tr>
<tr><td>12</td></tr>
<tr><td>2008</td></tr>
</table>

(Note: This piece is interesting over the passage of time. On one hand, I think the principal argument here is still correct—namely, it's harder to get and keep "1,000 true fans" than people think. Counterpointing this, however, is the rise of Kickstarter, Patreon and other self-funding schemes which do make it easier for creators to connect with fans and customers, and in most cases don't require a $100 buy-in as assumed here. Basically, this is one piece the times have caught up with, and, I think, have changed some ground assumptions.)

Former *Wired* Editor and current Web thinker Kevin Kelly recently caused the creative sectors of the Web to freak out a bit with his article "1,000 True Fans," in which he posits that what a creative person needs to do in order to have a fiscally comfortable life is not try for millions of fans but rather cultivate a thousand or so "true fans"—people who will spend about a day's worth of income ($100 is the example sum Kelly gives) a year to obtain your stuff. One thousand people spending $100 equals $100,000 for the artist, Kelly suggests, which is a tidy sum for an artistic type, many of whom spend years as ramen connoisseurs as they pursue their craft.

The reason the "1,000 True Fan" formulation sets folks on fire is pretty obvious: It seems like it's a reasonably realistic goal. All but the most deluded of artistic types realize that massive, earth-shaking fame (and the riches that come with it) is extraordinarily rare to achieve, and that along with talent one needs a heaping helping of luck to get there.

But 1,000 people—well, that seems doable on work alone. Plus now creative folks have lower cost and opportunity barriers for production and distribution, the Internet makes it easy to reach infinitely more folks, and so on and so forth. 1,000 people is a high school worth of people. It seems *reasonable* that you could be famous to a high school's worth of people, especially when those thousand people are spread out among the 300 million people in the US/1 billion people in the world who have Internet access.

Speaking as someone who is arguably at a 1KTF level of notoriety, I certainly think it's *possible* to gather a cabal of personal fandom to you and then ride them to a comfortably middle-class living. That said, it's not what I do, and I don't think it's as easy a task as some folks seem to be hoping it will be, either in the acquisition of or the maintenance of that trusty band of true believers. Nor do I think the reward will be what one expects.

Why not? Well, I'm glad you asked.

1. Gathering a thousand true fans is harder than it looks. Let's say for the sake of argument that I am indeed at the 1KTF level of fame, where I could get a thousand people to shell out $100 each, once a year. How did I reach this level?

* I built a daily audience of 30k–40k on this site—an audience that accreted here over the course of a decade (i.e., not quickly);

* I became a strong-selling author ("Strong selling" = six figure total units sold in 2007) in a literary genre well-known for its fandom.

Which is to say that before I could lay an arguable claim to having 1,000 "true fans," I needed to create an overall audience of at least tens of thousands of readers/fans. The conversion rate of reader/casual fan for me would seem to be in the single digit percentages at best. While other fandom-accruing artists may be more efficient in their conversion rate than I am, at the end of the day I think you need to have *already* generated a large audience in order to sift out the true fans therein. In other words: You already need to be at least a *little bit* famous.

And of course, there's the rub, since becoming even just a little bit famous takes some doing—in my case, my own meager ration of fame took ten years of blathering here and then another few years concurrently selling novels. Now, perhaps it's possible to do it another way—to sort of handcraft a "true fan" audience without first engaging a larger, less-committed audience—but off the top of my head I can't think of an artist who's really done it that way. Kevin Kelly sort of suggests it's not that hard: why, all you have to do is add just one fan a day! But it's not adding a fan, it's adding someone every day who is willing to give you $100. Which is a different thing altogether. Look: *I'm* not adding that sort of fan every day, and I've got a ten-year head start on you.

2. The available universe of "true fans" is not the entire US (or the entire Internet), but the subset of those who are willing/able to spend a significant sum of money on a single creative person. Ask yourself: Who among all the artists *you* enjoy/admire have you spent more than $100 on in the last year? I have a lot of people whose work I admire, and that I will happily buy. But in the last several years, the only time I've shelled out more than $100 for someone's creative output in a single year was when I drove a couple hundred miles and spotted a friend a ticket to come see the Crowded House show with me. Because it was their first time touring in a *dozen* years. I'm not spending $100 on Crowded House again any time soon. I also spent $100 on a Bob Eggleton sketch a little more than a year ago, but that was because the sketch was based on my wife, not because I'm a Bob Eggleton superfan (although, to be clear, I think he's great). And really, that's it—and in both cases there were unusual circumstances.

(Oh, wait. I *did* spend a metric shitload of money on a Donato Giancola original painting about three years ago—but that was because it was the cover artwork for my very first published novel. Again, *extraordinary* circumstances.)

There *are* people who will pay $100 or more for stuff—I know because people have bought lettered editions of books of mine that go for $250. I thank them from the bottom of my heart and hope they live long and fruitful lives. Bless them all their days. But it's not for nothing that really expensive lettered editions of my books come in *very small* quantities. That's because the universe of people willing to shell out *that* sum for my work is genuinely constrained.

Lots and lots of people will spend $20 a year to be someone's fan. A *much* smaller number will spend $100. An interesting question is whether there are enough of *those* people to go around. Which brings up another point:

3. Artists are likely competing for "true fans." Let's posit
that someone is willing to spend $100 a year on their favorite artist. How many of them are going to be willing to spend that sum on two different artists? On three? The further out you go on that, the smaller the numbers are likely to get.

And what this means is that artists will likely compete for these "true fans." As a science fiction writer, I share the same pool of "true fans" as, oh, let's say, Charles Stross and Neal Stephenson. Is someone going to be enough of a "true fan" to give us each $100 a year? Knowing the general financial disposition of SF fandom, I sort of doubt it. If any of us gets $100, it'll likely be one of us, and those others will be lucky to get a common book sale. Personally, I'd prefer we each get a book sale and then the fan has $40 left over for two more hardcovers from other writers, but then, I'm not particularly mercenary (and I'm a fan of both Charlie and Stephenson).

Additional point to make here: Charlie and Neal Stephenson and I are all much more likely to be choices for a "true fan" commitment than someone just starting out, because we all have track records that indicate some notable level of success: Award nominations, sales, etc. Once the "true fans" run the gauntlet of the artists they already *know* they like, there are likely substantially fewer to spread their largess amongst the previously untried.

4. "True Fans" may not stay true fans. Just because you've
managed to convince someone to shell out $100 to you in one year, doesn't mean they'll do it again next year. Your output might slip and they could decide to put their money somewhere else. Something you create might not appeal to them, and they choose not to renew their

"true fandom." Their incomes might drop. Maybe they have kids. Maybe they start playing more Xbox. Who knows. The point is, if you consider "True Fans" in a business sense, you'll have to expect a substantial amount of drop-off from year to year, and you'll have acquire more "true fans" to make up for those you lost. You have fun with that.

Finally, a financial note:

5. Just because a "true fan" spends $100 on you doesn't mean you get $100.

Remember those really excellent folks who spent $250 to buy a lettered limited edition of one of my books? Well, most of that money goes somewhere else other than my pocket—mostly to the publisher, who, to be fair, did have to pay to produce the book (I'm okay with this, incidentally). The kid who spends $100 on a concert and a t-shirt is giving most of her money to people other than the band she came to see, even when the band gets a cut of t-shirt sales. And so on. Short of 1,000 fans actually sending the artist $100 free and clear (and over and above whatever output of the artist they may purchase), the chances of an artist *grossing* $100,000 off of 1000 fans is pretty slim.

Now, having said that, there are lots of examples of artists saying to fans "help fund my next project," and then having fans pitch in a certain amount—basically, acting as commissioning agents for a work. I could see 1,000 fans pitching in $100 for something like that and then the artist using that money to create the work (provided, per point one, you have a large enough audience that you can sift through them to get these folks). But this isn't what Kevin Kelly's talking about when he's talking about that $100,000; he's clearly at least initially talking about that hundred grand as *income*: "If you have 1,000 fans that sums up to $100,000 per year, which minus some modest expenses, is a living for most folks," says the article.

But this formulation doesn't square. Even if an artist cuts out the middleman and sells everything direct, there's still going to be a huge difference between net and gross. Let's say that I write a book and publish it through Lulu.com. Lulu charges a certain amount for each book printed (the *Zoe's Tale* copies I made for myself there were $16 or so) and then charges for handling fulfillment (i.e., shipping and handling). Let's say I sell each copy for $20, minus postal charges. I'll only get $4 of the $20 the fan has paid for the work. I could possibly print them cheaper by not doing a publish on demand option, but I'd still have to pay a printer, pay for shipping materials, and (if I don't have a lot of space in the basement for dozens of cartons of books) pay for storage.

I'm using books as examples, but this problem crops up however an artist provides tangible goods or when there is some sort of production and/or distribution cost. No matter how you slice it, you're not getting $100,000 from your "true fans" unless they're giving you money with no expectation of recompense—which is not a great way to guarantee continued support.

Again: it's not impossible to get 1,000 "true fans." It can be done. The problem is that Kevin Kelly, in his enthusiasm, wants to make it seem that getting 1,000 people to give you $100 is no great trick. What I am telling you is that it actually *is*—it's a pretty damn *neat* trick, in point of fact. Even if you manage it, the financial reward is not likely to be anything close to what you had hoped for, nor will it likely be as permanent as Kelly seems to imply.

In other words: "1,000 true fans" is no real short cut to making a living off of your creative work. If you think it is, you're likely to be disappointed. And well short of 1,000 true fans.

A SMALL MEDITATION ON ART, COMMERCE AND IMPERMANENCE

Jan

30

2012

I'm going to touch on something that I've discussed briefly before but which I think is worth reheating into its own post. Here are the best-selling books in the US from 1912, which is (for those of you for whom math is not a strong suit) 100 years ago.

1. *The Harvester* by Gene Stratton-Porter
2. *The Street Called Straight* by Basil King
3. *Their Yesterdays* by Harold Bell Wright
4. *The Melting of Molly* by Maria Thompson Davies
5. *A Hoosier Chronicle* by Meredith Nicholson
6. *The Winning of Barbara Worth* by Harold Bell Wright
7. *The Just and the Unjust* by Vaughan Kester
8. *The Net* by Rex Beach
9. *Tante* by Anne Douglas Sedgwick
10. *Fran* by J. Breckenridge Ellis

Questions: How many of these have you read? How many of the author names do you recognize? How influential have these books been to modern literature, or at the very least, the literature you choose to read? Do you think these authors believed that their works would, in some way, survive them? I think it's fair to say that outside of a small group of academic specialists or enthusiasts, these books and their authors don't have much currency.

This isn't a slight on the authors or their works, mind you. If you look up some of these authors, they're pretty interesting. Gene Stratton-Porter was an early conservationist and owned her own movie studio. Meredith Nicholson was a US diplomat to several countries in South America and central America. Howard Bell Wright was reportedly the first author to make more than a million dollars writing fiction, and this was back in 1912, when a million was worth more than $22 million today. I don't doubt at least some of these books were well-regarded as art. And I would imagine, author egos being what they are, that at least a couple of them imagined that we would be talking about their works today, a hundred years later, as influences if nothing else.

We're not. Now, I imagine there's at least a couple people out there shaking their fists at me, wondering how I could not see Stratton-Porter (or whomever) as a towering figure in American literature. As noted above, I cede there is possibly academic or specialized interest. I'm talking about everyone else. I feel pretty confident of my basic knowledge of early 20th century literature, if nothing else than through my interest in HL Mencken, who was one of the preëminent literature critics of the day. If I'm coming up blank on these names and books, I feel reasonably confident in suggesting most readers these days—even the well-read ones—will do similarly.

If you're a writer, this might depress you. If the best-selling books of 1912 are largely forgotten, what chance do *your* books have in 2012, especially if they don't scale the heights of sales these books have? Surprise! Probably little. I mean, it's certainly possible they will survive: Neither Theodore Dreiser nor Sherwood Anderson got near the year-end bestseller lists between 1910 and 1919, but they are still taught and discussed, and in their way influence literature today. But, yeah. Don't count on it.

And that's fine. Relieve yourself of the illusion that you're writing for the ages. The ages will decide who is doing that on their own; you don't get a vote. I understand the temptation is to try to write something that will speak to the generations, but, look, in 1912 they hadn't even yet invented pre-sliced bread. If you aim for being relevant to the future, you're probably going to fail because you literally cannot imagine it, even if you write science fiction.

Forget even sliced bread; you can't imagine the values or interests or views on the world that people might have a century from now. Human nature as defined by biology doesn't change much over decades or centuries but the culture sure does, and it's a moving target in any event; there's no end point in attitudes and opinions. If I tried to explain a woman's place in 1912 United States to my daughter, she would *explode with outrage*. If a writer in 1912 tried to write specifically to my daughter (or anyone's daughter) 100 years hence, the disconnect would be impressive. If I tried to write for a thirteen-year-old girl in 2112, the same thing would happen.

If you *must* aim for relevance, try for being relevant *now*; it's a context you understand. We can still read (and do read) Shakespeare and Cervantes and Dickinson, and I think it's worth noting Shakespeare was busy trying to pack in the groundlings *today*, Cervantes was writing in no small part to criticize a then-currently popular form of fiction, and Dickinson was barely even publishing at all, i.e., not really caring about future readers. In other words, they were focused on their *now*. It's not a bad focus for anyone.

Will your work survive? Probably not, but so what? You won't survive, either. 100 years from now you're *very* likely to be dead. Even if your work survives, it won't do *you* much good. In the meantime that still leaves lots of people *today* to potentially read your stuff, argue about it, be inspired by it (or react against it) and generally make a lot of noise about it. You might even make a living at it, which is a bonus. Focus on those people today, and on today's times. Enjoy it all now. Enjoy it while it lasts. Then when it's over, you can say you had fun at the time.

THE STATE OF A GENRE TITLE, 2013

(Note: I did a similar piece to this in 2015, for my book Lock In. *But inasmuch as I didn't want two pieces here with the same theme and the points here stand, and it has a follow-up piece I wanted in the collection, this is the one I'm keeping in the collection.)*

Yesterday *Redshirts*, my most recent novel prior to *The Human Division*, was made available in trade paperback format, which formally ended its hardcover format era. There are still hardcover editions out there, but Tor isn't printing any more of them; from here on out its print presence will be in trade paperback. Aside from switching formats, this offers an interesting point in time to take a look at the *Redshirts* sales numbers and see what, if anything, they mean for me, and what, if anything, it means for the genre of science fiction in a general sense.

So, below, please find the North American sales numbers for *Redshirts*, dating from June 5, 2012 (the day of release) to January 14, 2013 (the last day of the hardcover run).

Hardcover: 26,604

eBook: 35,667

Audio: 17,008

For those who don't want to pull out your calculators, the sales total across every format—hardcover, eBook and audiobook, was 79,279.

Thoughts:

1. These are healthy sales, and importantly they are healthy and reasonably balanced across the formats the book was available in. This is an important thing because while people like to talk about eBooks being the future, or audiobooks increasing in popularity, the fact of the matter is that print sales continue to be important, and a solid author presence in physical book stores also continues to be important. For me to lose any of these formats—or to discount their importance—would represent a substantial loss of sales and income. I expect each of these formats to continue to be important to my overall sales for some time to come, and intend to make sure I'm adequately supported in each.

2. This sales profile also indicates to me that choosing to work with established publishers—in this case Tor (for print and eBooks) and Audible (for audiobooks)—is a smart decision for me. There are arguments made for self-publishing, and many people will make them, but at this point, for the majority of self-published authors, self-publishing primarily gains you access to eBook sales. Print sales are difficult (because it is difficult to place books into bookstores, particularly chains, on a non-returnable basis), and by and large self-pubbed audiobooks are still an emerging market. Working with established publishers gets my work into as many sales channels as possible. Aside from everything else they do—including editing, design, artwork, marketing and advertising (hey, did you see me on tour? Or see those *Redshirt* ads in Times Square?)—the market access these established publishers provide is reason enough to keep working with them.

3. The sales profile of *Redshirts* in its hardcover format run is vastly different than the sales profile of *Old Man's War*, released eight years ago this month. *Old Man's War* sales for its first year were totally supplied by hardcover sales, because neither the eBook version nor the audio version was available until years later, and both the eBook market and (to a lesser extent) the audiobook market were not as fully developed as they are today. It would be specious of me to make too many direct comparisons between my debut novel and my eighth, because my personal circumstances have changed significantly in the time between their publications. But a debut author today would still be very unlikely to have her book presented only in print format.

4. My sales profile here is nicely diversified, but it's also clear that the largest chunk of my sales are in eBook. I attribute this primarily to two factors: One, my personal presence and history online, which presents me as an "online native," with a core fanbase of similarly tech-savvy readers; Two, science fiction as a genre tends to have a tech-friendly readership, which is likely to have adopted electronic readers early. A third factor is that eBooks tend to be priced more cheaply than hardcovers, which is not insignificant. That said, the healthy sales of the *Redshirts* eBook at the $11.99 price point suggests that readers are willing to spend at that level, which argues for publishers to continue at least initially to peg their eBook prices to their hardcover prices, lowering them as the print format shifts.

(I would note, incidentally, that my eBook sales profile doesn't come as a surprise either to me or Tor; we've been watching these sales for a while now, and it's one of the reasons that we are initially sending *The Human Division* out in weekly eBook episodes. But also note that we are very quickly following up to serve the print market with the compiled novel—because print is important *now* and will continue to be in the future.)

5. My audiobook sales I attribute to a number of factors: One, healthy sales of previous audiobook titles; Two, an excellent and marketable narrator (Wil Wheaton) who has his own significant fanbase; Three, a strong marketing push by Audible for me and the book. It's clear to me that audio is not just an aside to my print and eBook versions but a core aspect of my sales profile, which needs to be considered and tended to.

6. My own guess, based on watching my sales profile over the years, is that print, eBook and audiobook do not inherently cannibalize each others' sales—it seems to me that for each there is a class of reader that is "native" to each—that is, there is a group of readers who strongly prefers print over eBook or audio, another group who prefers eBook strongly to the other formats, and a third group (correlated, I imagine, with people who have long commutes) who strongly prefer audiobook. I don't think I lose a print sale by selling in eBook, or an eBook sale by selling in audio—rather, that selling in each of these formats is allowing me to expand my overall audience. Once again, this is an argument for remaining actively involved in all of the formats rather than throwing one (or more) overboard and putting all my chips on a single format.

7. This is a bit of inside pool but it's a significant point and it matters: The fact that the absolute majority of my *Redshirts* sales came in formats other than hardcover means that the large majority of my sales were not tracked by Bookscan, the service offered by Nielsen that tracks book sales primarily at various brick-and-mortar stores. Bookscan tracked just under two-thirds of my hardcover sales, which is par for the service (a number of independent bookstores don't report to the service, and I sell reasonably strongly in those stores). But overall it tracked just 21% of *Redshirts'* total sales, missing almost all the electronic and audiobook sales.

The reason this is significant is that Bookscan vastly underreports my sales record as an author—and yet Bookscan is the primary point of reference for sales for publishers and booksellers. I'm not in the market for a new publisher at the moment, but if I were, Bookscan's report of my sales wouldn't be doing me any favors. It also doesn't do me favors with booksellers today when it comes to them making decisions about which books to stock. If bookstores look at numbers that don't even accurately estimate how I sell *in* bookstores—much less my overall sales (which are indicative of a larger, overall sales potential), then my job selling to them gets tougher.

While my total sales profile is in many ways idiosyncratic to me, I suspect that science fiction, as a genre, is likely finding its sales underreported by Bookscan in a general sense, primarily because of lack of information about electronic sales. To be clear, as I understand it this is not solely the fault of Nielsen/Bookscan, as it's difficult to report electronic sales if certain significant retailers are not exactly forthcoming with the data (and this is a whole other level of bad, because it makes it even tougher for authors to get an accurate idea of their sales—but I'll address that some other time). But it does suggest that if one is looking at science fiction sales only through the lens of Bookscan, the image one is getting is distorted indeed.

8. For those who are curious, I gross roughly the same for each format (I believe that I gross more from audiobook for each individual sale because the unit price is higher but I would have to dig out a contract to check). So from a financial point of view it's all the same to me whether you prefer hardcover or eBook or audio. Get the format you prefer. One nice thing for me on the royalty side of things is that the book went into the black in the first week of sales—this was a side effect of using *Redshirts* to cash out a long-unfulfilled contract for a different book I never wrote (on account of someone else publishing a book with almost exactly the same idea first). It was nice to have the book earn out that early.

9. On the personal side of things, I have a number of takeaway points from the sales of *Redshirts* during its hardcover run, of which I will now highlight two. The first is that I think I've successfully posted a relevant data point against a longstanding shibboleth that—aside from *The Hitchhikers Guide to the Galaxy*—humorous science fiction won't sell well. Clearly, it sells just fine, or at least *can*. I like this because I have some more humorous ideas I want to turn into novels.

The second is that my basic philosophy of writing accessible science fiction, stuff you can follow even if you're not a dyed-in-the-wool literary science fiction fan, is one that continues to work out pretty well for me. *Redshirts* is obviously designed to tickle the pleasure centers of geeks, but it was also designed to bring in the people who consume geek culture without identifying as geeks themselves—the same people who go see science fiction films in the theaters or watch *Big Bang Theory* at home or play *Mass Effect* or *Bioshock*, but don't carry that geek enjoyment into other aspects of their lives. I'm happy to make the argument to these folks that they can enjoy science fiction books as much as they enjoy other forms of science fiction entertainment. It's working so far.

10. Science fiction books often sell more in paperback. I won't mind if that's true here, too.

The eBook Path to Riches: Possibly Steeper Than Assumed

Jan

23

2013

comment in my "The State of a Genre Title" post reads:

Wow, if you would've published that book yourself, you would've made over $300K from the ebook alone.

Actually, probably I would not have. And here's why.

The poster of the comment is, I assume, taking his number from the idea that I would earn a 70% royalty from my self-published eBook version of *Redshirts*. In the timeframe noted in the entry, I sold 35,667 eBook versions at $11.99. And quick math shows that 70% of that gross is $299,353. Which is just under rather than just over $300k, but close enough. But:

1. Assuming that one is distributing through Amazon (the largest retailer of eBooks worldwide at the moment), one gets the 70% royalty rate from the company only if one agrees to certain things, like an agreement to price the eBook within in specific price band, the top price of which is $9.99. So already the maximum gross for that number of sales drops, from $299k to just under $250,000. Still not bad, but also not $300,000. At the 70% royalty, Amazon also charges a download fee against royalties, to the tune of 15 cents per megabyte download. *Redshirts* is 449kb (just under half a MB), so that's $2,407 shaved right off the top. That's 1% of my gross, but, hey, $2,400 pays a lot of bills. There are other details that can also drive down gross here, but you get the idea.

2. If I don't agree to Amazon's demands for the 70% royalty tier, then I drop to the 35% royalty tier. The good news here is that (on Amazon, anyway) I can now price the book above $9.99, so let's bring that sale price back up to $11.99. At that rate, a 35% royalty nets me $149,676. Again, totally not chicken feed, and well done me. But it's also less than half the $300,000 I was told I would get, and that's not trivial in the slightest.

3. All of this assumes, of course, that I could, on my own, shift 35,667 eBooks in the timeframe discussed. I would like to think I could, because we'd all like to think that. But it's worth noting that some non-trivial fraction of those sales happened in part because of large chunk of marketing and advertising provided me by my publishers (Tor and Audible for the audiobook), and that some chunk of those sales happened because of the incidental benefits accrued by being traditionally published. Hitting the *New York Times* hardcover bestseller list (which happened without the eBook sales at all, by definition) led to profiles and interviews with the *Times* and NPR and other mainstream outlets. Those wouldn't have happened with eBook only. I had *Redshirts* advertised everywhere from *Locus* to *The New Yorker*—again, not something I could have accomplished on my own.

Yes, I am a well-known writer with a large footprint online, and that doesn't hurt. But simply being well-known does not automatically equate to massive book sales. It's pretty obvious I think well of myself, but ego aside I am skeptical that I would have sold 35k worth of books at an $11.99 price point on my own.

4. This leads to the obvious question of whether I would sell more if I chose to sell at a lower price point; say, oh, $4.99. The answer here is of course it's possible, although it's not guaranteed. But to reach the vaunted $300k gross at that price point, I would need to sell roughly 87,500 copies, if I was using the 70% royalty, and obviously about twice that for the 35% royalty. That's a lot of books to sell with only myself for marketing muscle. And obviously, the lower I price the book, the less I gross per sale and the more I have to sell to get to the goal. And, again, clearly, if I didn't sell a larger number of books, my takehome would be commensurately lower.

5. Yes, but, what about [insert favorite eBook success story here], who made tons of money without all that, and so on, etc? This is where I remind people of the fact that exceptional cases are not a great place to argue from. I know that directly since I've been lucky enough to be an exceptional case, and I cringe every time someone points to me and says, more or less, "*There's* my argument." Exceptional cases are, by definition, rare and not representative.

6. And beyond all of that, if I published on my own I would have to do all the work aside from writing, or (because I'm lazy and in some areas not competent) hire people to do it for me, so what I publish looks professional and not like a crap. That's money I'd need to put out up front on the hope of getting those hundreds of thousands of dollars in ebook sales. I'm okay with someone paying me to do all the work.

So could I have made $300,000 if I had self-published *Redshirts* as an eBook? Well, it's *possible* I could have. But it seems to me *very unlikely*. And regardless if I had made that money, it would have required much more time and effort from me than I would have wanted to exchange. And at the end of the day, the way I did publish is going to do just fine for me. So I am comfortable with the publishing choices I made, and am *very happy* and genuinely grateful I have the opportunity to make those choices at all.

Twitter Thoughts, April 2014

Apr
2
2014

see a lot of people obsessing about Twitter these days, with particular emphasis on who one should follow, or not follow, and why. Occasionally these conversations touch on me, sometimes as a positive example, and sometimes not (such as the random person purporting to be a writer attempting to lecture me on not following everyone who follows me—he's been blocked, because, really, fuck *off*, dude). So I thought it might be useful to offer up a few thoughts on how I use Twitter these days, and why.

Obvious note: This is what works for me, and may not work for you, etc, blah blah blah. As a general rule, please note that anyone who tells you that you are doing Twitter wrong is probably an asshole who you can ignore (exception: When you use Twitter specifically to troll and attack people. It is almost always you who are the asshole then, and you should probably fall down some stairs).

The salient rule for Twitter and any other social media is: Are you using it in a way that you enjoy and makes you happy? If the answer is "yes," then keep doing it that way.

Now, then:

I use Twitter largely for three purposes, and they are, in roughly descending order of importance: to keep up with friends, to blather in short form about topics which interest and/or amuse me, and to inform both fans and overly-committed haters what I am up to, careerwise.

Although I use Twitter to keep up with friends, I am well aware that the vast majority of people who follow me are people who I *don't* know, and who follow me because they are fans/interested in my work/ decided I was amusing on Twitter—in other words, that for the majority of people who follow me, I am *entertainment*, to a greater or lesser degree (my friends may also be entertained by me, but that's secondary).

This does have some bearing on my Twitter presence, and is also of value to me as someone who is in fact a professional entertainer of the writing sort. My Twitter presence is largely a public-oriented performance; save when I am talking to a friend through a direct message, I am always aware there is an audience for my tweets, regardless of who I am speaking to and what I am saying. I suspect many of the people with whom I regularly chat on Twitter are also aware of this "public performance" aspect.

Does this make our Twitter chatting "inauthentic"? I don't think so; it merely means we're aware we're in public and that when we're having a conversation on Twitter, that people are listening in over our shoulders—and will feel free to comment or repeat what we've said to others.

As a result, when I am on Twitter, I do what I do on the blog, which is to be "personable but not personal"—I have a voice that is familiar and friendly, and will share stuff I deem to be amusing or pertinent, but I will rarely if ever share anything from the sphere of topics I deem to be too personal. I don't share everything, and have no interest in sharing everything—not everything needs to be shared to or known by people who I don't, in fact, have any relationship other than that I exist as entertainment for them.

For all that I am aware of the public nature of my Twitter feed, and that for the large percentage of my followers I exist as entertainment, I don't generally go out of my way to strategize the commercial application of my Twitter feed as a writer, i.e., how to convert every single follower into a paying customer of my books or whatever. The reasons for this are simple. One, that sort of thing bores the shit out of me. I have things I want to do with my life, but obsessing whether my Twitter feed is selling my work is not really one of them. Two, overthinking that sort of thing makes one's Twitter feed boring, because you're not doing it to enjoy it, you're doing it to manipulate people. Three, I think a lot of the people who *do* spend too much of their time worrying about how their Twitter feed is working for them give off an unpleasant, metallic whiff of desperation, and why would I want to be or do that?

This is why the jerk who tried to upbraid me for not following everyone who follows me found his way into my block queue: What he was saying was YOU ARE NOT OPTIMIZING YOUR TWITTER FEED TO MAKE EVERYONE ON IT MARGINALLY FEEL MORE SPECIAL AND THUS MORE LIKELY TO BUY YOUR THINGS HOW DARE YOU SIR. And well, you know. That's not how I use Twitter, nor is it how I want to use Twitter. My career has gotten along fine *without* having HOW WILL THIS MAKE YOU WANT TO BUY ALL MY THINGS as the guiding principle for every single human interaction I have, online or off. Seeing every other human being as a mark is no way to go through life. It's tiring, it's insulting, and it's no fun on either side of that exchange.

In terms of who I follow on Twitter, it susses out something like this: People I know in the real world as friends or colleagues (I'd say about 90% of my follow list), friends of friends who I find to be particularly clever, who I (happily) then often later get to know in real life (about 8% or so), and the occasional person who I don't know but of whom I am a fan of their work (the remainder).

Note that the vast majority of people I follow are people I actually know. That's a personal choice; I'm interested in the goings-on of people who are friends. One reason for that is that my friends tend to be far-flung—or more accurately, as I live in rural Ohio, I am far flung from them. Another reason is that my friends are entertaining and I like playing with them on Twitter. A third reason is that while I have my own (small) list of people I follow because I am a fan, at the end of the day my primary interest is the people I know and care about because of my personal history with them.

(Now, as it happens, because of who I am and the circles in which I run, some of the people I am friends with happen to be notable to one degree or another, particularly in geek fields. However, I don't follow them on Twitter because they are notable. I follow them because they are my friends. It's a difference which may mean little, looking in from the outside, but means a fair bit from the inside.)

It's theoretically *possible* for me to follow everyone who follows me, but then I would have a Twitter feed that that would be useless for what I want it to do, which is to keep me up to date with my friends and what they are doing. There are 319 people on my follow list now, and I have a hard time keeping up with all of them as it is. Moreover, and this sounds a little mean, but come on, we're grownups here, just because someone is interested in following me on Twitter doesn't mean I'll be interested in following them. Because I usually don't *know* them, nor am I a fan of them or their work. It doesn't mean they aren't wonderful, interesting people with cool lives, etc. But I don't *know* them, see. And that matters to me for my follow list.

This doesn't mean I don't interact with the people who follow me, or who directly address me on Twitter. I do a lot of both as people either respond to what I've written or want to ask me something. It's fun and part of Twitter's conversational style. But I think that's to the point, here—you *don't* need to follow someone to talk to them on Twitter. You just ping a comment to their handle. Follow who you want to; don't follow the people you don't. Simple enough.

On the flip side of following, there are the people I block or mute ("mute" being a function where they are not barred from following you or even responding to you, but you don't see what they're saying). I block real people rarely (as opposed to spambots, which I block all the time), but I *do* block, because some people are real shitheads and I don't mind letting them know I think so.

I mostly mute people, because it's quieter (people don't know that they're being muted) and because it's flexible—the Twitter client I use, Janetter, allows you to mute people for times ranging from 30 minutes to forever. That's useful when I post something contentious and someone follows up with something I find dumb; I (usually) put them in the timeout box for a day rather than snark at them, and the next time they comment to me, I've forgotten they annoyed me, which benefits both of us. There are some people I've permanently muted; I don't miss them.

Muting is useful not only for people who annoy me, but for people I genuinely like but who are on a momentary hobby horse I don't want cluttering up my follow feed. When that happens I'll mute them for an hour or three while they rant and then later they are back to their usual selves. Or when two friends are being contentious to each other, I'll sometimes mute them both for an hour, because watching my friends argue all over my Twitter feed is awkward. Muting them while they argue is the Twitter equivalent of seeing friends argue at a party and deciding to go into the next room and chat with other people, who are currently *not* arguing.

(Do people who follow me mute *me*? Oh, probably. I can be annoying on Twitter from time to time.)

As much time as I spend on Twitter, there's no way for me to respond to everything, either on my Twitter feed or when people tweet at me. I can't imagine how my friends who have substantially more followers than I manage it.

Twitter is a fast-moving stream, basically. I enjoy it—a lot—but I also know there's only so much I can do with it. So I do with it what I enjoy, and which makes me happy. You should do the same, however that is for you. Again: Simple enough.

THE VIEW FROM THE TOP OF AMAZON'S HEAP

Feb

12

2017

(Note: As of this moment—1:50 p.m., June 20, 2017—my Amazon Author Ranking is #469, and #66 in Science Fiction and Fantasy. Fame is fleeting.)

Yesterday nine of my novels were on sale for $2.99 in ebook format, across a bunch of different retailers, but most prominently on Amazon, because, well, Amazon. Amazon has a number of different ways to make authors feel competitive and neurotic, one of which is its "Amazon Author Rank," which tells you where you fit in the grand hierarchy of authors on Amazon, based (to some extent) on sales and/or downloads via Amazon's subscription reading service. And yesterday, I got to the top of it—#1 in the category of science fiction and fantasy, and was #4 overall, behind JK Rowling and two dudes who co-write business books. Yes, I was (and am still! At this writing!) among the elite of the elite in the Amazon Author Ranks, surveying my realm *as unto a god.*

And now, thoughts!

1. To begin, it won't last. The thing that got me into the upper echelons of the Amazon rankings was an unusual sale of a large number of my books for what is (for me) a very low price point, and that sale is meant to be of a short duration, i.e., one day. When that price point goes away, my Amazon sales will go back to their usual level, and my Amazon Author Rank will decline to its usual ranking, which is— well, it kind of bounces around a bit, because honestly that's what most

Amazon Author Rankings *do*. I'm often somewhere in the top 100 for science fiction, but I'm often somewhere *not* in the top 100, either.

2. Why? Got me, and this is the point I often make to people about Amazon Author Rankings (and other various rankings on the site): They're super opaque. I mean, in this case, there's a direct correlation between my $2.99 sale and the boost in my author ranking. But it's also the case that *sales* are not the only criterion—a large number of top Amazon authors are ones who sign their books up for Amazon's subscription service, for which they don't make sales, but make money based on however Amazon decides to track engagement with the book via Kindle. How much is *that* criterion weighted versus sales? I don't know, nor, I suspect, does anyone outside Amazon, nor do we know what other criteria go into the rankings.

3. This opacity works for Amazon because it keeps authors engaged, watching their Amazon Author Rankings go up and down, and getting little spikes or little stabs as their rankings bounce around. I mean, hell, *I* think it's neat to have a high ranking, and I know it's basically nonsense! But I do think it's important for authors to remember not to get too invested in the rankings because **a)** if you don't know how it works, you don't know why you rank as you do, at any particular time, **b)** it's foolish to be invested in a ranking whose mechanism is unknown to you, **c)** outside of Amazon, the ranking has no relevance.

4. Which is also a point I think people forget about: Amazon, despite its dominant position in the bookselling industry (particularly in eBook), is not the entire market. Regardless of my day-to-day Amazon ranking, I generally sell pretty well and pretty steadily in book stores and other eBook retailers, and in audio and in translation, none of which is tracked by Amazon for its rankings. Most authors who are not wholly committed to Amazon via its subscription service likewise have outside sales and attention channels. It's in Amazon's interest to keep authors' gaze on it, and especially to have authors sign on to its subscription service, with a bump in Amazon Author ranking a potential and implicit part of that deal.

5. This doesn't make Amazon *malign*, incidentally. Amazon's gonna Amazon. And in a mild defense of Amazon, one reason that

Amazon's rankings, of authors and books, weighs so heavily on the psyches (and neuroses) of authors is that author-related data in publishing is often either equally opaque (in the case of publishers) or effectively non-existent (in the case of self-publishing, which would rely on thousands of authors accurately self-reporting data to some informational clearinghouse). I mean, here's Amazon saying "Look! We have rankings! Tons of rankings! Rankings for every possible subdivision of writing! And your book is probably a top ten bestseller in one of those!" Amazon *gets* authors. Authors love validation, even if that validation comes in the form of a "bestseller" label in a genre subdivision so finely chopped that the ranking is effectively a participation ribbon. As I write this, *Old Man's War* is #1 in the following Amazon subdivision: "Kindle Store > Kindle eBooks > Science Fiction & Fantasy > Science Fiction > Military > Space Fleet" That's pretty finely chopped, and I might argue not especially useful (there's not really a "space fleet" subgenre in SF). But if I were a newer author, I'd be thrilled! Even as an established author, it doesn't suck! Hell yeah, *space fleets!*

6. The flip side of all of this is that it's very easy, if you're the sort of personality inclined to do so, to transmorgify your Amazon ranking into a dick-waving contest. Every now and again I see authors who don't like me much crow about beating me or one of my books in an Amazon ranking, as if this were a sort of personal victory against me. My responses to this tend to be, **a)** congrats, **b)** you know it's not actually a contest, right, **c)** and if you want to assert that it is anyway, well, then, bless your heart. If you believe the world is truly a zero-sum contest in which evanescent book/author rankings promulgated by a corporation for its own interests represent the final word on your self-worth, which apparently must be assessed in relation to *me* (or any other author you might have a bug up your ass about), then please, take this victory. I want you to have it. Everyone else should maybe not do that.

7. Which is not to say one shouldn't have *fun* with rankings, when the opportunity presents itself, such as when I was number 9 on the Amazon rankings and Neil Gaiman was number 8, and my Amazon avatar appeared to be staring directly into his nostrils. We had a nice twitter moment about that, we did.

8. And that's really the point of Amazon Author Rankings (and other rankings Amazon might offer): Enjoy them when they're up but don't stress about them when they're down. One's writing career will have many moving parts, and Amazon's rankings are only about Amazon's part in that, and then only opaquely. I'm having fun being at the top of Amazon's heap. It won't last, and when it doesn't, I'll still be fine. And I'll still be writing.

Who We Are Online, Who We Are Offline, How They're Different and How They're the Same

O ver on Facebook, a person who claims to have met and interacted with me (and he may have! I meet and interact with a lot of people) suggests that he wouldn't want to associate with me because, among other things, there's a difference between how I present myself online and how I present myself offline, which this fellow takes to mean that I say things *here*, that I wouldn't say *there*. Which means, apparently, that I'm false/dissembling/a coward and so on.

This is interesting to me! I have thoughts on this! I am going to share them with you now!

One: Of course, and I think obviously, people who don't want to associate with me should not associate with me. Whatever reason you have for not wanting to associate with me—including having no reason at all!—is perfectly acceptable. It's your life, and life is too short to associate with people with whom you have no desire to spend time, even if that person is me. Maybe I'll be sad about that, if you are someone I like or admire or thought I might one day like to get to know. But I'll just have to be sad about that. If you don't want to associate with me, I celebrate your choice. Go! Be associative with others who are not me.

Two: Also of course I am quite happy to say in the offline world the things that I say when I am online—in point of fact I do that *all the time*, because frequently, in both public and private conversation, people want to talk to me about things I've said online. Why? Well, for one thing, that's how a lot of people *know* me, either through this blog or through my various social media presences. So naturally that's going to be an entryway for actual conversation, or, when I'm doing a public event, a way for people to get me to further expound on a subject. I'm *frequently* saying offline what I've said online. It's actually quite common.

Three: But what I suspect this fellow means is that I wouldn't say *negative* things I might say about someone online to their face offline. For example, upon meeting, say, Ted Cruz, I wouldn't, to his face, call him "a jowly gobbet of tubercular phlegm," or "a necrotic self-regarding blight on the face of American politics," which are things I've called him here. And here's the truth of it: If, in fact, circumstances required that I *had* to meet Senator Cruz, and I couldn't get out of it by saying "I'd prefer not to meet him" or alternately by faking a massive head injury, when the moment came that I was required to speak with him, I would say, "Hello, Senator," and try to keep it to that. But if Cruz then said to me, "Hey, aren't you the fellow who called me 'an odious fistula that walks the earth in a human skin?' I would say, 'Why, yes, Senator Cruz. Indeed, I called you just that thing.'"

But I wouldn't *lead* with it, because, you know. I'm not *that* kind of asshole. Unless I am specifically and affirmatively going to meet someone with the intent of telling them how much I dislike or oppose them—which is *very* rare, because there's usually something better to do—I'm happy to be courteous and civil with the people that I disagree with or have arguments with, online or off. Why not? It'll let everyone get through the day without being pissed off (more). And, here's the thing—if someone I've had arguments with online shows civility and courtesy to me offline, in the world, *good for them*. Rather than chalk it up to cowardice or hypocrisy, I'm going to give them credit for understanding that context has a bearing on discourse. It doesn't mean I forget the things they've said about me, or the things I might have said about them. It does mean we both understand that going after each other with hammers in one medium does not necessitate all hammers, all the time. You get credit in my book if you understand that.

("But Scalzi," you might say. "Aren't you the one that says that the person who is an asshole online and polite offline is still an asshole?" Yes! Yes, I did. That goes for me as well—if your opinion of my online presentation is "what an asshole," then no matter what you think of my offline public presentation, it's perfectly valid for you to continue to have "asshole" as part of the foundation of your opinion of me. I'm okay with you thinking I'm an asshole. But in public, in the real world, I do try to be a decently socialized asshole.)

Be that as it may, if you're determined to have me say to your face what I wrote about you online, then yes, in fact, I will absolutely say it to you, to your face. Why wouldn't I? I wouldn't have written it if I didn't mean it—or at least, didn't mean it at the time. It's possible that over time I might have changed my opinion, and if that's the case, I'd say that too. And if in time I decided that what I said was wrong, I would apologize, to you, *to your face!* (Yes, I've done that before.) But if I wrote something about you, and it still stood, and you asked me to repeat it to you, to your face, then, yup, that'll happen.

Four: I should note that for my own self *I* don't go out asking the people who say horrible things about me online to repeat them to my face. First, why would I willingly want to spend any time with people who say horrible things about me? I'm forty-seven, man. More years behind than ahead. I endeavor to spend that time with people who actually *like* me. Second, in the cases where I am in the same space as they are for whatever reason, I generally try not to be the one determined to drop a turd in the punch bowl. Third, I don't automatically assume that just because someone appears entirely jerky to me online, they will be the same way offline, because, again, most people understand context and are socialized, and who knows? Maybe we'll get along otherwise. It's happened before! Fourth, running around being an exposed nerve all the time is tiring. And fifth, generally speaking, people are entitled to their opinion of me, even if it's not a nice one.

Five: This person who says he won't associate with me rather proudly asserts his presentation is the same online or off. He seems to think this is a virtue, which is his right. I think it suggests an unsophisticated understanding of how people present themselves in the world, online and off, and how we tune ourselves for different contexts and different purposes. My online presentation, as I've noted numerous times, is a version of me tuned for performance—I'm usually telling you what I think, in a hopefully entertaining way. It's *me*, but it's me in a way designed for a specific declamatory purpose. If I used the same version of me in one-on-one conversation, it'd be fucking awful. The version of me for that context is tuned very differently—again, still me, but in a context that's not all *about* me.

I have different modes: One for when I'm doing public events, one for when I'm at home with family, one for conversation with friends, one for meeting strangers one on one, one for when I'm collaborating with people on work, and so on. I don't think this is a particular revelation for anyone, in no small part because I talk about it as a thing I do, but also because pretty much everyone does it; everyone presents differently in different circumstances. I suspect this fellow who maintains he's the same online and offline is wrong about that, but if he's not, then he's a rare individual who perhaps should be studied by sociologists.

The larger point here is that it's not (necessarily) insincere or *bad* if your presentation in one medium varies from your presentation in another. Certainly one *can* have a presentation of self that is false or hypocritical, or have such a wide variance between one presentation and the other that it gives the appearance of either (or both). But there's a ways to go before you get to that point. I don't tend to think my presentation in any circumstance is false, although I admit ego and self-interest keeps me from being a perfect observer of me (and sometimes I will willingly lie to people if I think it's in my interest to do so. Hello, I'm a human and that means I'm complicated). But generally speaking, however I tune me ends up being me. I think this fellow who apparently doesn't tune himself to circumstances may be making life unduly harder on himself.

Six: There certainly are people I wouldn't associate with willingly but generally speaking I don't make a public spectacle out of it. I just… don't *meet* them. It's a big world and one can do a pretty good job of avoiding people if one likes. One can even be at the same convention or in the same building or even at the same party and still do a good job of not spending time with people if one wants. Likewise, I have a (very) small list of people who, if they went out of their way to get into my face, I would tell them to fuck right off. The list is small because **a)** most people, like me, tend to avoid people they don't want to associate with, **b)** my life is good and part of the reason it's good is that generally

I don't let the assholes get to me. But it's also small because, again, most people are reasonably socialized and can be polite to each other, even if they're otherwise at odds. Civility! It can happen.

Seven: To sum up: I totally will in fact say to your face what I say online, but I'm also happy not to unless you decide to make a *thing* out of it. I suspect most people are that way, and that's not a bad thing. Also, go ahead and avoid me if you must, I'm cool with that.

WHY IN FACT PUBLISHING WILL NOT GO AWAY ANYTIME SOON: A DEEPLY SLANTED PLAY IN THREE ACTS

Feb
3
2010

CHARACTERS:

ELTON P. STRAÜMANN, *a modern-thinking man with exciting ideas*
JOHN SCALZI, *a humble writer*
KRISTINE SCALZI, *the wife of a humble writer*

ACT I
SCENE OPENS ON STRAÜMANN and SCALZI, standing.

STRAÜMANN:
The publishing world is changing! In the future, authors will no longer need those fat cat middle men known as "publishers" to get in the way of their art! It will just be the author and his audience!

SCALZI:
Won't I need an editor? Or a copy editor? Or a cover artist? Or a book designer? Or a publicist? Or someone to print the book and get it into stores?

STRAÜMANN
(waves hand, testily):
Yes, yes. But all those things you can do *yourself.*

SCALZI:
And I'm supposed to write the book, too?

STRAÜMANN
(snorts):
As if writing was *hard.* Now go! And write your novel!

SCALZI goes off to write his novel. STRAÜMANN stands, alone, on stage, for several months. Eventually SCALZI returns, with a book.

STRAÜMANN:
You again! What took you so long?

SCALZI:
Well, I had write the book. Then I had to edit it, copy edit it, do the cover, do the book design, have it printed, act as my own distributor and send out press releases. It cost me thousands of dollars out of my own pocket and the better part of a year. But look! Here's the book!

STRAÜMANN
(pulls out his electronic reader):
I'm sorry, I only read on *this.*

SCALZI sighs, slinks off the stage.

STRAÜMANN
(yelling after SCALZI):
And where's the sequel? *Why aren't you writing more?!?*

ACT II

It is A YEAR LATER. SCENE OPENS on STRAÜMANN and SCALZI, standing.

STRAÜMANN:
I'm still waiting for that sequel, you know.

SCALZI:
I spent all my money last year making that first book. And it didn't sell very well.

STRAÜMANN
(sneers):
Well, what did you expect? The editing was sloppy, the copy editing was *atrocious*, the layout was amateurish and the cover art looked like it was Photoshopped by a *dog*. Who would want to buy *that*?

SCALZI
(dejected):
I know.

STRAÜMANN:
Seriously, what were you *thinking*.

SCALZI:
But that's my point! I want to get professional editing and copy editing and book design and cover art, but I just can't afford it.

STRAÜMANN

(smiles):

Scalzi, you naive fool. Don't you realize that thanks to the current economy we live in, editors and copy editors and artists are desperately looking for work! Surely some of them will work for almost nothing! Scratch that—they'll work for *exactly* nothing!

SCALZI:

Is that ethical? To get work from people without paying them?

STRAÜMANN:

Of *course* it is. They'll profit from the *exposure*.

SCALZI:

I don't think a printer is going to want to be paid in exposure.

STRAÜMANN:

Then release the book electronically to skip on all those printing costs!

SCALZI:

Yes! And then sell it for a reasonable price!

STRAÜMANN

(shrugs):

Well, do what you want. I'll be getting it off a torrent.

SCALZI:

What?

STRAÜMANN

(brandishing his electronic reader):

I paid $300 for this thing! Honestly, how much do you expect me to pay to *fill* it?

SCALZI:

So, pay people nothing to help me create a book I make nothing on, for people who will refuse to pay for it.

STRAÜMANN:

I wouldn't put it *that* way. But yes.

STRAÜMANN and SCALZI stand for a moment, silent.

SCALZI:

I'm trying to remember if you voted for Obama.

STRAÜMANN

(snorts):

As if I'd vote for a *Communist*.

ACT III

SEVERAL MONTHS have passed. SCENE OPENS on STRAÜMANN and SCALZI, standing.

STRAÜMANN:

Dude, where the fuck is that sequel? I'm dying over here.

SCALZI:

Well, I was going to write it, but when I tried to find editors and artists to work on it for free, I kind of hit a road block. The ones who were good wouldn't work for free, and the ones that were free weren't good.

STRAÜMANN
(rolls his eyes):
Well, duh. I could have told you that.

SCALZI:

But…

STRAÜMANN:

But that's not *important* now. What's important is that we get you writing again.

SCALZI:

But I don't have the money to make another book with professional help, and I don't have the time to make another book on my own.

STRAÜMANN:

As it happens, I have a solution for you. And look, here she is.

ENTER KRISTINE SCALZI from STAGE LEFT.

STRAÜMANN:

Mrs. Scalzi, a word, please.

KRISTINE:

Yes?

STRAÜMANN:

As you may know, your husband is a writer. But he is finding it difficult to do writing recently because of issues of cost and time. I know that you are the organized, financially-minded person in your relationship, so allow me to suggest to you that you become his publisher. While he writes, you locate and pay for an editor, a copy editor, a cover artist, a book designer, a publicist, a printer and a distributor. This will leave him free to focus on his craft, and the sequel I so desire.

KRISTINE:

I see. And you propose I fund these people how?

STRAÜMANN:

Well, I'm sure I don't *know*, Mrs. Scalzi, but I have faith in your ability to do so.

KRISTINE:

So to recap, you want me to quit my full-time job and devote all my time to my husband's career.

STRAÜMANN:

Of course not! I never said for you to *quit your job*. You need the health insurance.

KRISTINE:

Ah. Could you come over here for just a second?

STRAÜMANN
(walks toward KRISTINE):

Yes?

KRISTINE clocks STRAÜMANN in the head, stunning him, then rips off his testicles, stuffs them into his mouth and sets him on fire while he chokes on them. STRAÜMANN dies.

KRISTINE
(to SCALZI):
You. Find a *fucking publisher.*

SCALZI:

Yes, dear.

CURTAIN FALLS.

Why New Novelists Are Kinda Old, or, Hey, Publishing is Slow

Jun

24

2009

rom the e-mail pile today:

Whenever I hear about a "new" novelist, they turn out to be in their 30s. Why is that? It seems like you hear about new musicians and actors and other creative people when they are in their 20s.

Excellent question. Leaving aside the mechanics of why it pays to be young in the music and acting industries, here's what's up with those old new novelists:

1. Writing an entire novel is something most people have to work up to. Because you know what? Writing sixty to one hundred thousand words of fiction is not something most people cannonball through, even if they assure you, with the appropriate amount of false modesty, that they're really better at long-form fiction. Maybe they are, but they still had a long walk to get there. *I'm* better at long-form and it took me until I was twenty-eight before I could do it. Meanwhile I'd been writing short for years up to that point, in the form of reviews and columns and humor pieces and (yes) occasional attempts at short fiction that I mostly abandoned after a page or two. Lots of people in their teens and early twenties start novels; rather fewer finish them.

Why? Well, some of them start novels and finish short stories, which is a surprise both for the would-be novelist and the would-be novel.

Others (and this included me in my twenties) start writing something that they thought might be a book-length idea, only to find not only did it not qualify as a short story, it was better for everyone involved if the stunted, weird thing was taken behind the tool shed, whacked with a shovel and buried without anyone else knowing it ever existed.

Some others actually finish a whole novel-length pile of words whose best quality, alas, is that it gave its author a chance to exercise his or her fingers. The erstwhile author realizes that making it into a novel would require pulling it apart and starting over, and the thought of doing so fills them with the same joy as they might get from sucking down a Dran-O mojito. So the not-actually-a-novel gets stuffed into the proverbial drawer or trunk, never again to see the light of day.

All of this, incidentally, is *perfectly fine*. Craftsmen don't make their masterpiece the first time they approach a potter's wheel (or whatever). Most writers aren't going to write a brilliant or even passable novel the first time they sit down in front of a keyboard and intone (to themselves if no one else) that today is the day they will commit *art*, in a convenient, novel-sized package. They usually have to work up to it, one way or another. That takes time, just as learning any craft takes time.

And when people do finally manage to write something that is actually identifiable to anyone else but the author as a novel, guess what?

2. Most people's first novels well and truly suck. Oh my,
yes they *do*. Which again is perfectly fine. Writing anything over 60,000 words that still recognizably tells one single story is a hell of an achievement in itself. Asking that it also be *good* is just being mean to the author, and the novel. It's like watching someone run their first full-length marathon, ever, and criticizing them for not finishing in the top ten. I mean, shit. That can be the goal for the *second* race, right?

Most first novels are no damn good. Second ones are often better, but not always, and often not by much. Third and fourth novels, the same thing. Fact is—and this should not be news at this late date—ask most debut novelists how many novels they wrote before they got one published, and you'll find out the answer is: two, three, four—sometimes more. Debut novels are almost never first novels; they're just the first novels *you* see. And all those other novels you will never know about? They took lots of time to write, too.

Which brings us to the next point:

3. The physical act of writing a novel takes a long time. Yes, we all know of the authors who can crank out a perfectly publishable novel of 60, or 80, or 100,000 words in just under six weeks. But there are two things to note. First, most of those hyperkinetic authors are not newbie novelists; they're people who have been writing long enough that certain aspects of novel writing are encoded into their brain's muscle memory. Second, if you're a would-be novelist, you'll probably never be one of those people anyway.

No, I'm not intending to insult you. Most currently published authors don't write that quickly either. I know successful, working authors who are happy to get 250 words of fiction a day, because that's 90,000 words a year: A full-sized novel. But consider that there are any number of writers who have trouble getting out *that* much out a year, because—surprise!—a novel is usually more than just sitting down and cranking out a word count. There are those little things like plot, and character, and pacing, and dialogue and so on and so forth. All of those things take time to develop.

Note also that while you're doing all of this as a budding novelist, you are also most likely doing all the other things in your life that constitute *your life*: A day job, spouse and family, hobbies and friends, reading and television and video games and even (wait for it) sleep. It all adds up—and it all subtracts from the amount of time you have to write.

What all this means is that writing those three or four novels an average writer has to burn through before they write a publishable novel will likely take years.

But hey! A budding novelist has put in the time and the work and the effort and has sacrificed numerous innocent, trusting pizzas to the Gods of Writing, and has finally got a novel good enough to sell. Good for them. Now it's time for the next point:

4. Selling a novel takes a long time. At this point, like the Game of Life™, there are two paths a would-be novelist can go by. The first path is the path of Finding an Agent. This path takes more time but potentially opens the door to more publishers, because most publishers these days require agented submissions.

Finding an agent is a slog. One has to query the agent, wait to see if the query is accepted, and then if it is sample chapters and an outline go out in the mail. Then more waiting to see if the agent asks for more. If he or she does, it's time to send the whole manuscript and then wait again to see if he or she thinks the writer is worth their time to represent. At any point the agent can say "no," at which point our budding novelist will have to start over again.

But if the agent says "yes," then comes the part where he or she starts schlepping the novel to publishers. Presuming the agent gets a publishing house interested in looking at the manuscript, it could be weeks or even months before there's response, either positive or negative. If it's the latter, it's on to the next publisher.

The second path is the Path of the Slush Pile. This gets the work out there quicker but fewer publishers still accept unagented manuscripts, and as you might guess from the name "slush pile," the rate at which editors work through the slush pile is pretty slow. Baen Books, which accepts unagented manuscripts, lists their response time as nine to twelve months: Yes, you could make a baby (if you *can* make a baby) before our poor theoretical writer here would hear back about their literary child. And if at the end of those nine months to a year Baen (or whomever) says no, the poor writer has to start all over again.

And along either path, there's no assurance that the novel—despite being of publishable quality—will sell. This means that at some point the writer may have to give up the ghost on this particular novel and move on to try to sell the next one—which of course, they were busy writing while they were waiting for that other one to sell.

All of this—you are sensing the theme by now—takes lots of time.

But wait! Despite the myriad challenges, a novel has actually been sold! Excellent. Now guess what?

5. Publishing a novel often takes a long time. Once a book has an offer, there's the time it takes to work through the contract. Then the editing process begins—it's very likely the editor working with the writer will want tweaks and edits to the novel. This round of editing takes time, depending both on how much work the book needs and how well the writer takes direction during the editing process. After that comes the copy editing, with the writer required to go through the manuscript, answering copy editor queries and signing off on the edits. And beyond this is all the production stuff the writer is not directly involved with, like cover art, interior and cover design, and so on and so forth. This, yes, takes time.

But even when that's done there's more waiting! That's because the publisher will need to find a spot for the novel on its release schedule, one that allows it to highlight the work and also gives it time to secure publicity and advance reviews and all that good stuff. That spot on the release schedule may be a year or even two in the future. This is the part that really drives writers nuts: Everything's done and yet, no book. It's *madness*, I tell you.

So, let's recap: It takes time for most people to learn how to write to novel-length. It takes time to write well at that length. It takes time to write *to* that length. It takes time to land a publisher and it takes time to get that novel to market. And suddenly, it makes sense why so many debut novelists just happen to be in their thirties.

You want a real world example, you say. Fine, take me. I'll note my own path to publication has some irregularities in it, but overall it works well enough for these purposes. Ready? Here it is. The number at the end of each line tells you how old I was each step of the way:

1969 – 1997: Time spent learning to write well enough to write a novel (28).

1997: Wrote first complete novel (28)

1997 – 2001: Life intervenes and keeps me away from fiction (32)

2001: Wrote second novel (32)

2002: Offer made on second novel, now my debut novel (33)

2003: Contract signed for debut novel (33)

2004: Editing and early publicity for debut novel (35)

2005: Debut novel published (35)

2006: Won the John W. Campbell Award for Best New Writer (37)

So, eight years from first completed novel to having a debut novel in the bookstores, and four years between completing the debut novel and it being published in book form. And if you think it's ironic to win a "Best New Writer" award at the ripe old age of thirty-seven, consider that thirty-seven is pretty much the average age of the Campbell winners over the last thirty-five years. "New" does not equal "young."

Having said all of that, it's worth noting that a whole stack of writers have managed to get novels published while they were in their twenties—it's not *that* huge a trick to do so. These debuts are not necessarily any worse (or better) than those of authors who debut in their thirties or later. Some writers are publishable more quickly, some are in the right place at the right time with the right books, and some people are simply unfathomably lucky.

Also, at this point in time there are more authors who are willing to attempt self-publishing—either online or through print-on-demand—thus avoiding the whole "finding a publisher" time suck. We could have a debate on whether this is wise, from the point of view of distribution, publicity, marketing and/or writers debuting before their work is worth *reading*, but that's a debate for another entry. The fact of the matter is that if you self-publish, your debut as a novelist will undoubtedly come sooner.

But for the folks who do it the old-fashioned way—and, currently, the way that still affords them the best chance for notoriety and a chance at a long-term career as a novelist—the combination of writing skill development and the mechanics of contemporary publishing conspires to drive the age of most debut novelists into the thirties. It doesn't seem likely to change anytime soon.

Yog's Law and
Self-Publishing

Jun

20

2014

Many years ago, writer Jim Macdonald postulated "Yog's Law," a handy rule of thumb for writers about the direction money is meant to flow in publishing:

"Money flows *toward* the writer."

This is handy because it will give the writer pause when she has a publisher (or agent, or editor) who says that in order to get published, the author needs to lay out some cash up front, and to that publisher/agent/editor. The author can step back, say, huh, *this is not how Yog's Law says it's supposed to go,* and then surmise, generally correctly, that the publisher/agent/editor in question is a scam artist and that she should run away as fast as her feet will carry her.

But does Yog's Law apply in an age where many writers—and some even successfully—are self-publishing via digital? In self-publishing, authors are on the financial hook for the editorial services that publishers usually do: Editing, copy-editing, page and cover design and art, marketing, publicity and so on. In this case, unless the author does everything (which is possible but not advised if one want's a professional-looking product), money is going to have to flow away from the writer, as he hired people to do work for him.

Does this mean Yog's Law is now dead? Author Harry Connolly, who has published traditionally and also self-publishes, thinks so; a summation of his argument is here:

> Yog's Law comes from a time when people offering self-publishing
> services were largely preying on people who would pay significant
> sums to third parties for books that would be throttled by a distribution
> system that was not open to them, and what's more, those third-parties
> largely knew this and did their best to hide the fact. But distribution
> has changed and Yog's Law no longer holds.

Connolly is correct that the rise of digital self-publishing puts a new wrinkle on things. I disagree, however, that it means Yog's Law no longer generally holds. I think it does, but with a corollary for self-publishers:

Yog's Law: Money flows *toward* the writer.

Self-Pub Corollary to Yog's Law: While in the process of self-publishing, money and rights are *controlled* by the writer.

Which is to say that when the self-published writer pays for editorial services, she's at the head of the process; she's employing the editor or copy editor or cover artist or whomever, and she's calling the shots. If she's smart she's listening to them and allowing them to do the job she's paid them for, but at the end of the day the buck stops—literally—with her. This differs from the various scammy publishers, who would take the money and the author's work, and then would effectively disappear down a dark hole, with the writer entirely out of the loop on what was going on (what as going on: generally, almost nothing).

This corollary, I think, is useful for self-publishers because there are still lots of ways for self-publishers to use their money foolishly, primarily by losing control of how it gets spent and by whom. If at any step the self-published author asks, *who controls this money I am about to spend?* and the answer is not "me," that's a flag on the field. Likewise, if control of the work is somehow compromised by the process, that's another flag.

And of course outside the self-publishing process, i.e., when the work is out there in the world, Yog's Law continues to apply. It continues to apply however the work is published, actually.

So, Yog's Law: Still not just a law, but a good idea. The self-publishing corollary to Yog's Law: Also, I think, a good idea.

This is the Section Where Scalzi Snarks on People More Famous Than He Is, So Get Out Your Popcorn, or, Thoughts on Writers and Other Notables

DURAN DURAN,
NEIL GAIMAN,
AND BEGINNINGS

Sep
22
2015

'm both a friend and fan of Neil Gaiman, and a former music critic. So for years I've known about, but had never seen, Neil's very first published book, the 1984 quickie biography of Duran Duran, arguably the biggest band to emerge from the first era of MTV ("You know! Back when they actually *played music!*" the 80s kids grouse, shaking their canes in unison). It's a difficult find because a) it was a quickie bio of a pop band, not exactly meant to survive through the ages, b) apparently the company that published it went under shortly after it was published, so there were never that many copies to begin with. The fact that Neil's become NEIL GAIMAN also adds to the rarity as collectors snap them up. Decent copies of the book fetch hundreds of dollars; at this moment on eBay there's a copy whose description all but implies the tattered book is smudged with a then-14-year-old girl's kisses which is being offered for $130. And while I like Neil, I'm not sure I'm willing to part with that much in order to see the thing.

Fortunately, there's now a "Neil Gaiman Rarities" eBook Humble Bundle, and Neil stuck in the bio as part of the bundle. As soon as I saw that it was in there, I slapped down my money (more than the $15 required to unlock the tier that included the bio, I'll note) and made a beeline to download the pdf version.

How is it?

Oh, my friends. It is *glorious.*

It is glorious primarily because it is a triple-treat bit of nostalgia. One, it's a nostalgia piece for the 80s, and of a certain stripe of 80s British music journalism, a tone and feel I personally most associate with *Smash Hits,* the magazine me and all my we-want-to-be-too-cool friends in high school would read to find out what Morrissey and Pete Burns were up to (apparently they were friends! Pete would come round for tea! or so I recall). Two, obviously, it's a nostalgia piece for Duran Duran, who when the book came out were at their most Duran-iest, which is to say, with the original line-up, before Andy and Roger left, with those first three studio albums and all those Russell Mulcahy videos.

Three, it's a nostalgia piece for Neil, although I suspect as much or more so for him as the rest of us, because here Neil is twenty-four years old and a journalist and almost no one has the slightest idea who he is. He hasn't become NEIL GAIMAN and won't start being that guy for a few more years yet, when *Sandman* kicks in. Nevertheless this is a reminder that everyone who is someone comes from somewhere and starts with something; this is where Neil begins as an author of books. For anyone who is a published author, a book like this is going to be evocative of their own first book, however many years back in the timestream that is.

Yes, yes, you say. Fine, nostalgia, whatever. Is the book itself any good? It's Neil Gaiman writing but can we see the NEIL GAIMAN he became in it?

Maybe a little? I think maybe there's some expectation management that needs to be put in place. To wit: it's a quickie bio of a pop band. The thing is 132 pages long, and most of that is pictures. It ain't exactly *Mystery Train*, nor would it be fair to suggest it was supposed to be. I don't know the specifics of its compilation, but I would be a bit surprised if Neil had more than a couple of months to cobble the thing together with bits and anecdotes from newspaper and magazine articles. There's nothing in the text to suggest that Neil spent any time with the band itself, back when the thing was put together (he does go to a concert, however, where he's frustrated by the inarticulateness of the band's fans, which leads, somewhat amusingly, to him being upbraided for his snobbishness by a fan on a train, after the concert).

The nature of bio—short, full of facty tidbits rather than personal connection, probably written fast—mitigates against actual, shall we say, *art*. Neil gets in a clever line here and there, and his penchant for sardonicism via phrasing and pacing is in embryonic form in the text. If you know Neil Gaiman's mature writing, you can see some of what he does in that, here. If you were reading it cold, I don't know, *maybe* you'd see it? It's hard to say.

As noted above, the tone of the text owes as much to a certain style of journalism as it does to Neil's native writing gifts and discipline. I doubt that anyone who read this in 1984 slammed it down on completion and said "My God, *this* is the voice of a man who will become one of the most beloved fantasy authors of our time!" On the other hand, I doubt that if you got into a time machine and told that same 1984 reader that Neil *did* go on to become one of the most beloved fantasy authors of our time, they would look at you in horror and wonder what sort of dystopian hellscape allowed such a thing to occur. I suspect they would go "Really? Huh," and then ask you why, if you indeed had the privilege of a time machine, you would waste it on such a trivial errand.

Which is to say: The bio's not bad. It's competent—possibly more competent than its editing, which occasionally allows for paragraphs to appear more than once. It's light and it's a quick, mildly informative read. Neil jams in the Duran Duran trivia (you can tell it's the eighties because we learn all the band members' astrological signs) and even attempts a bit of criticism with the albums and the videos, although none of the criticism is really that critical; there are a couple places where Neil is all "well, that one was a bit dodgy, wasn't it?" but that's about it. This is not an actual complaint on my part, because again: quick bio of a pop band, aimed at its fans. If Neil had gone off on a rant about how none of the lyrics of *Seven and the Ragged Tiger* actually mean *a single goddamn thing Jesus what the hell is going on in Simon Le Bon's head besides cocaine and Cristal* I suspect his editors would have pulled him aside to let him know to trim it up otherwise he'd be murdered by a roving pack of Duran Duran fans. And thus would the history of comic books and fantasy literature have been irrevocably changed.

(Although, seriously: *Seven and the Ragged Tiger*. Nothing there makes even the slightest lick of sense. "The Union of the Snake" is just friggin *word salad*, man. We can say it now, here in 2015.)

But, you know. I didn't read it expecting it to be brilliant stuff, and I don't find it glorious because of its prose. I find it glorious (aside from the nostalgia value) because it's 2015 and I know who that twenty-four-year-old writer is going to become one day, even if he doesn't. I know that thirty-one years down the line, the kid writing about these other vastly more famous kids—Neil is the same age as the Duran Duran members—is going to be in his way just as famous as any of them, individually or possibly even together, and he has *absolutely no idea*. It's probably not even on his radar, because how would it be? All he knows is that someone said (more or less): "Hey kid, write a book on Duran Duran," and he said "Yeah, okay, I can do that," and inside he was probably thinking *this is it. I'm on my way*. Because when you get your first book, that's what you think: *Here we go*.

I wish I could get back in that time machine to 1984 and tell twenty-four-year-old Neil about this. "Neil!" I would say. "In 2015 you will have sixteen times as many Twitter followers as Simon Le Bon!" And he would say "Those words all make sense individually but not as a sentence," as politely as possible and then he would back away quickly from the very odd American blathering nonsensical terms like "blog" and "Internet," who is telling him something about people named "Amanda" and "Anthony" (two people named Anthony, actually) and suggesting that black really *is* going to be a good look for him, just wait and see. Poor twenty-four-year-old Neil, accosted by creepy balding Americans from the future. Perhaps best to let him be.

I also find it glorious because twenty-four-year-old me was not at all unlike twenty-four-year-old Neil: A journalist, writing about famous people and not really knowing how vastly different his future was going to be from his then-present. In fact, one of the famous people the twenty-four-year-old me wrote about and interviewed was a guy named Neil Gaiman; I wrote a whole newspaper story about the hip new medium of graphic novels just so I could have an excuse to call him up and talk to him (I didn't know how to pronounce his last name so when his daughter picked up the phone and I asked to speak to him, I could hear her say "Hey dad, someone wants to talk to Neil *GUY*-man!"). My own first published book wasn't a quickie bio, but a book on online finance, now also out of print and utterly unrelated to the sort of work I would become known for (it's also competent and a quick, informative read).

I don't want to press the comparison too heavily, mind you; Neil's, uh, a *little bit* further along than I am (and Simon Le Bon has twice the Twitter followers I do). But I am saying when I read the Duran Duran bio, I smiled, because I remember being someplace very similar to where that kid was, back then.

As I said, the Duran Duran book is an exercise in nostalgia. But a nostalgia that does not suggest that the past was a better time than now; just a different time, gone but not entirely forgotten. Here in the present, within days of each other, Duran Duran, thirty-five years into a career, put out a new album, and Neil has put out a new edition of his own (in collaboration with Amanda, his beloved wife). Times have changed, and times are good. The bio chronicles the start of a band and of a writer, and both are still going strong. I like that I've seen the beginning, and the latest, from each. The world has not heard the last of either.

And Now, an Incomplete List of Women Writers Who Inspire Me

Apr

4

2016

(Note: In 2016 Gay Talese, in an interview, was asked about women authors who inspired him and came up with zip. Later, after the uproar, he released a backtracking statement. Good for him.)

"Incomplete" because I'm doing it off the top of my head. Also, in no particular order. Ready? Here we go:

Dorothy Parker

Molly Ivins

Elaine May

Madeleine L'Engle

Nora Ephron

Susan Cooper

Hannah Arendt

Ursula Le Guin

N.K. Jemisin

Beverly Cleary

Sheri Tepper

Jenny Lawson

Kelly Sue Deconnick

Emma Thompson (Yes, she's a writer. Won an Oscar for it, too)

Caroline Thompson (no relation to above)

Amy Wallace

Melissa Matheson

Erma Bombeck

Mallory Ortberg

Pauline Kael

There are more, but as I said: Off the top of my head. And these are just the ones I find *inspiring*—that is, the ones whose work I looked at some point or another in my life and came out of the experience wanting to write and/or to have my own work to be *better*. If you were to ask for the list of women writers who I like, enjoy or admire, well. We'd be here all day. And that, again, would be for the ones I could list right off the top of my head.

Which is the point. Gay Talese, who inspired this particular list, couldn't think of a single woman writer who inspires him or whose work he loves, when asked in an interview. That unfortunate man. Maybe he needs to read more widely. For a start.

Dan Brown and Me

May

14

2013

A couple of weeks ago I was contacted by a journalist who was doing a story about authors who have a book coming out on the same day as Dan Brown's new book *Inferno*, presumably because it will be amusing to hear us wail and gnash our teeth about that particular juggernaut crushing our books. I wasn't home when he called and he never got back to me about it, so I will not be in that article. But if I had been, what I would have said is this:

I am in fact entirely unconcerned. I have no doubt that *Inferno* will sell rather more copies than *The Human Division*, but I doubt seriously that it will take away any sales *from* my book; which is to say I doubt that someone is going to walk into a book store, see Brown's book and mine, and have a great existential crisis about only being able to choose one or the other. There may be overlap between our audiences, but I suspect that the overlap we have would choose to get both.

This would be the place to say something snarky about Brown, but I have nothing snarky to say about the dude. I read one of his books; it was entertaining and I was entertained and if there was anything about the book that was supposed to be deeper than that it went right past me. Being cranky about a Dan Brown book not being high literature is like yelling at a cupcake for not being a salad; it's really missing the point. You don't want the cupcake? Don't eat the cupcake. Apparently lots of people like cupcakes. They don't care that you want them to eat salad. *You* eat salad, if it's so important to you.

But beyond this, I suspect that the article this journalist fellow was writing might have been predicated on a zero-sum thinking, which is that the money spent on Dan Brown today takes money from other writers. It doesn't actually work that way. There are a certain number of Dan Brown readers who read one book a year, and the book they read this year is his. Bluntly put, that's not money taken from me or other writers because we were never in contention for that cash. There is the another category of Dan Brown reader, which are the sort of people who love to read books, and also read Dan Brown. Someone in that category is going to cruise through *Inferno* in a couple of days and be on to the next book—perhaps mine, perhaps someone else's. The point is in this scenario Dan Brown doesn't take money away from any other writer in any significant way, because people who love reading read a lot of books.

And then there's a third scenario in which people who didn't know they like to read, read a Dan Brown book, enjoy it and then say "what else is out there?" In which case Dan Brown just did me and every other author a favor, because now there's a new reader to shop our wares to. This is one reason why you won't hear me gripe about Dan Brown, or E.L. James, or Stephenie Meyer or [insert frequently maligned author here]. They don't hurt my career, and have the potential to benefit it.

So good luck to Dan Brown on his sales today, not that I think he will need it. And good luck to me, too. I suspect when the day is over, both of us will be perfectly happy with how it's turned out.

Diversity,
Appropriation,
Canada (and Me)

<table>
<tr><td>May</td></tr>
<tr><td>13</td></tr>
<tr><td>2017</td></tr>
</table>

So, I've been following this thing that's been happening in Canada, where (briefly), Hal Niedzviecki, a white editor of a writer's magazine, in an edition of the magazine focusing on the indigenous writers of Canada, wrote an editorial in which he encouraged white writers to include characters who weren't like them, saying "I'd go so far as to say that there should even be an award for doing so—the Appropriation Prize for best book by an author who writes about people who aren't even remotely like her or him."

This outraged a bunch of folks, and Niedzviecki ended up apologizing and resigning, which in turn outraged a bunch of other (mostly white) literary and journalistic folks, some of whom briefly started going about on social media about actually trying to fund an "Appropriation Prize" before at least a few of them realized that maybe they shouldn't be doing that and started backtracking as fast as they could.

As I've been reading this, I think I have a reasonably good idea of what was going on in the mind of Niedzviecki. I suspect it was something along the line of, "Hey, in this special edition of this magazine featuring voices my magazine's reading audience of mostly white writers doesn't see enough of, I want to encourage the writing of a diversity of characters even among my readership of mostly white writers, and I want to say it in a clever, punchy way that will really drive the message home."

Which seems laudable enough! And indeed, in and of itself, encouraging white, middle-class writers out of their comfort zones in terms of writing characters different from them and their lived experience is a perfectly fine goal. I encourage it. Other people I know encourage it. There's more to life than middle-class white people, and writing can and should reflect that.

But it wasn't "in and of itself," and here's where Niedviecki screwed up, as far as I can see:

1. In an edition of his magazine about indigenous writing in Canada, his essay pulled focus away from indigenous writers to focus on white, middle-class writers, (probably unintentionally) signaling who was really more important here.

2. He tried to be clever about it, too, and the failure mode of "clever" is "asshole." Specifically, the crack about the "Appropriation Prize," which probably sounded great in his head, and by all indications sounded pretty great to a bunch of other mostly white Canadian authors and journalists.

3. Which is a point in itself, i.e., the easy conflation of "diversity of characters" with "appropriation." *Very* basically, the former says "I as a writer acknowledge there's more to the world than me and people like me and I will strive to represent that as best I can," and the latter says "The imaginary version of people I'm not like, that I have created in my head, is as valid as the lived experience of the actual people I claim to represent in my writing." And, yeah. *Maybe* these two should not be conflated, even if it makes for a punchy, memorable line in an essay. Also, if you genuinely can't tell the difference between these two states, you might have work to do.

(This is why the white Canadian authors/journalists yakking about funding an Appropriation Prize are particularly clueless; they're essentially saying "Hey! Let's give money to white writers for the best fake version of people they're not!" Which is not a good look, folks, really. Words *do* mean things, and "appropriation" doesn't mean a good thing in this context.)

This whole event really appears to fall into the category of "Well-meaning person does something they thought would help and instead makes things worse." Niedzviecki thought he was championing diversity in Canadian writing—because (I have no doubt) he actually *does* wish to champion diversity in Canadian writing—and instead blundered into controversy because lack of understanding about what he was doing, or at least, lack of understanding of how what he was doing would look outside of his own circle of experience. He meant well! But he showed his ass anyway.

And, well. Join the party, Mr. Niedzviecki! There are many of us here in the "We Showed Our Ass" club. And judging from the response to the piece, and Mr. Niedzviecki's decision to resign his post, more are joining as we speak. "Cultural Appropriation: Why Can't We Debate It?" asks one Canadian newspaper column headline, from another white writer who clearly doesn't understand what "cultural appropriation" actually means and seems confused why other people are upset by it. Niedzviecki, to his credit, seems to have picked up the clue. Some others seem determined not to. And, look. We all show our ass. The question is whether we then try to pull our pants back up, or keep scrunching them down to our ankles, and then poop all over them and ourselves.

....

Now, related but slightly set apart (which is why I've separated this part off with asterisks), let me address this issue of diversity of characters in writing, using myself as an example, and moving on from there.

I'm a white male writer of North American middle-class sensibility, and I try from time to time to write characters that are not like me, because it reflects the reality of the world to do so, and because in science fiction I believe we write the futures we want to see, and I want to see diversity. How do I do, writing these characters who are not like me? Well, that's for other people to decide. But here is my thought on doing it, which I take from Mary Anne Mohanraj's essays on the subject:

a) I should write diverse characters.

b) I'll screw up sometimes, and when I do people with the lived experience I'm trying to represent will let me know.

c) I'll learn and when I write diverse characters again, I'll try to do better. If I make mistakes again, they'll be new ones, not the same ones over again.

d) Repeat until dead (or I quit writing, which I suspect will happen simultaneously).

With that said, while I think it's useful for me to have diverse characters in my writing, I also think it's even *more* useful for publishing to have diverse writers. This is not just because of some box checking sensibility but because other writers tell stories, create characters and interrogate writing in ways *I would never think to*. I'm a pretty good storyteller, folks. But my way of storytelling isn't the only way it gets done. As a reader I like what I like, but I also like finding out about what I didn't know I'd like, and I even occasionally like reading something and going "wow, that was *so* not for me but I get that it's for *someone*."

This is relevant because even when I write diverse characters, they get filtered through *me*, and while that's fine and I think necessary, in a larger sense it's not sufficient. I'm not running me down here. I give good character. But as a writer I know where my weaknesses are. Some characters I will likely never explore as deeply as they could be explored by other writers, because I am not able to write those characters as well as others could. I strive for diversity in my writing. But my writing won't ever reflect the diversity that literature in general should be capable of. You need writers whose lives are not like mine for that.

White writers adding a diversity of characters into their work is one thing. Publishers seeking out and publishing a diversity of writers is another. A fall down happens when people—writers, editors, and publishers—appear to think having the former is somehow *equivalent* to the latter, or that having the former is *sufficient*, so that the latter is optional, if the former is present. It's not. The former can be laudable (if it doesn't fall over into appropriation, which it can, and when it does is its own bag of issues), but it's not and *never is* sufficient. A field of literature that comes only from one direction is bad literature because it's *incomplete* literature. There's more to it and it's being missed out on. And that's a much larger issue.

So, yes. Good on me and any white writer for having diverse characters. Go us! But if your argument about diversity in writing and publishing is centered on that, and not on an *actual* diversity of writers, you're missing the point in an obvious way. Everyone who isn't a white writer is going to notice.

THE FULL-TIME SF NOVELIST: PROBABLY NOT AS ENDANGERED AS YOU THINK

Jun

30

2010

In e-mail, I'm asked if I have any comments about Robert J. Sawyer's recent blog post, in which he worries that within a decade, it will be impossible to make a living solely as a science fiction novelist.

It's a fair concern! I have thoughts!

To begin, it's worth noting for clarity's sake that the vast majority of science fiction novelists *already* live in a world in which it's not possible to be a full-time novelist, and have for as long as the genre has existed. It's not just science fiction novelists who have always lived in that world, but novelists in general. Full-time novelists have always been a fortunate minority, and that minority would get even smaller if you only counted the ones who made enough from their novel writing to support themselves and their family, rather than having that income thrown into a larger pool of household income into which their spouse or spousal equivalent was also contributing.

As far as science fiction was concerned, at any time in the history of the genre the number of full-time novelists supporting themselves from their novels was a slim number—indeed smaller than the number of actual full-time novelists, since not a few of these writers, some of them now quite famous, lived all or part of their careers in a poverty that's not as romantic to live in as it is to read about. Science fiction is genre writing, and genre writing has always paid poorly relative to other sorts of writing, and *this* is nothing new, either; Robert Heinlein's famous invasion of *Saturday Evening Post* and *Colliers* back in the 40s was motivated in no small part because the man wanted and needed to be paid real money for his work.

When Rob's worrying about the death of science fiction novel-writing as a full-time endeavor, he's discussing what is and has always been fundamentally a high-class problem, and one most science fiction novelists of *any* era would love to have been in a position to worry about. To recast it a different way, you could very easily say that Rob's concerned that within a decade, the very top tier of science fiction novelists will be forced to do what every other science fiction novelist out there has already done: get a job.

This isn't to minimize Rob's concern—it's actually not a trivial concern, either for him personally or anyone who hopes to write science fiction/fantasy novels full-time—but it is to give it context. When Rob worries about the possibility of anyone making a full-time living writing science fiction novels a decade from now, implicit in this is the idea that anyone *can* make a living writing science fiction novels now. Well, theoretically anyone can; as a practical matter very few do, or ever have.

More generally, Rob's piece is a meditation on the fact that the business model of the industry is changing and the ways that authors get paid for their work is changing with it, and leaving aside the issue of full-time novelists, this is a matter of no little concern for anyone who wants to get paid for their writing. I'm not going to gainsay Rob's concerns, and certainly he's not alone in these concerns. I will say my own perspective on the matter is more optimistic than his appears to be. 2010 is not 2000, the publishing industry for all its faults is not the music industry, and its reaction to electronic media has not been what the music industry's reaction was a decade ago, which was to shit itself in a panic and demand everything go back to the way it was before.

If nothing else (and it's not a "if nothing else" situation), it's worth noting that *every* major eBook reader on the market connects directly and seamlessly to a bookstore, and that to date the major battle in eBook sector was over *how much* eBooks should cost on release and who should dictate those prices, not whether eBooks should cost anything at all. There's a secondary and pertinent question regarding whether ten years from now writers will need publishers in the same ways and for the same things as they do now; while that's an interesting question, it's not necessarily here or there about whether authors themselves will be able to support themselves on their fiction, or on their science fiction particularly. There are lots of challenges to this task, some specific to this particular era. Every era has its own set of specific challenges.

My personal prediction for science fiction authors a decade from now is this: There will be a few who will be able to support themselves full time on their science fiction writing, but the large majority won't. Which is to say it'll be pretty much like it is today. Some things will very likely change, including *which* science fiction writers will be able to write full-time; some pulling it off today won't be doing so in ten years, while others we haven't heard of will be at or near the top of the heap (said the Hugo-winning, *New York Times* best-selling incoming President of SFWA who no one in science fiction *even knew was alive* in the year 2000). It's also possible that what we consider a novel will have changed somewhat, just as today's 100,000-word standard for a novel is different than the 60,000 word (or less) standard of a few decades ago. And so on. The details will change, as they've changed before, and will yet again, even after the digital switchover becomes old news.

But at the end of the day, a few science fiction writers will be lucky enough not to have to do anything else with their time, while everyone else will have to do it *also*, meaning they do something else *too*. Just like now.

JAY LAKE,
REMEMBERED

Jun

1

2014

(Note: Jay Lake, Campbell Award-winning writer and novelist.)

I can't actually remember when it was that I first met Jay Lake, which is an unusual thing for me. I can often tell you the exact time and place I met most people I care about, from my oldest friend Kyle (on the bus on the first day of second grade) onward. I suspect my memory of meeting Jay is more diffuse because I first knew so many people who knew Jay, so that by the time we had our first meeting it felt, by commutative property, that I already knew him. I'm racking my brain here and coming up with nothing. From the point of view of my memory, Jay just *was*.

One of the last times I saw Jay was the 2013 Nebula Awards Weekend. I have picture of him and me; in it, he's licking my head because he's attempting to taste my brain, and I am both alarmed and intrigued by the attempt. Because, you know: Jay. That's him. A big goof in a Hawaiian shirt.

In between the nebulous start of our friendship and that brain tasting. I am happy to say I got a good amount of quality time with Jay. We shared many conversations about writing and the sf/f community and other things. We collaborated together on a project. I blurbed one of his books. He and Elizabeth Bear instigated the Campbell Tiara, a piece of jewelry for Campbell Award winners which I was honored to be the first (but not the last) to wear. Indeed, "instigating" is a thing he did a lot of, both for good and for fun. I was happy to be an occasional participant of the instigations.

He was my friend, in short. In moments like these I always feel like I need to be careful about overstating the friendship; I don't want to claim a special status. So many more people are ahead of me in the line for Jay's affections, starting with his partner, and his daughter, his family, and then moving down the line. Nevertheless we were friends, and there was mutual affection. I am happy to have shared in his life in the amount I have been able.

Of the many things I admired about Jay, his ability to write, in *astoundingly huge gouts,* was chief among them. He had nine novels and *three hundred* short stories published during his career, during which he also maintained a full-time job and, alas, had to fight against the cancer that would eventually take him from us. It's not necessarily a smart thing to compare one writer's process with another's, so I never compared my output to Jay's. But one thing I *did* do, whenever I was having a little pity party for myself about how *hard* my writing life was at the moment, was to remind myself of Jay's work ethic, even in the face of everything he had to deal with. Writers write.

Jay was an excellent writer—the winner of the Campbell award and a nominee for the Hugo and the Nebula (among others)—and he was a person who was open about so much of his life. When it came to his cancer, it was no surprise that he would write about it and write about it nakedly, chronicling what seemed almost every aspect of his fight with the disease with a lack of personal vanity. Jay never painted himself a noble sufferer as far as I could see. He was *pissed* that he had cancer, angry about what it was taking from him, and apprehensive about the end of the only life he would have.

He was, in a word, human about it. I like so many others in science fiction and fantasy read these posts—not only because Jay offered them like signposts, letting us know where he was in his journey, but because, I think, Jay was asking us to stand witness to his life. I tried to be the witness I thought he was asking me to be. I think many of us did.

Now the witnessing is over and Jay is gone and there is a life complete. It is a good one, as far as I can see. Jay was and is a man of complexity; my picture of him is incomplete and narrow but hopefully not less true because of it. I'm happy I am his friend and glad for the times I had with him. I'm glad he shared part of his life with me, through his writing and through his company. I'm glad he shared part of his life with all of us.

Goodbye, Jay. You are remembered, and loved.

Jonathan Franzen Shakes His Fist at the Clouds, Especially the Virtual Ones

Jan

30

2012

Q uestion, which seems apt considering the previous post today:

Any thoughts on Jonathan Franzen's opinions about eBooks?

For those of you who have not seen them, here's a quote from Mr. Franzen on the matter:

> *Maybe nobody will care about printed books 50 years from now, but I do. When I read a book, I'm handling a specific object in a specific time and place. The fact that when I take the book off the shelf it still says the same thing—that's reassuring...Someone worked really hard to make the language just right, just the way they wanted it. They were so sure of it that they printed it in ink, on paper. A screen always feels like we could delete that, change that, move it around. So for a literature-crazed person like me, it's just not permanent enough.*

On one hand I get what he's saying, because I do love physical books. Today I got copies of the Spanish language version of *Fuzzy Nation*, and holding the physical printed object brings home the point that yes, someone bought the book, yes, someone printed it, and yes, people will read the thing (in another language, even!). A printed physical object ties into my personal sense of accomplishment when it comes to books. It's like, *here it is. In the real world. Finally.* I think the love of books as tactile objects is something that's going to be around for a while, and not just because writers need to be assured there is a (presumably) permanent, unalterable record.

On the other hand I suspect Franzen overprivileges the permanence of the book as a physical object to a considerable degree, and if you want to know why I think that, try reading an original science fiction pulp paperback from the 70s or earlier. They were printed on crappy acidic paper that started turning yellow nearly the moment they got off the printing press, the glue on the spine crumbles, and the thing starts falling apart the second you look at it too hard. You can *hold* one of these books, but if you try to *read* it, you run a really good chance of destroying it in the process. Bibliophiles—the ones who love physical books at least—are aware that physical books are anything but permanent. There are lots of ways for them to go away.

Here's another way of looking at it. I have a copy of China Mieville's *Perdido Street Station* on my shelf (it's the gorgeous limited edition by Subterranean Press). I also have a digital copy of it on my Nook. Which is more permanent? One is a physical object, but that physical object could be lost or stolen, or destroyed if, say, my house burned down to the ground, taking my library with it. The digital object, on the other hand, is hard to lose because it can be in multiple places; I can read it on my computer, or my eReader, or my cell phone or my computer tablet; indeed, I can read it one one, set that down and fire it up on the other and have the book open to the very spot I stopped reading it before. If my house burns up, my digital copy of *Perdido* will still be there to comfort me. But if Barnes & Noble goes out of business—and it might—then I may be screwed, because there's no guarantee the access to the book file will survive Barnes & Noble as a company (I have some useless DRMed audio files on my computer as testament of that).

There are other ways that both physical books and digital books can go away, but you get my point, I trust, which is that neither physical books nor digital books have any claim on permanence that can't be immediately refuted in significant ways. The one unassailable advantage physical books have or digital books is that they don't require an intermediary piece of hardware to access them—all you need is your eyeballs—and given the turnover in tech hardware, that's not insignificant. But it doesn't argue for permanence; it argues for a potentially longer window for information decay.

(Franzen's also incorrect that physical copies somehow limit the alterations that can be made to texts after the fact; Compare early versions of Ray Bradbury's *The Martian Chronicles* with later versions and you'll see what I mean. There's an excellent chance people who have read the later versions are entirely unaware that the text has been significantly altered. Franzen's also apparently charmingly naive about the number of copy errors that make it through the editorial process, despite everyone's best efforts.)

Franzen's dislike of eBooks appears essentially to be an appeal to the romanticism of physical books, which is nice and about which I can sympathize with him, although only up to a point. Ultimately, however, my more pragmatic side comes through, and it says "You want this book in [x] format? You'll pay me money for it? Here you go." Which is why my books are variously in hardcover, trade paperback, mass market paperback, eBook (in various formats) and audio (also in various formats), depending on their place in the production cycle and the agreements I have in place with publishers.

Outside of the desire to see my local indie bookstore stay in business, because they are awesome folks and it's a great shop, and in a larger sense for bookstores to survive because of what I see as the long terms social benefits of having booksellers as part of the matrix of commerce, I'm agnostic regarding format. The words—my words—are the same across all the formats, and it's those words that matter; the container, less so. I'd note Franzen's work is out there for electronic consumption, so it seems at the end of the day he is pragmatic about this at well, at least on a contractual level.

LIVING LIKE FITZGERALD

With a hat tip to the estimable Walter Jon Williams, I note an article which examines the tax returns of one F. Scott Fitzgerald, of whom you may have heard, over the length of his writing career from 1919 through 1940. It turns out that during those years, Fitzgerald more or less consistently clocked $24,000 in writing income, which the author of the article, employing a 20:1 ratio of money values then to money values now, offers as the equivalent of making $500,000 a year in today's dollars. This is a nice income if you can get it, and Fitzgerald got it in an era in which his tax rate was something on the order of 8%.

What's interesting for modern writers, however, are the little tidbits that let you know how much things have changed—and how much, alas, things have stayed the same.

For example, here's one fun fact: The engine of Fitzgerald's income (at least until he went to Hollywood) was not his novels but his short stories. He considered them his "day job," a thing to be endured because writing them would allow him the financial wherewithal to write the novels he preferred to do. And how much did he make for these short stories? Well, in 1920, he sold eleven of them to various magazines for $3,975. This averages to about $360 per story, and (assuming an average length of about 6,000 words) roughly six cents a word.

To flag my own genre here, "Six cents a word," should sound vaguely familiar to science fiction and fantasy writers, as that's the *current* going rate at the "Big Three" science fiction magazines here in the US: *Analog* (which pays six to eight cents a word), *Asimov's* (six cents a word "for beginners") and *Fantasy & Science Fiction* (six to nine cents a word). So, sf/f writers, in one sense you can truly say you're getting paid just as well as F. Scott Fitzgerald did; but in another, more relevant, "adjusted for inflation" sense, you're making five cents to every one of Fitzy's dollars. Which basically sucks. This is just one reason why making a living writing short fiction is not something you should be counting on these days.

(Mind you, science fiction writers of the 1920s weren't making what Fitzgerald did, either—indeed, if they were writing for *Amazing Stories* (the first SF magazine, which debuted in 1926), it was an open question as to whether they'd get paid at all; publisher Hugo Gernsback loved his "scientifiction" but he had liquidity problems, which is why he lost control of the magazine in 1929.)

In 1920, Fitzgerald also had his first novel published: *This Side of Paradise*. He made $6,200 on it for the year, from a royalty rate of 10% (later bumped up to 15%), on a cover price of $1.75. Using the 20:1 multiplier, we can say hardcovers in the US, at least, have gotten a lot cheaper, but that royalty rates for authors are essentially unchanged 90 years later; I myself make a 10% – 15% royalty on my books.

It's also interesting to note that *Paradise* was Fitzgerald's bestselling book while he was still alive, and that it sold less than 50,000 copies at the time. This would be similar to someone selling 150,000 copies of their book today: A solid seller, to be sure (I wouldn't turn down sales like that) but no *Twilight*, or even *The Secret History*. It's also a reminder that the main portion of Fitzgerald's literary fame had to wait until he was dead and unable to appreciate it—*The Great Gatsby* regularly sells in excess of 200,000 copies a year these days (hello, high school reading lists!), but sold only 25,000 copies while Fitzgerald was alive. I'm sure Fitzgerald would be happy being considered a writer for the ages—he was somewhat embittered at the end of his life that his literary star had fallen so dramatically—but I also suspect he wouldn't have minded all those yearly sales happening today occurring while he was still alive and having use of the money. He certainly could have used it.

Which is of course the other thing; in this era or the 1920s, a half million dollars (or its real money equivalent) is not an inconsiderable sum—and yet Fitzgerald had a hard time keeping it. Much of that was due the cost of tending to Zelda, his increasingly mentally erratic wife, who was frequently in psychiatric hospitals—yes! Health care was expensive then, too!—but some of it was just money just leaking out all over the place, as money seems to do around those creative types. And then there was Fitzgerald's desire to live well, with servants and nice houses and such, and his wee problem with alcohol. Eventually Fitzgerald's financial issues became significant enough that he felt obliged to work in Hollywood—*Hollywood!* of all places—which he found remunerative but degrading.

The lessons here: Do keep track of your money, try to live within your means, avoid debilitating addictions if at all possible and, for the nonce at least, try to have decent health insurance. That'll help you keep your cash as a writer, whether you're making $24,000 a year from your writing, or $500,000.

On my end of things, while I wouldn't mind getting paid like Fitzgerald (in the "half a million" sense, not the "$24,000" sense), I don't think I'd want to *live* like him. Aside from the fact that I'd have less than four years left on my life, he doesn't seem to have been very happy in his life while he lived it, and that wasn't something that having a significant income was going to fix. I might have wished for him a little less money (and the need to acquire it), and a little more peace of mind.

THE MAN
IN THE FREY
FLANNEL SUIT

Nov

13

2010

Folks from all over are sending along e-mails asking me what I think of the story in *New York* magazine about author James Frey's book packaging shop, in which Frey trolls classrooms full of impressionable MFA candidates and/or aspiring authors to get them to give him their ideas, in return offering them a contract that is a high water mark in being a complete asshole:

> *In exchange for delivering a finished book within a set number of months, the writer would receive $250 (some contracts allowed for another $250 upon completion), along with a percentage of all revenue generated by the project, including television, film, and merchandise rights—30 percent if the idea was originally Frey's, 40 percent if it was originally the writer's. The writer would be financially responsible for any legal action brought against the book but would not own its copyright. Full Fathom Five could use the writer's name or a pseudonym without his or her permission, even if the writer was no longer involved with the series, and the company could substitute the writer's full name for a pseudonym at any point in the future. The writer was forbidden from signing contracts that would "conflict" with the project; what that might be wasn't specified. The writer would not have approval over his or her publicity, pictures, or biographical materials. There was a $50,000 penalty if the writer publicly admitted to working with Full Fathom Five without permission.*

Just to be clear, if James Frey (or anyone else) tried to offer me this contract to write a book, here's what I would do: Have my agent schedule a meeting with him for the clear and specific purpose of kicking him hard and square in the balls.

But then again, James Frey would never offer *me* this sort of contract. I'm too old and ossified (read: agented and with knowledge of the publishing industry) for him. He doesn't want to deal with writers who know the appropriate response to this contract is to knee him in the groin. For Frey's scheme to work, he needs writers who don't know better, and apparently our nation's MFA programs don't actually have classes on contracts or how the publishing industry works, so they make fertile ground for a huckster intent on dazzling the kids. You can't say Frey doesn't know his target audience.

Seriously, people. $500 and unauditable net points for a novel? That contract probably also specifies that the writer has to spring for the lube.

The lamentable rejoinder to this is that some people will think that it's worth it for the exposure to the film industry or publishing industry or whatever. Folks: being an anonymous, uncredited cog in a book packaging scheme doesn't actually get you exposure to *anything*, except to the fact that you're working for peanuts for The Man, and The Man is a rich bearded hipster who walks around in socks, and doesn't care about you, just what you can do for him. Congratulations: you're the man in the Frey Flannel Suit. Not that you could afford a suit on what you're being paid.

Writers: This contract would be appalling and egregious regardless of who was offering it. A story idea good enough for James Frey to sell to Hollywood would be good enough to sell to Hollywood without James Frey. Write your story, get an agent, and sell your work with your own name on it and all your rights to the work intact. It may take more time, but it will be worth it. Have more respect for yourself and your work than quite obviously James Frey will have.

An Open Letter
to MFA Writing
Programs (and
Their Students)

Dear MFA writing programs (and their students):
Recently *New York* magazine published a story, in which
Columbia University's graduate writing program invited James
Frey to come chat with its students on the subject of "Can Truth Be Told?"
during which Frey mentioned a book packaging scheme that he had
cooked up. The contractual terms of that book packaging scheme are now
famously known to be egregious—it's the sort of contract, in fact, that
you would sign only if you were as ignorant as a chicken, and with about
as much common sense—and yet it seems that Frey did not have any
problem getting people to sign on, most, it appears, students of MFA programs. Frey is clearly selecting for his scheme writers who should know
better, but don't—and there's apparently a high correlation between being
ignorant that his contract is horrible and being an MFA writing student.

I don't blame Columbia University's graduate writing program for
inviting James Frey over to talk to its students about "truth." If there's
anyone who knows about the word *truth* contained between ironic quo-
tation marks, it'd be James Frey, and it's probably not a bad idea for the
kids to see a prevaricating hustler up close to observe how one of his
kind can rationalize bad actions and even poorer ethics as transgressive
attempts at literature. It's always a joy to see how a master of bullshit
spins himself up; publishing and literature being what they are, the students should probably learn to recognize this species sooner than later,
all the better to move their wallets to their front pockets when such a
creature stands before them.

What does bother me, however, is that Frey apparently quite intentionally was working his way through MFA programs recruiting writers for his book packaging scheme. You could say there's an obvious reason for this, which is that MFA writing students are likely more competent at writing than your average schmoe writer on the street (this is a highly arguable contention, but never mind that now), and they're all in one place, which makes for easier recruiting. But I suspect there's another reason as well, which is that in general it appears MFA writing programs don't go out of their way to educate their students on the publishing industry, or contracts, or much about the actual business of writing.

And so when someone like James Frey breezes in and starts blowing smoke about collaborations, the response is this—

> We were desperate to be published, any way we could. We were spending $45,000 on tuition, some of us without financial aid, and many taking out loans that were lining us up to graduate six figures in debt. A deal like the one Frey was offering could potentially pay off our loans and provide an income for the next decade. Do a little commercial work under a pseudonym, sell the movie rights, and never have to suffer as a writer in New York. We wouldn't even need day jobs.

—followed by a number of students receiving and then signing a contract that pays them next to nothing, and offers a deal so constrictive that by the terms of the contract Frey could publish works under their names and keep them from publishing again (via a gloriously vague "non-compete" clause). Frey was no doubt counting on the students being starry-eyed at the presence of a real-live bestselling author (even a disgraced one) who was waving a movie deal in their faces, but one reason he *could* count on it was because he was speaking to an audience whose formal educations did not include learning how to spot a crappy deal.

So, MFA writing programs, allow me to make a suggestion. Sometime before you hand over that sheepskin with the words "Master of Fine Arts" on it, for which your students may have just paid tens of thousands of dollars (or more), offer them a class on the business of

204

the publishing industry, including an intensive look at contracts. Why? Because, Holy God, *they will need it.*

Now, perhaps you are saying, "We focus on the art of writing, not the business." My answer to that is, please, pull your head out. Your students are not paying as much money as they do for your program strictly for the *theoretical* joys of writing. They are paying so they can publish, and it's a pretty good bet, considering how many of those Columbia folks scrambled to pitch to Frey, that they actually want to be published *commercially*, not just in university presses, in which (sorry) low advances and small print runs don't matter since it's just another line on the CV. Yes, you are teaching an art, but whether you like it or not you're also teaching a trade—or at the very least many of your students are coming to learn a trade, and put up with the art portion of it as part of the deal. Teaching them something about the trade will not hurt your program.

And then you might say, "there's no point in teaching them about the business because if they go the commercial publishing route they'll have agents." To which I would say, wow, really? "Other people will handle the dirty money part" is a response that **a)** shows a certain amount of snobbery, **b)** sets up a writer to be dependent on others because she is ignorant of the particulars of her own business. You know how every year you hear about an actor or musician who has been screwed by his accountant or business manager? That's what happens when you don't pay attention—or more relevantly don't have the *knowledge* to pay attention.

To be clear, I don't want to paint literary agents, *et al* as suspicious and shady characters; I have two literary agents (one for fiction and one for non-fiction) and they are super-smart and do a great job for me, and I'm glad they do their job and leave me to do mine, which is writing. But you know what? Part of the reason I know they're doing a good job is because I know my own business, which makes it easier for me to know what they are doing. It also means they know that they can discuss business with me on a realistic and sensible level. Beyond that, not everyone has an agent, or (alas) a good one if they have one.

Finally, you may say "We don't have anyone on our faculty who can/wants to teach that course." Well, presuming that your university doesn't have a business or law school on campus, from whom you might borrow an appropriate professor every now and again, I can't help but notice that adjunct professors are very popular in academia these days, and I'm guessing that maybe you could find someone. Try a working agent, maybe. Point is, if you wanted to offer this class, you could.

There is no reason not to offer a class on this stuff. And maybe students will choose not to take that class. But if that's the case, at least *then it's all on them.* Your students are all presumably adults and are responsible for their own actions, to be sure. But if you're not giving them the tools to know when a huckster is hucking in their direction, if they get hulled, some of that's on you.

Speaking of which, let me know turn my attention away from the MFA writing programs and to the writing grad students themselves:

Dudes. *Learn about the industry,* already, *before* you sign a contract. Otherwise you're going to get shaved by the first jackass who waves a publishing deal in your face. Yes, I know, you're smart and clever and you write really well. You know what, your belief in your intelligence and your cleverness and your writing ability as a proxy for knowing everything you need to know about the world is *exactly* what's going to get you screwed. Because being smart and clever and writing well has *nothing* to do with the backend business of the publishing industry or reading a contract knowledgeably and dispassionately. Think about those MFA students who are now slaving away for Frey on the worst contract just about anyone in publishing has ever seen. I'm pretty sure they all think they are smart and clever and write well, too.

If your MFA program doesn't have a class on contracts and the publishing industry, ask for one. Because, Jesus, you're spending enough for your education. You might want to get some practical knowledge out of it as well. If it can't or won't offer that class to you, **a)** complain and **b)** seek out that information. The writers' organization to which I belong, SFWA, sponsors the Web site Writer Beware, which offers some of the basics about avoiding scams and bad practices, and has an informational area which includes sample contracts. Other writers' organizations also have information for you, and most bookstores will have sections on writing and the business of writing. Find that information, learn it, and use it before you have anything to do with anyone trying to make a deal with you.

But why you should have to pay extra for this essential bit of education, or search for it outside your writing program, mind you, positively baffles me.

MFA PROGRAMS AND COMMERCIAL PUBLISHING

Nov

17

2010

Elise Blackwell, author and director of the MFA program at the University of South Carolina, offers in *The Chronicle of Higher Education* a rebuttal to my suggestion that MFA writing programs offer a course on contracts and the publishing industry. Her position is that the goal of MFA programs is "not to grow hothouse flowers but to protect writers for two or three short years so that they [can] write a book without distraction," and notes that one real issue is MFA programs which charge large sums for tuition, thus adding additional pressure on their students to find a way to defray their debt load as soon as possible—and thus making them more susceptible to hucksters like James Frey. Her problem with the Columbia MFA program is not so much that it doesn't offer a business/contracts course, but that it costs close to $50k a year to attend (the MFA program Blackwell attended, at UC Irvine, apparently funded its students).

I encourage you to read the article, which I think is an interesting and useful perspective from the other side of the MFA fence. That said, I (naturally) have some quibbles with the article, and here they are.

• Blackwell and I are certainly in agreement that $50k a year for an MFA is a ridiculous sum on its face, and I agree that staring at that debt load is bound to make a writer quiver. But as I've noted elsewhere, part of the reason one pays for a degree from an elite institution is not just for the degree but for everything else such a degree confers, including connections, a robust alumni/elite school network, and an (at least initial) economic leg up on other folks with an equal or comparable degree from schools perceived as less elite. I remember the editor who hired me for my first job telling me that my degree from the University of Chicago was "impressive;" I'm pretty sure that the same degree from Fresno State would not have elicited the same response. And I of course was happy to let that editor be impressed. I wanted the gig. But beyond that, that was one of the things a U of C degree was *supposed* to do for me, and did. That made it, both short and long term, worth the cost.

Let us stipulate that a writer who is accepted into Columbia's graduate writing program very likely had her choice of other programs to attend, including ones substantially less expensive. One reason to choose Columbia despite the cost is for these ancillary benefits. This is not to defend the actual price tag of $50k, which I think is a silly amount. It is to suggest there is a rational reason to make that expensive choice.

It's also worth noting that those students who make that choice for that reason are *already* looking beyond the classroom to their overall careers. So while the MFA program can offer a safe harbor to focus on writing and study, that's not the only (and perhaps not even the primary) reason students are in the program. In which case, a little practical knowledge would not be a bad thing.

• Likewise, I suspect that Blackwell rather overadvantages the idea of the MFA writing program as a cloister for the life of the mind, with students inwardly turned to the program rather than outward facing into the world. She and I certainly do not disagree that there are advantages to the former, nor do I think it's wrong for an MFA writing program to say to its students "your head should be *here*, now" and to tell editors and agents hovering by the door to piss off. That said, I think a program should be realistic about the latter at the same time, because, surprise, whether in theory an MFA writing program is about literature and the life of the mind, in practice people want to be publishing sooner than later—maybe not for good reasons and maybe before they should, but, well. That's ambition for you, and that ambition will be there regardless of the cost of the program.

That being the case, the argument for a business/contracts class is as much about *protecting* the "hothouse flowers" who are anxious to jump the fence into commercial writing as it is *preparing* the people who have stuck with the program to make their first sales. A practical understanding of the traps and disadvantageous things writers both do and let slip past them in contracts can be a useful cautionary tale that feeds into the overall goal of the MFA program of keeping its student's head in the program, not craning out to a hustler with a genuinely crappy contracts.

• Speaking of which, I think Blackwell is rather too dismissive that the awfulness of Frey's Full Fathom Five contract. She writes:

> *Some suggest that Frey's "victims" were made vulnerable by MFA programs that didn't educate them about publishing, but it requires little training to identify Frey's contracts as absurd. (Does anyone really think $250 is fair market value for a commercially viable novel or that letting someone else use your name as they please is smart?) The writers who signed those contracts weren't acting out of ignorance but from some combination of desperation, hope, and a sense of exceptionalism that writers need to get out of bed. ("I know James Joyce died in poverty, Kafka worked a desk job, and Dan Brown can't coax a sentence out of a bag, but I can be brilliant and rich.") Some of them were just taking a flyer.*

The issue with that awful, awful contract isn't what's obvious, but what's *not*. Sure, anyone with a brain could see that $250 for a novel is terrible, but what those damnably ignorant MFA students were looking at *wasn't* the $250; they were looking at the alleged 40% of backend, which includes (cue Klieg lights and orchestra) *sweet, rich, movie option money!!!!!!!!* And what they *don't* know, or undervalue because reading contracts is difficult when you've not done it before and no one's explained them to you, is that it's not really 40% of everything, it's 40% of whatever Frey *decides to give you* after he's trimmed off his share, and, oh yeah, you have to take his word for it because you're not allowed an audit. So yes, the $250 (or $500) for a book is awful and obvious. But it's everything else about that contract which is truly rapacious, as it appears to promise *so much more*, and it all seems perfectly reasonable when you don't have the experience to know what a horror it is.

Beyond this, of course: Has anyone told the MFA students holding those contracts the odds of a book making it through the production gauntlet, even when they're from best selling authors? Has anyone told them how much the average film option is for (hint: Not a lot) or that it's not paid all at once but often in installments that dribble out over years? Or that the real payday is not up front, but on the back end—*if* the property ever goes into production, which it probably won't—and in the meantime they will still have to eat? Does anyone expect *James Frey* to be honest to them about all of this? No, what they can expect from James Frey is what he no doubt says: "I'm offering you not a lot now but there's a huge potential later." Which is perfectly accurate as far as it goes. It just doesn't go very far.

So, yes: Blackwell is wrong, here. It doesn't take training to see the parts that are obviously bad, but the obviously bad parts are easily rationalized away. It *does* take training and experience to see the parts that are genuinely egregious, and to know why they are so. If an MFA program is going to let a snake into the garden, as Columbia did when it dropped James Frey into that classroom, then it should damn well have some antivenom on hand.

• Finally, I found this bit egregiously classist:

> M.F.A. programs are about the creation and study of literature, and it's worth reminding people that you don't need any degree to be a writer. A young writer whose central goal is commercial success should skip graduate school. (You don't apprentice at an opera company and expect to be introduced to Nashville music producers, which I say with no disrespect to either milieu.)

Opera companies aren't interested in commercial success? Nashville music producers can't or don't create art? I have news for Ms. Blackwell on both counts. Overt and woefully uninformed personal musical snobbery aside, it appears she's confusing how each of these musical genres currently generally acquires funding with whether they are concerned with commercial success. This is not a good comparison.

On the same token, I can very easily picture a writer who has commercial motivations going to graduate school for writing because he has adjudged his own personal success as a writer depending on honing his own skills in a setting of collaboration and instruction. To suggest such a writer deprive himself of these advantages simply because he also dreams of best seller lists seems a bit dismissive. I certainly agree one does not need a degree to be a writer (hello!), but if Blackwell's classmate Mr. Chabon is any indication (or indeed Ms. Blackwell herself), neither must an MFA doom one to a life of academic publishing and/or obscurity.

A love of literature and the study thereof, and a desire for commercial success for one's own writing and art, are not either/or propositions. Even for MFA writing students.

MFAs, Writing
and Teacher Guilt

Apr

21

2010

Via Galleycat, today we learn that bestselling author Lionel Shriver doubts the value of an MFA degree, even thought she has one herself (and from Columbia, to boot):

> *I can't say that I regret it exactly...But I sometimes feel in retrospect that I should have gotten a proper education in something like history, something substantive. If I'm going to be honest, what I really needed in my early 20s was an audience; I wasn't developed enough as a writer to be publishing. So I couldn't achieve that audience through getting short stories in The New Yorker...*
>
> *So it is not a dumb thing for me to do. And therefore I can't really tell other people who were in a similar situation and have a similar need to have people read their work that they shouldn't do it. But it does have a kind of indulgent, middle-class gestalt. The grim truth is that most people who get MFAs will not go on to be professional writers and therefore when I've been on the other side of it and occasionally taught creative writing, I felt a little bit guilty because so many of the people that you should be encouraging, because there's no point to it if you're not encouraging, are not going to make it.*

This is an interesting perspective to me on a couple of grounds. The obvious one is that I share Ms. Shriver's ambivalence about writing MFAs; they're not necessary to be a published writer or author, and they take up time that a budding writer could be using gathering experience in other aspects of the world outside of safely cloistered academia. For myself, in my last year of college, I never considered going on from there into an MFA program; I wanted to get out there and get an actual writing job, because **a)** the thought of someone paying me to write had its appeal, **b)** if I went into an MFA program I'd still have to get a job anyway, so why not just get a job and keep the money for myself.

But then, I've also always had a wide blue-collar streak to my writing ethos—writing is work and a job, not (just) an art and a calling—which was undoubtedly fueled by the fact that so many of my early writing idols were newspapermen and/or science fiction writers, many if not most of whom simply got out there and *wrote* for a living, rather than taking the time to take a degree in it. Anyone who knows me knows I take very nearly as much pride in the fact I earn a living writing as I do in the works I write, and that I don't scorn the writer whose work pays for the roof over her head or the food on her table, even if the writing itself will never win a literary award. Given this, it's not entirely surprising I find an MFA optional at best and a somewhat frivolous expenditure of time and money at worst (especially if, like Shriver, all you really want is an audience). Naturally, your mileage may vary on this opinion.

So there's perhaps some measure of irony—if not to say bald contradiction—for me to note that even though I share Shriver's ambivalence on the value of a writing MFA, I disagree with her ambivalence (or more accurately, guilt) about the value of teaching writing to people even if the majority of the people you teach don't go on to be professional writers. Indeed, I think her feeling guilty about it is a little silly.

Why? Because that's not her problem. Her problem is to teach well; everything else is on the student and up to forces mostly beyond the control of either of them. Shriner is almost certainly correct that most people in MFA programs will not become professional writers. Nor will most people who go to writing workshops, or take undergraduate Creative Writing degrees, or show up at the Learning Annex for a six-hour crash course, or whatever. They might not become pro writers because they're not good enough. They might not because there's a recession going on. They might not because the particular sort of thing they like to write is obscure and has no commercial market. They might not because they decide there's something else they want to do more. They might not because they never intended to, they just wanted to learn for their own pleasure (it happens). They might not because on the way home from class, they fall down a manhole and are eaten by the CHUDs. Lots of things could occur that could keep these prospective writers from going pro.

And none of it is anything Shriner (or anyone who teaches, writing or otherwise) has to worry their head about. Their gig is handing out tools; what the students do with the tools is up to them. And the tools in themselves have value—that is to say there's a value to learning that extends beyond the rather limited gauge of what that learning will do for you in a direct commercial fashion. You know, I have a degree in philosophy: Should my teachers feel even a little bit guilty that I am not a professional philosopher? I don't suspect they do feel guilty, and if they do they shouldn't. The degree has been useful to me in other ways.

So, again, the interesting conundrum of someone offering genuine value by teaching in a program of debatable value for the student. But perhaps not so much a conundrum if you remember these are two different things, and if you grant that the student is capable of making an informed choice about the program and what they're really getting out of it at the end of the day. That makes things a lot simpler, it does. And a lot less guilt inducing.

My Schadenfreude Phaser is Set to "Meh"

May
9
2012

Peaple are (rather gleefully, I suspect) sending me a story about conservative writer Jonah Goldberg getting dinged for the jacket flap bio of his latest book, which incorrectly states that Goldberg has been twice nominated for the Pulitzer. In fact it appears he's been twice submitted for consideration, which involves no special skill other than filling out an application and sending the $50 fee. When called on it, both Goldberg and his publisher said "whoops, that's an error" and backtracked on it, both suggesting it was an innocent mistake.

Well, it's definitely a mistake. I'm not sure it was "innocent" in the sense of "unintentional," although it might be in the sense of "non-malicious," since no one gets hurt when Goldberg overinflates his accomplishments. But as publishing sins go, it's pretty venial. It's not like *plagiarism*.

Also, from a certain pathetic point of view, it's not an actual *lie*. It's *stupid*, and it's something you can get called on so easily that it's foolish to do it. But just as Bill Clinton wanted to parse what "is" is, Goldberg appears to have been hanging his hat on what the word "nominated" means.

In this case Goldberg seems to have been using the word "nominated" in the sense of "proposed for consideration," which if you're a word dork who hauls out the dictionary every time someone points out you're using a word in a non-conventional manner, is not incorrect: Goldberg's publishers did propose him (and/or his work) by filling out the forms and sending along the money. Goldberg's initial response to being called on his use of the word "nominated" in at least one of his various bios—"Nominated by the Tribune syndicate. Never said I was a finalist. There's a distinction"—makes it clear that's why Goldberg went with the wording.

And in his defense, he's not alone. I've had people proudly note to me that they've been nominated for a Pushcart Prize (again, by a publisher sending in an application) or for Hugos or Nebulas (by a member of the voting pool offering a recommendation and/or submitting their name or work on the initial nominating ballot) or for other awards. Again, in a strict dictionary sense, they're not wrong. It's a nomination—they or their work has been named for consideration.

In the practical, real world sense, however, it's *totally incorrect;* the common usage of the "nominated" when in comes to awards is those works that have made a short list prior to the naming of a winner (or, in the case of the Pulitzer and a few other awards, noted as being part of the final selection pool after the award is announced). What's more, I rather suspect a large number of the people who announce their work is "nominated" in the dictionary sense are well aware that people who see the word in the context of award immediately go to the "short list" meaning of the word. Which is why they use it at all—or at the very least allow it not to be corrected.

This is, incidentally, why it doesn't pay to be a dictionary dork if you don't understand that dictionary definitions are descriptive, not pre-scriptive; you can be literally correct about the definition of a word, but still be contextually wrong and look silly in the real world. I mean, look: I'm pretty certain at least a couple of people nominated *Fuzzy Nation* for the Best Novel Hugo Award this year. If I went around saying it was nominated for Best Novel because of that, I'd have my ass handed to me. And rightly so, because it's not correct, even if by the *dictionary defini-tion* I've been nominated. The dictionary is not your friend in situations like these.

Why didn't Goldberg correct this until he got called on it? You got me. I don't buy that Goldberg was unaware of the notations. He prob-ably didn't write his jacket bio copy (I don't write mine) but he almost certainly got jacket proofs, and it's incumbent on him to correct errors.

This would have been an easy fix. The obvious answer is that he didn't correct it because he didn't want to or that he genuinely believed that it wasn't a big deal to say "nominated" when "submitted for consideration" was more correct. Maybe to his audience it doesn't matter, or he didn't believe his audience would know anything about the Pulitzer process. Which may be correct since he was ultimately called on it by another journalist. It was still kind of dumb of him.

My problem is that I can't work up a real sense of *schadenfreude* on this because, really, it's just kind of amateur hour. I'm no fan of Goldberg, who strikes me as a slap-dash researcher and whose political rhetoric runs the gamut from "fatuous" to "shallow," but the dude's been in the grown-up publishing world for a couple of decades now and has shipped hundreds of thousands of books. You'll likely never see me write these words in the context of Goldberg ever again, but he's *better* than this sort of penny-ante silliness, or at least he should *know* better. It's like watching an NBA player trip over untied shoelaces. It's not as much fun as it could be.

THE MYTH OF SF/F
PUBLISHING HOUSE
EXCEPTIONALISM

May

1

2015

(Note: For this piece, it's useful to know that in the mid-2010s there was much of a to-do made by science fiction authors of politically conservative leanings about "Social Justice Warriors," which in this particular case meant science fiction fans and writers with liberal political leanings, imagined or otherwise. This culminated in a long, messy and ultimately futile attempt by conservative and/or "alt-right" writers and their fans (calling themselves "Sad Puppies" and "Rabid Puppies") to flood the Hugo Awards with their chosen nominees, many of which were chosen purely to annoy other voters. This nonsense appears to have receded for the moment, at least in science fiction.

Baen, a very fine house publishing house offering some very fine science fiction and fantasy, is the publishing home of a number of conservative authors, some of whom found themselves caught up (and in some cases originating) this agitation. Don't worry, we'll come back to this later.)

Recently author John Ringo (in a Facebook post previously available to the public but since made private) recently asserted that every science fiction house has seen a continuous drop in sales since the 1970s—with the exception of Baen (his publisher), which has only seen an increase across the board. This argument was refuted by author Jason Sanford, who mined through the last couple of years of bestseller lists (Locus lists specifically, which generate data by polling

SF/F specialty bookstores) and noted that out of 25 available bestselling slots across several formats in every monthly edition of Locus magazine, Baen captures either one or none of the slots every month—therefore the argument that Baen is at the top of the sales heap is not borne out by the actual, verifiable bestseller data.

(This is all related tangentially to the current Hugo nonsense, as Ringo wanted to make a point about Social Justice Warriors and how they've tainted science fiction in general, except for Baen, apparently the lone SJW-free SF/F publisher, whose political/social purity is thus being financially rewarded.)

Sanford is correct in his point that as a matter of books from Baen whose individual sales can compete with the sales of individual books from other science fiction publishers on a month-to-month basis, as charted by the *Locus* list, Baen's showing is modest (the May *Locus* lists, incidentally, show no Baen books, whereas Tor shows up five times, Orbit five times, DAW four times, Del Rey three times, Ace and Harper Voyager once each, and non-genre-specific publishers like Bantam and Morrow taking the rest of the slots).

But does that mean Ringo's larger assertion (sales of SF/F publishing houses are down since the 70s except for Baen) is false? Not necessarily! Here are some reasons Ringo might still be right:

1. Ringo's first assertion (SF/F publishing houses sales down since the 70s) is *independent* of how any individual title by any publishing house stacks up against any other title by any publishing house in the month-to-month or week-to-week horse races known as the best-seller lists. That a book is #1 on the *Locus* list one month does not mean it sold the same number of books as any previous #1; nor does it speak to the overall sales of any particular publishing house.

2. Bestseller lists don't (generally) track backlist sales or month-to-month sales of books that don't hit the lists but nevertheless sell steadily. A book that initially sells modestly but keeps selling regularly can (and sometimes does) eventually sell more than a book that cracks the best-seller lists but then falls off precipitately. If Baen books are good backlist sellers—and better so than other publishers' books—then Ringo's assertion could be correct.

3. Publishing houses expand and contract all the time, and some years are better than others. If you're charting the existence of a publishing house over forty years—genre or otherwise—then its sales history is going to reflect that. It's possible Baen's own history has been one of consistent (although, if so, I would suspect very modest) growth, as it's stuck to its knitting, specializing largely but not exclusively in specific sub-genres of science fiction and fantasy.

Now, in order for Ringo's assertion to be proven true, he'd need to provide actual data that show all of these things, otherwise, he's just asserting. Does he have that data? Well, hold up for a moment, because I have some other things I want to get to first.

Ringo's assertion *could* be correct. But here are some various ways that Ringo could be—intentionally or otherwise—putting his thumb on the scale:

1. Baen has only been in business since 1983; comparing its sales history to a house like, say, Ace, which was founded thirty years prior and whose own sales history went through a couple of boom-and-bust cycles (not to mention changes in ownership) before Baen even came into being, not to mention other publishers who participated in the business cycles of the 70s that Baen did not, *might* be misleading.

2. If Baen's initial sales were modest, then growth from that modest number would not necessarily be all that impressive; one can grow from modest numbers to only slightly less modest numbers and still see significant growth, percentage wise. Likewise, continued growth can be fractionally modest and still be growth. "Growth" without context is not a useful metric.

3. Additionally, "growth" in itself doesn't necessarily mean that what Baen publishes does particularly well in sales, either by itself or in competition with other publishers. Scale is important. If Baen sells "X" books one year, and another publisher sells 3X, and then next year Baen sells X+1% while the other publisher sells 3X-1%, then Baen has experienced growth where the other publisher hasn't—and the other publisher is still selling a healthy multiple of Baen.

4. Likewise, "growth," while a nice thing, does not necessarily directly equate to success as a publisher. A publisher could shrink the number of titles it sells but end up making more money than it did with a larger list by focusing on core titles, paring off costs associated with selling an extended list (marketing, touring, advances, etc) and negotiating better deals with retailers, etc. Whereas growth, unchecked and unplanned, can lead to ruin; off the top of my head I can think of at least a couple of publishers in the genre who experienced enviable growth and then fell on their ass because their businesses didn't scale.

5. Ringo's focus on SF/F publishers elides that other non-SF specific houses have done a very good job selling science fiction and fantasy in recent years. *The Martian*, arguably the best-selling adult science fiction book of the last year, is published by Broadway. Ernie Cline, whose *Ready Player One* sells very well, is published by Crown. Neil Gaiman is published by Morrow. George R. R. Martin is published in paperback by Bantam. Lev Grossman is published by Viking. It also elides the entire YA market, which is a huge market for SF/F, almost all of which is published by YA-specific imprints rather than SF/F-specific imprints. So even if Ringo's claim were broadly true, with regard to specific SF/F houses, the claim is so narrowly tailored with regard to how SF/F written work sells today—and by whom, and *to* whom—that it is of dubious utility.

6. Finally, Ringo appears to fall prey to the old "correlation is not causation" thing, in that even if Baen is experiencing growth where other SF/F houses are not, it's not necessarily the case that it's because its authors (or stories) are "SJW-free."

Ringo appears wants to make to two arguments: One, that Baen has experienced consistent, across-the-board growth in its sales where other SF/F publishers have not. Two, that this is due to Baen not publishing authors or tales that are "SJW"-y; only "cracking good tales" allowed, the definition of which apparently preclude any Social Justice Warrior-ness (although apparently may include any number of conservative/reactionary tropes).

The first of these, naturally, would appear to be the easiest to prove or disprove. Here's what you would need: Baen's complete sales numbers from 1983 onward, and every other publisher's sales numbers, since 1970 (or whenever they started business).

You'd need the first to establish that Baen's sales have indeed always shown an upward trajectory of growth, which is to say 32 years of absolutely unbroken sales increases (and you'd need to make sure that sales were *actual sales*—i.e., exchange of money as opposed to downloading freely available ebooks, which Baen laudably offered well before anyone else). I'm going to go on record saying that while this is certainly *possible*, I suspect it's unlikely; if nothing else there's likely to have been a divot in 2008/2009, when the world economy crashed and everyone freaked out. But it could be true! And if so, good for them.

Then you'd need the second to establish that every other publisher in the genre has seen *continuous* decreased sales since the 1970s. This will be more difficult. Some of the most prominent publishers in the genre weren't around in the 1970s; Tor, the largest US SF/F publisher, as an example, wasn't founded until 1980. Others have almost certainly seen their sales expand as their reach has expanded; for example Orbit, which was founded in 1974 in the UK but which is now an international house with the distribution might of Hachette behind it. Still others have probably seen their sales grow since their founding simply because they are new houses; Saga Press, Simon and Schuster's new SF/F imprint, will see *infinite percentage sales growth* this year because it literally did not exist last year. That alone, I would note, would invalidate Ringo's assertion.

(And in all cases, again, you would have to show that the drop was *continuous*—that is, no uptick in sales at any point by any of these publisher in at least thirty-five years. Which seems, well. *Unlikely*.)

This is of course where the quibbles and caveats would come, but, you know. Words do mean things. If you're going to say without qualification that every single SF/F publisher except one has seen continuous sales drops for decades, while that lone exception has seen a continuous increase in the same timeframe, it'd be nice to see the evidence of that assertion. Actual data, please!

Which might be hard to come by, as several SF/F publishers are owned by, or are themselves, privately owned companies. Baen is; so is, if memory serves, Tor Books. They are under no obligation to offer sales data to the public. Also, what sales data is publicly available is often incomplete—Bookscan, the most prominent book sales tracking apparatus in the US, does not track all sales (I've noted before that it tracks only a small percentage of my own overall sales). Authors can eventually learn their own total sales, but the key word here is "eventually," as royalty statements can arrive semi-annually, and record sales with a six month lag. And of course authors themselves have no requirement to accurately report their specific sales to anyone.

All of which is to say that I wish John Ringo joy in actually proving his assertion. It's rather easier to disprove.

The second part of Ringo's assertion, the implication that Baen's continuous sales upswing is due to cracking good SJW-free tales, I'm not going to bother to address seriously, because what a "Social Justice Warrior" is at this point is something of a moving target, the most consistent definition of which appears to be "Anyone left of Ted Cruz who certain politically conservative authors want to whack on in order to make whatever dubious, self-serving, fact-free point they wish to make at the moment." I believe George R. R. Martin has recently been relegated to SJW status for being upset with the action of the Puppy slates and the Hugos; this is a curious maneuver if we're talking "cracking good tales" and sales numbers as a proxy for...well, whatever they're meant to be a proxy for.

It's also bunk because while Baen is being used by Ringo as a synecdoche for a certain subgenres of science fiction (and the non-SJW agendas of the authors who produce it and the readers who read it), I have to wonder whether Baen itself wants that responsibility or affiliation.

I mean, as just one example, we're all aware that Baen published *Joanna Russ*, yes? More than once? Joanna Russ, part of the "new wave" of science fiction that Ringo identifies as a proto-SJW movement? Joanna Russ, who was the very definition of what is labeled a Social Justice Warrior before any conservative or reactionary person even thought to spit such an epithet from out between their lips? *That* Joanna Russ? The only way that Joanna Russ does *not* fully qualify for retroactive SJW status is if the definition of "SJW" *actually includes* "cannot be published by Baen Books." And yet, apparently, she could tell a "cracking good tale," because that's what Baen publishes. Strange!

You know, here's a thing. I am published by, and frequently associated with, Tor Books. I have a pretty good idea of how the place works. I *do not* presume to talk for them, or to suggest how they might proceed with their business, other than in the most general terms of "They're going to mostly buy and sell science fiction and fantasy." Why? Because that's not my gig. I think if I *started* to tell people what sort of science fiction Tor is only going to sell, or who it will publish and who it will not, it might eventually get back to me that I should maybe *not* do that.

Because who knows how that would play out? What authors who might be a great success at Tor—and for whom Tor could do a great job—would shy away from the house because I flapped my gums in apparent certain knowledge of what my editor and publisher wanted? What damage might I do associating the publishing house with politics and personalities they might wish to stay far away from? How uncomfortable might I make other authors my publisher works with by asserting what will and will not be published there? And how foolish would I look if I asserted something about what the publishing house would never do—and then the publishing house went and did it?

That previous paragraph is not entirely directed at Ringo, incidentally. I've seen a number of authors published by Baen asserting what the house would or would not do, with regard to stories and books and authors, and what is and would be published, and what is and would not, and to whom any of the above is sold. I can't help wonder how many of them will be surprised one day. Baen is a house that publishes some very good science fiction, mostly of a certain type, and, one presumes, largely to a certain audience. But I would submit that the type of science fiction, and the audience for it, is rather more varied than is currently being asserted. I can scan my own shelves and find a *whole lot* of Baen, and a whole lot of other publishers. It all goes into the pot for me. I suspect that it might irritate or annoy certain folks (*not* Ringo, but some others, I feel sure) that I like, read and promote Baen Books, but you know. The hell with that stupidity. Being a "social justice warrior" means I get to read (and incidentally, vote for on award ballots) what I want, rather than waiting to be told by someone else what I should like and what I shouldn't.

In any event: Let's put to rest the myth of exceptionalism of Baen Books. It's like Tor, or Ace, or Orbit or Del Rey or lots of other SF/F houses (and other publishers) you might care to name. It's in the businesses of selling books. Sometimes it has good years, sometimes it has less good years. Sometimes its authors win awards, sometimes they don't. At the end of the day, however, it does the same thing as any publisher: It publishes books that it hopes, when you get to the end of them, you say "I'd like to read more like *that*." Good for them. Good for any publisher who does that.

A Note On
a Jackass
Getting Booted
From Twitter

Milo Yiannopoulos, aka Nero aka some real basic garbage in human form, got the boot from Twitter last night as a result of encouraging his racist and/or sexist and/or alt-right pals to go after actress Leslie Jones, who starred in the new *Ghostbusters*, aka the film sexist manboys wailed was ruining their childhood. Jones was subjected to more than a day of appalling abuse, Yiannopoulos chortled about it like the troll he is and cheered his minions on, and Twitter finally decided he was a liability and permanently dumped his ass.

So, some thoughts on this:

1. Yiannopoulos and his party pals are now mewling about this being some horrible violation of free speech, so let's recall that **a)** Twitter is not the US or any other government and **b)** is a private entity and **c)** essentially reserves the right to boot anyone from their service for whatever reason, so, really, *waaaaaaaah,* and also, no. Yiannopoulos still has a platform for his nonsense on Breitbart, aka where journalism goes to drill holes in its temple and then cover itself in its own poop, so anyone who wants him can go there (Please go there. Please stay there). He hasn't been censored; he's just been told to take a hike.

2. Yiannopoulos and his party pals will also want to claim this is about him being conservative, and again, no. There's nothing inherent in holding to a conservative philosophy that requires one, in their interactions with others online, to be a raging shithole, or to encourage others to be the same. Millions of conservatives use Twitter every day without being raging shitholes. Conversely, there's nothing about a *liberal* philosophy that means you can't be a raging shithole; I just the other day muted a liberal turd over there because I didn't want to be bothered with his smug dickery any further. Being an asshole is orthogonal to political philosophy. Yiannopoulos' public persona is centered on being an asshole in order to serve a market of assholes. That's pretty obvious.

3. When Yiannopoulos was booted off of Twitter, some folks wrenched their hands and said "But that's what he wants! It'll just serve his narrative of persecution!" Well, one, no, it's not what he wanted. This is a fellow who, when given an opportunity to ask a question in the White House press room, querulously whined about losing his "verified" checkmark on Twitter. Being booted from the service is not an actual win for him. Two, *of course* he'll spin it like a win anyway, because as with other dipshits of his sort, everything must always be spun as, not only a victory, but as a victory that is unfolding *exactly to plan*. Yiannopoulos could trip down a flight of stairs mouth first and he'd crawl himself up a wall at the landing, turn to you with a mouth full of broken teeth and try to convince you that he meant to do that. If you know that about him (and other dipshits like him), it becomes easy to ignore the "that's what he wants" aspect and do what you need to do.

4. "But he's gay!" Yes, Yiannopoulos is gay. He's also an asshole who points other assholes at people to harass and terrorize them. He got booted off Twitter for the latter; the former doesn't excuse it. Being an asshole is orthogonal to sexuality as well as political philosophy.

5. It's good that Twitter punted Yiannopoulos, but let's not pretend that it doesn't look like Twitter did some celebrity calculus there. Yiannopoulos and pals had a nice long run pointing themselves at all other manner of people they didn't like, for whatever reason, and essentially Twitter didn't say "boo" about it. But then they harass a movie star with movie star friends, many of whom are Twitter users with large numbers of followers, and whose complaints about Twitter and the harassment of their friend get play in major news outlets, and Twitter *finally* boots the ringleader of that shitty little circus.

So the math there at least appears pretty obvious from the outside. You can punch *down* on Twitter and get away with it, but don't punch *up*, and punch up enough to make Twitter look *bad*, or you'll get in trouble (after more than a day). Is this actually the way it works? I'm not at Twitter so I can't say. I *can* say I do know enough women of all sorts who have gotten all manner of shit by creeps on Twitter, but who weren't in a movie and had movie star friends or got press play for their harassment. And they basically had to suck it up. So, yeah, from the outside it looks like Twitter made their decision on this based on optics rather than the general well-being of their users.

6. Which is a recurring theme with Twitter (and other social media services, but also, of Twitter): Not much gets done until the service looks bad, and then what gets done is cosmetic rather than useful. Don't get me wrong, Twitter punting Yiannopoulos is a good thing; he deserved it and has done for a while. But Yiannopoulos didn't get to the point where he needed the boot all by himself. He happily exploited the weaknesses of Twitter—weaknesses Twitter could have dealt with years ago—to become one of the service's leading shitlords. And getting rid of the shitlord doesn't mean the shitty little minions he gathered to himself still aren't on the service and happy to continue their shitty ways. Which is fine if they keep to themselves; less so when they're shitty to others, as they are likely to be.

Twitter can do more to make it easier for users to route around awful people and to get them off the service if they won't let themselves be routed around. Twitter's been promising for years that they're going to make better strides in this department—and is promising more in the coming weeks—and yet here we are in 2016 and still it takes someone with a number two box office film to her name *and all her famous friends* to get the service to do something it should have done long ago. Yiannopoulos is giant turd of human, to be sure. But Twitter did its part in letting him get that way. Maybe they should do more to avoid let turd buildup happen from here on out.

They say they're going to do it. Prove it, Twitter.

ON HOW MANY TIMES I SHOULD GET PAID FOR A BOOK (BY READERS)

Apr

7

2010

Randy Cohen, who writes the "Ethicist" column at the *New York Times*, caused a minor fracas this week when he told someone who had purchased a hardcover copy of Stephen King's *Under the Dome* and then also downloaded a pirated electronic copy for travel purposes, that they were ethically in the clear for the illegal download. Cohen's reasoning is, hey, the guy *paid* for the thing, and because he paid for it once, he should have the right to enjoy it in whatever format he likes. Therefore the download, while illegal, was not unethical.

Personally I think Cohen is pretty much correct. Speaking for myself (and *only* for myself), when I put out a book and you buy it for yourself in whatever format you choose to buy it in, the transactional aspect of our relationship is, to my mind, fulfilled. You bought the book once and I got paid once; after that if you get the book in some other format for your own personal use, and I don't get paid a second time, *eh*, that's life.

So, as examples: If you bought the paperback copy of one of my books and then liked it so much that you pick up a cheap remaindered hardcover edition for archival purposes, great. If you buy a hardcover copy, lose track of it, and then pick up a used paperback copy for re-reading, groovy. If you buy a trade paperback edition of one of my books and then happen to find a free electronic version of the same book, which you then download onto your cell phone for travel purposes, that seems reasonable to me.

Now, in each case, if you *decided* to pay me or any author a second time, I wouldn't complain—indeed, please do! Athena's college fund thanks you. And it's what I do; for example I recently paid for and downloaded an authorized electronic copy of China Miéville's *Perdido Street Station* because I wanted to read it again and my trade paper copy is currently in a box in my basement. I didn't want to bother to dig it out, I didn't want to have to troll the underside of Teh Internets for a pirate copy, I can afford the $6.39 authorized copy cost, and I like paying authors. Likewise I usually buy new editions of books I've lost or displaced, again because I can afford it and because philosophically I am inclined to do so.

I pay the authors more than once, because I can and I think I should. However, I also put such actions in the ethical category of "morally praiseworthy but not morally obligatory"—that is, I believe my transactional responsibility to the author was fulfilled the first time I paid her. Additional payments to the author are optional, and indeed are sometimes transactionally difficult. If a book is out of print I may have no choice but to buy a used physical copy, for which an author gets nothing, or acquire an unauthorized electronic edition, which again gives nothing to the author.

The moral issue with unauthorized/pirated electronic copies of works has to do with the fact that **a)** they were put out online by people who didn't have permission to do so, and **b)** that it makes it easy for people who haven't paid for the work and have no intention of paying for it to acquire it and share it with other people who *also* have no intention of paying for it. These are *separate moral issues* than the issue of whether someone who has paid full freight for an author's work should feel bad about acquiring a second copy of the work for personal use without additional financial benefit to the author.

To be *very* clear, I think the person who puts an unauthorized edition of a work of mine online is ethically and legally wrong to do so; that guy is ripping me off. I don't take kindly to it and neither do my publishers, who have lots of lawyers. Please don't post my work online without permission, and please don't share unauthorized copies with others. I thank you in advance for your sterling morals in this area.

But if that work *is* out there online, and the guy who just bought an authorized version—thus paying me and the people who worked on the book—downloads it for his personal use, am I going to be pissed at him? No, I don't really have the time or inclination. Maybe it would have been marginally more ethical for the fellow to have, say, scanned in each individual page and OCR'd it himself, thus making the personal copy he's allowed to make under law, rather than looking for it online. And maybe I'd ask him how it was he got so knowledgeable in the ways of the dirty, dirty undernet, where pure and innocent books are exposed to bad people, and suggest to him that he get his computer checked for viruses. But at the end of the day, he *did* pay me, and paid my publisher.

(That said, I do think there are limits to this. For example, I think an audio book and a text book are two separate things, because a significant part of the audio book is the performance of the reader, an aspect that is not there in the original book. Likewise buying a book doesn't give you a free pass to torrent the movie version of the book; alternately, having bought a Halo video game doesn't give you a moral green light to snarf down a Halo novel. Etc.)

If I had my way about these things, I'd be doing with books what movie companies are now doing with DVDs and blu-rays, which is to bundle a legal electronic copy of the work in with the hardcover release. There are distribution issues with doing something like this (unlike physical movie media, books are typically sold unsealed) but these aren't unsolvable; I think in a later post I'll talk about this in more detail.

But the point to make here is that these days, people are deciding that when they buy a book or a movie or a piece of music, they're buying the content, not the format. As a writer I don't have a philosophical problem with this, since I write content, not format, even if publishers want that content to fit a particular format. And as a consumer, I think there's a certain point at which you get to say "you know what, I've *paid* for this already, and I'm done paying any more for it." Both of these are why I say that if you've paid me once for a book I've written and what you've enjoyed, we're good. Pay me again if you like; I won't complain. But once is enough.

RICHARD STERN, RIP

Jan

29

2013

There's an obit in the *New York Times* for author Richard Stern, who passed away last week from cancer at the nicely advanced age of eighty-four. Fans of literature will remember him (as the obit notes) as a somewhat obscure part of a coterie of writers which included Saul Bellow and Phillip Roth, the author of books like *Golk*, *Stitch* and *Noble Rot*, and the recipient of both the O. Henry award for short fiction and the Medal of Merit for the Novel. He also somewhat infamously panned the novel *Catch 22* in the *New York Times*, a review which probably became as well known as his novels.

I remember Stern because when I was a first-year student at the University of Chicago, I somewhat arrogantly marched into his upper-level creative writing class and demanded to be let in; Stern, who I think among other things was amused at my impertinence and ego, allowed me to be in it, warning that he intended to cut me no slack. He lived up to his word on that, since of the several pieces I turned in for the class, he liked only one, and that just mildly: A brief character piece about a grandfather who was disappointed in a grandson but was trying to hide it from the younger man, perhaps not successfully.

Remembering the pieces I turned in, Stern was unsurprisingly correct: The pieces were clever but not good, the work of someone who had some facility for dialogue but not much of an idea for how people talked. Inasmuch as this continues to be the direction in which my writing tends to fail, he was on to something. It's a bit of a shame it took me nearly a decade after I left his class to clue in on this.

I had problems with Stern's class. My first problem was that on the first day of class, Stern said to us that he wouldn't be reading any science fiction stories, as he felt, basically, that they were childish and inauthentic. As a longtime reader of science fiction at that point, I bristled at that approximation (and, well, obviously, still do). I also suspect I know what he was trying to get at: he wanted the writers in the class to deal with people and character interactions, and a lot of student-level science fiction is focused on (supposedly) nifty futuristic ideas first, and people second. Fair enough, although I think (and continue to think) he was using science fiction as a stalking horse for the general idea of putting characters first.

My second problem was not about Stern, but about my classmates, whose stories drove me batty. This was late 1987, and Bret Easton Ellis' *Less Than Zero* and Jay McInerney's *Bright Lights, Big City* were all the rage, so the class was full of students sharing stories of dissolution, drug use and dorm room bisexuality. It wasn't that I was opposed to any of those things, *per se*, just that they got awfully tiring to read about over and over (there was one girl who wrote something else; I liked it so much I begged for a copy of the story. I still have it). I remember snapping one class session and chewing out the rest of my classmates about their tiresome written exercises in ennui; they looked at me like I had sprouted a second head. I think I remember Stern grinning as I lost it, however.

(There is some irony in that as far as I know I am the only published author from that particular class. I remember sending Stern a copy of *Old Man's War*, since I imagined it might annoy him that it was a science fiction novel. If I had to do it again, I'd send him *Redshirts* instead. Stern's first novel, *Golk*, was about television's more surreal aspects; I think he might find several points in common between our novels.)

In the end I didn't get much out of the class, other than a strong belief that creative writing classes and I were destined not to agree with each other. For a fairly long period of time I suspected that Stern had not been a particularly good teacher; these days I suspect more that I was not a particularly good student. As a young writer I was very arrogant—even more so than now, without the attendant track record to back me up. If I could go back now I imagine I'd tell the younger me to relax and stop trying to suggest he was the most awesome writer in the room; I'm equally sure the younger me wouldn't bother to listen. I was that guy. I know how I was.

Nevertheless, looking back I wish I had been a better student and had listened to what Stern had to say rather than focused on being an arrogant twit. I don't know that it would have made me a better or worse writer in the grand scheme of things, but it seems a shame I mostly missed out on an opportunity to learn more from a writer held in such esteem by other writers. I hope I'm smarter, or at least less arrogant, now.

SIZE MATTERS NOT

Nov

12

2015

Larry Correia has just come back from a book tour, and on his site he reported that he generally had a good time and had good crowds along the way, which is nice. Near the end of the post he wrote about the tour he notes that after his Portland stop, some Twitter commenter gave him stick about the size of his crowd (which eventually topped up at over forty fans) and how *real* successful authors pull larger crowds, and so on. Larry responded as Larry does, and that's fine for Larry, but as a general topic of interest, let me add a few additional cents.

First, an anecdote. Back in 2006, I was at the Worldcon in Anaheim and I gave a reading, and I pulled in, oh, about, forty people to the room. A little earlier than that, I walked past a room where George R. R. Martin was doing a reading, and that room had maybe ten people in it, listening to George read. From these numbers, can we assume that in 2006, I was four times as popular as George?

Answer: No, don't be stupid. The reason I had more people than George at my reading is that at the 2006 Worldcon, the rooms where the authors were holding their readings were really difficult to find— in a hotel, on a somewhat inaccessible floor, away from the main convention—and if you didn't tell people how to get to the rooms, they may not have found them. I had a signing just before my reading and I told *every single person in my signing line* how to find my reading. That's why I had as many people as I did at my reading. I don't assume George did the same thing, so I suspect that's why he had fewer (seriously, those rooms were hard to find. If I hadn't scouted the room before my reading, I'm not sure *I* would have found my way to my own reading).

Moral to this anecdote: It's not a good idea to make assumptions of a writer's popularity from a sample size of a single reading.

Indeed, speaking from some experience, it's also not a great idea to make assumptions of a writer's popularity—as it is expressed by overall number of books sold—by how many people show up, on average, for their book events, no matter how many of them you string together. Why? Well, because it all depends on the writer, and the book. Some writers are *good* at book events and pull in a crowd disproportionately large to the number of books they sell in general; some aren't and do the opposite. Sometimes the book subject doesn't lend itself to people showing up in a bookstore. Sometimes most of the readers of a book might be in a demographic that doesn't correlate to going out to events.

In terms of single events, sometimes your event is counterscheduled against something huge going on in town. Sometimes it's scheduled in the middle of weather that is likely to kill people if they go out in it. Sometimes the bookstore, who is supposed to promote the event, did a bad job of it (although in my experience this is rare; bookstores are usually on it). Sometimes it's at an odd time of day where people can't get away to a event. Sometimes you do everything right, and people just don't show up anyway. There are lots of reasons why people don't go to book events, in other words, even if the books sell just fine. These reasons often have nothing to do with the author themselves.

I've been actively touring novels since 2007, when Tor put me on tour for *The Last Colony*. Since that time, across several tours, I'd say my largest tour event had several hundred people at it, and my smallest event had…three. Yes, three. I was at the time a *New York Times* best selling, award-winning author, and yet *three people* showed up to a tour event of mine. And they were lovely people! And we had a fine time of it, the three of them and I. But still: Three.

Because sometimes that happens. And it happens to every writer. Ask nearly any writer who has done an event, and they will tell you a tale of at least one of their events populated by crickets and *nothing else*. Yes, even the best sellers. And here's the thing about that: Even with the best sellers, it's an event often in the not-too-recent past. Every time you do an event, you roll the dice. Sometimes you win and get a lot of people showing up. Sometimes you lose and you spend an awkward hour talking to the embarrassed bookstore staff. Either way, you deal with it, and then it's off to the next one.

Also, tangentially: the dude on Twitter trying to plink one off of Larry because of the size of his event crowd? Kind of a dick. For all the reasons noted above, but also because the size of the audience has *nothing to do* with the quality of the event. Larry and I have our various differences, but I've seen enough of him up close to know the dude has a work ethic and that he values his fans. If he had seven or eight or forty or however many people in attendance, I'm pretty sure he did his best to make them feel like they made the right choice by showing up. I have no doubt they had a good time.

And then those seven or eight or forty or however many people will go home feeling valued by Larry, and they'll keep buying his books and keep recommending them to friends and others. Because *that's the point* and that's how it's done. The value of doing a book event is not only about who is in the crowd that day. It's the knock-on effect from there—building relationships with fans and booksellers, and benefiting when they talk you up to friends and customers and so on. I know it, publishers know it, booksellers know it. I'd be very surprised if Larry doesn't know it. We *all* know it.

Which is why I'm fairly certain that however many people showed up to Larry's event, he entertained them and they had a ball. Just like I do my best to give people who show up to my events a good time, no matter the number. Just like pretty much *any* writer does.

That's what makes a successful author event: What the author puts into it and what people who showed up came away with. Not the gross number of people who show up.

A Small
Observation
Regarding Words
and Releases

I've noted before that comparing one author's process and career with another's is a situation fraught with difficulty (and often, some stupidity), so take the following with a grain of salt. That said, for everyone who ever bitched about George Martin taking so damn long to write *A Dance With Dragons*, allow me to make the following observation:

George Martin's previous novel, *A Feast for Crows*, came out in 2005, the same year as my novel *Old Man's War*. Since OMW, I have written *The Ghost Brigades*, *The Last Colony*, *Zoe's Tale*, *Fuzzy Nation*, and my upcoming 2012 novel (*Agent to the Stars* and *The Android's Dream* were written prior to 2005). Martin's written *A Dance With Dragons*. So I get credited with being reasonably prolific whilst Martin gets slammed by the more poorly socialized members of his fan base for slacking about.

The Ghost Brigades is about 95,000 words. So is *The Last Colony*. *Zoe's Tale* is about 90,000. *Fuzzy Nation* and the 2012 novel are about 80,000. Add all those up, and I've written roughly 440,000 words worth of novels since 2005. *A Dance With Dragons*, so I am told, clocks in at 416,000 words. So, in terms of total novel words written for publication since 2005 (and omitting excised material), there's a 5.5% difference between the amount that I have written for novels and what Martin has. If we're talking about the actual words *published*, written since 2005, there's a 13.5% difference—in Martin's favor, because my 2012 novel won't be published until, well, 2012.

Shorter version: During those years the unsocialized were snarling at Martin for being lazy or procrastinating or indolent or whatever, he wrote about as many words for novels as I had. By this superficial but easy-to-quantify metric, on the novel front he was as productive as I was, and most people seem to agree that I've been pretty productive these last six years. I just spread my words around five novels while he poured all of his into one.

Yes, but—some of you are about to say. To which I say, yes but *what?* Martin should have been releasing the story in smaller chunks? Well, and if he did, how much crap would he have gotten for milking his fanbase and releasing books that weren't sufficiently complete as stories in themselves? The publisher should have sat on him to write faster? To what end? So he could have sold more books? Look, I'm a *New York Times* bestselling author and I sell perfectly well, thanks for asking, and by the end of its first week of sales, it's entirely likely *A Dance With Dragons* will sell more hardcover copies in the US than I have sold of all my novels, in every printed format, since *Old Man's War* came out in 2005. How many *more* books can one human reasonably be expected to sell? Waiting six years and releasing a novel large enough to herniate a small human *works just fine* for Martin. His publisher would be foolish to mess with that. And so on. Any "yes, but—" argument one can make can be refuted on entirely practical terms.

In the end it comes to this: Why did it take six years for *A Dance With Dragons* to come out? *Because that's how long it took.* Martin wasn't being lazy, any more than I or any other author lucky enough to be regularly published these days has been. One hopes that those who are already primed to bitch at Martin about why *The Winds of Winter* isn't instantly on their shelves will keep this in mind. Martin's writing as much as anyone. He's just writing *big.*

TERRY PRATCHETT AND THE MOMENT HE GAVE ME

Mar

12

2015

I t's being reported that Sir Terry Pratchett has died. Which means that it's a very sad day for lovers of fantasy and science fiction. Sir Terry (which I will call him here rather than "Pratchett" because, hey, have *you* been knighted?) had been dealing with Alzheimer's for some time now, and his public journey with it, I think, did more to demystify the disease than anything else has in recent times.

More selfishly, he was the co-author of one of my favorite fantasy books of all time: *Good Omens*. I love that book insensibly.

I met Sir Terry only once and that fleetingly, but that encounter left me with a good story to tell, and I will share it now. It was at the 2004 Worldcon in Boston, where Sir Terry was the Guest of Honor. He was on a panel called "Looking Backward: the 20th Century," along with Esther Friesner, Craig Gardner and me. I was definitely the junior member of this crew—*Old Man's War* had not been published yet—and in retrospect I vaguely wonder whose idea it was to put a complete unknown on a panel with the convention's GoH (whoever it was—thank you).

The discussion was far-ranging, and because we were talking about the 20th Century in the past tense, we started talking about what future archeologists would make of the century, with the notation that trash heaps were invaluable for archeological purposes; after all, everything everyone uses sooner or later is turned into trash. This prompted Sir Terry to note that archeologists in Jerusalem very recently came across two-thousand-year-old cloacae (i.e., latrines), which, because they were in an anaerobic environment, their contents were perfectly preserved from when they were, uh, deposited, two millennia ago.

To which I replied, "Holy shit."

And for which I was rewarded with still the largest laugh I've ever gotten at a convention, much less a Worldcon.

Mind you, the reason I got a laugh that large was because hundreds of people filled a room to see Sir Terry, not me. But for that moment, I got to share. And if memory serves, Sir Terry gave me a little duck of the head after I said it, as if to say, *well played*.

It's one of my favorite moments of all my time in science fiction and fantasy, and it would not have happened without him. For that alone, he would be forever enshrined fondly in my memory. It is *not* that for that alone that he is fondly enshrined there.

My good thoughts and condolences to Sir Terry's family, friends and fans. He is not replaceable, but we were gifted by the time he was here. May his memory, and his writing, be a comfort to all.

THOUGHTS ON
SELLING OUT

<table>
<tr><td>Jan</td></tr>
<tr><td>8</td></tr>
<tr><td>2013</td></tr>
</table>

Over at io9, Charlie Jane Anders meditates on what it means to "sell out," inspired by a Twitter conversation between (among others) Paolo Bacigalupi, Tim Pratt and myself. I put in a comment over there, but I have a couple more thoughts about selling out, through the prism of my own experience, so let me run them out to you guys here. These thoughts are in no particular order and a bit rambly.

First, I don't think the sell out comes when you do things for money/fame, or mostly because of the money/fame, or even *solely* for the money/fame. If the desire for money/fame is intentionally and actively part of your career calculus, then the criticism or worry that you're doing something for money/fame is a little stupid. Because, duh, that was always part of the plan, and thus always an option.

Occasionally I've had people gripe that my books are explicitly commercial, which they don't like, and that's fine. But I've also had people gripe that I'm a sell out because of that aspect of the books. Those people I look at like they've turned into a farting fungus. Dudes: I intentionally write approachable books designed to sell in large numbers, constructed to make that goal as *easy to achieve as possible*. That's not selling out, that's *the actual plan*. Intentionality is an affirmative defense. I'm open to accusations of being a *hack*, which is fair enough (I would disagree, but then I *would*, wouldn't I). Sell out? I'm more dubious.

I think a major part of selling out has to do with fear. Specifically the fear that if you don't take a particular action (write a particular book, record a particular song, do a particular role, take on a particular gig, etc), your career will suffer, and you along with it. It can also have to do with desperation and exhaustion—the idea that despite all your efforts, other options are closed, and the sell out option is the only option left. That's another fear. Finally it has something to do with desire; not usually for the work you do but for what the work can bring: Money, fame, respect, opportunities and so on. Selling out is what you do when you're afraid. Sometimes—not always, but more often than it appears from the outside—it's not unreasonable to be afraid.

This is why, I will note, that I find it difficult to hold "selling out" against artists one way or another. I have been astoundingly fortunate in my career *so far*; I have never been in a position where I had to choose between what I thought was the integrity of my work, and the future of my career and (in a larger sense) my personal happiness. But I know people who have, and I know how much they've beaten themselves up about it.

What gets missed is the fact that work is work, and that we as humans live in the real world, and sometimes we have to make less than optimal choices in order to keep going. It's easy enough for someone on the outside to mock a musician for doing the state fair circuit, or an actor for showing up in an appallingly terrible film, or an author for writing yet another book featuring a protagonist you think is past her prime— or whatever. But people have to work and eat and keep moving, looking for their chances. I'm not going to dump on them or judge them for that.

It's also worth noting that what looks like a sell out to an artist and what looks like a sell out to a fan or other observer can be two entirely separate things. Artists, if they have any sort of success, often have opportunities fall into their laps they might not otherwise have gotten. The upside of these opportunities can be high. From their point of view they'd be foolish not to take them. From the point of view of a fan, however, the choice can be puzzling—a deviation from the thing that made that person a fan, and therefore (from their point of view) a waste of time and something to be resented. Cue "selling out." Alternately, popularity breeds contempt in some quarters.

Over on the io9 comment thread, there's some (perfectly civil and readable) discussion on whether—and under what circumstances—my selling the motion picture rights to *Old Man's War* could be considered a sell out. I find it interesting because my standard as to what constitutes a "sell out" is vastly removed from that of the conversation there, in part based on my own knowledge of the movie industry and my own pull relative to those who would make a film. For me, for a film, a sell out would have come from grabbing at option money from anyone, just to have it and just to say we did it. We waited instead for the right people to come along—people with good commercial and/or artistic track records, who could actually get a film made—worked out the best deal possible and then got out of their way to let them do what they do. I'm here when they need me, and they keep me in the loop, and that's pretty much how we work with each other and everyone's happy with that. So perspectives are different depending on where you stand.

I don't consider myself a sell out, and I think the logic behind the suggestion that I am is probably flawed—but at the same time I recognize that I give people lots of opportunities to label me as one. *Old Man's War* has four sequels now, which (fairly) opens me up to questions as to whether I'm just grinding out the books. *Fuzzy Nation* was a reboot of someone else's story, which can (and has been) seen as cynical appropriation for the cash. *Redshirts*—well, come on: *Star Trek* much, Scalzi? And so on. Add these to my public and enthusiastic embrace of the idea that writing to make money is not a bad thing, and I'm a fairly ripe target. And again: Fair enough. I would disagree but I wouldn't deny the argument is there, nor that it could be defensible.

On my end, however, I know what projects I've turned down despite the money, and what projects I've walked away from because I felt the other party was trying to trade on my fear of what would happen if I walked away from the table. I know what I *won't* do. In my mind, at least, it keeps me from worrying about whether I am a sell out. You can think as you like, of course.

What I Should Have Sent to Roger Ebert

Apr

4

2013

I can't say that I ever spoke to Roger Ebert, but I can say I was once in the same room with him—specifically, the critics' screening room in Chicago, where as the entertainment editor for my college newspaper I watched a terrible movie called *Farewell to the King*, and he and Gene Siskel were there as well, sitting, if I remember correctly, in the back of the little theater. Other critics were snarking and catcalling the screen (I mentioned it wasn't a very good film), and either Siskel or Ebert (it was dark and I was facing the screen) told them to shut it. They shut it. After the movie was done I rode down in the elevator with him. And that was my brush with greatness, film critic style.

For all that I consider Ebert to be one of my most important writing teachers. He was my teacher in a real and practical sense—I was hired at age twenty-two to be a newspaper film critic, with very little direct practical experience in film criticism (not withstanding *Farewell to the King*, I mostly reviewed music for my college paper). I was hired in May of 1991, but wouldn't start until September, which left me the summer to get up to speed. I did it by watching three classic movies a night (to the delight of my then-roommates), and by buying every single review book Roger Ebert had out and reading every single review in them.

He was a great teacher. He was passionate about film—not just *knowledgeable* about films and directors and actors, but in love with the form, in a way that came through in every review. Even when a movie was bad, you could tell that at least part of the reason Ebert was annoyed was because the film failed its medium, which could achieve amazing things. But as passionate as he was about film, he wasn't *precious* about it. Ebert loved film, but what I think he loved most of all was the fact that it entertained him so. He loved being entertained, and he loved telling people, in language which was direct and to the point (he worked for the *Sun-Times*, the blue collar paper in town) what about the films was so entertaining. What he taught me about film criticism is that film criticism isn't about showing off what you know about film, it was about sharing what made you love film.

I saw how much Roger Ebert loved film that summer, through his reviews and his words. By the end of the summer, I loved film too. And I wanted to do what he did: Share that love and make people excited about going to the movies, sitting there with their popcorn, waiting to be entertained in the way only film can entertain you.

I left newspaper film criticism—not entirely voluntarily—but even after I left that grind I still loved writing about film and went back to it when I could. I wrote freelance reviews for newspapers, magazines and online sites; I've published two books about film. Every year I make predictions about the Oscars here on the site. And I can tell you (roughly) the domestic box office of just about every studio film since 1991. All of that flows back to sitting there with Roger Ebert's words, catching the film bug from him. There are other great film critics, of course (I also have a soft spot for Pauline Kael, which is not entirely surprising), but Ebert was the one I related to the most, and learned the most from.

In these later years and after everything that he'd been through with cancer and with losing the ability to physically speak, I read and was contemplative about the essays and pieces he put up on his Web site. Much of that had nothing to do with film criticism, but was a matter of him writing...well, whatever. Which meant it was something I could identify with to a significant degree, since that is what I do here. It would be foolish to say that Ebert losing his physical voice freed him to find his voice elsewhere. What I think may be more accurate was that losing his physical voice reminded Ebert that he still had things he wanted to say before he ran out of time to say them.

His Web essays have a sharp, bright but autumnal quality to them; the leaves were still on the trees but the colors were changing and the snap was in the air. It seemed to me Ebert wrote them with the joy of living while there is still life left. I loved these essays but they also made me sad. I knew as a reader they couldn't last. And of course they didn't.

I had always meant to send Ebert a copy of *Old Man's War*, for no other reason than as a token of appreciation. I knew he was a science fiction geek through and through (he had a penchant for giving science fiction films an extra star if they were especially groovy in the departments of effects and atmosphere). I wanted to sign the book to him and let him know how much his work meant to me—and for him to have the experience of the book before the movie, whenever that might be. I tried getting in touch with one of his editors at the *Sun-Times*, who I used to freelance for in college, to get it to him, but never heard back from her. Later it would turn out he and I had the same film/tv agent, who offered to forward on the book for me. I kept meaning to send off the book. I never did. I regret it now.

Although he can't know it now, I still think it's worth saying: Thank you, Roger Ebert, for being my teacher and for being such a good writer, critic and observer of the world. You made a difference in my life, and it is richer for having your words in it.

WHO WILL
BE THE NEXT
DOUGLAS ADAMS?
HOPEFULLY, NOBODY

Mar

11

2013

O ver at the *Guardian*, David Barnett is asking why, a dozen years since his passing, Douglas Adams (whose 61st birthday would be today) is still considered the "king of comic science fiction." He mentions some pretenders to the throne—including me, which I appreciate—but considers none of us quite up to the task, although he hopes Neil Gaiman might take a crack at it, on the basis of *Good Omens,* the comedic fantasy work he wrote with Terry Pratchett.

Barnett offers some reasons, but also makes an assertion that I'm not 100% on board with:

> *Adams ultimately succeeded in mining a very rare yet rich seam of comedy that meant he was loved by both the science fiction community and the mainstream book audience who might not consider themselves science fiction readers. It's hard to fathom what his secret was—if we could, then more people would be doing the same.*

I'll go at this backwards. First off, it's not difficult at all to fathom what Douglas Adams' secret was. What Douglas Adams was doing was farce—a very specific, British version of it. *Hitchhiker* was right down the street from Monty Python, and both desperately beloved by nerds. My personal belief as to why this is has to do with the Python/Hitchhiker being very obviously comedy (i.e., even the most socially clueless nerds could see that it was broadly funny) and for being literate in a highly quotable way (i.e., easy to share and get a laugh from your friends with).

It's why so many of us dig Eddie Izzard today—he's all that farce-y stuff and a bag of chips.

The reason more people aren't doing the same is not because they don't know what it is but because it is *so amazingly hard to do.* Any sort of comedy or humor is difficult to write, mind you; it just looks easy (or at the very least is *supposed* to look easy). But to do a very *specific* type of humor—in this case British farce—is even harder to do, especially if one is not already a practitioner of the form. Douglas Adams was: the man got credited for a Monty Python TV bit, one of only two non-Pythons to claim that honor (the other being Neil Innes), and outside of Python he wrote with Graham Chapman.

Unfortunately for most science fiction/fantasy authors who would later attempt Adam's brand of comedy, they weren't practiced British farcisists, and their attempts at the form would fall flat. In my opinion, only Gaiman and Pratchett's *Good Omens* comes even close to the form, and the two of them are British, so that certainly helps (but, obviously, is not sufficient in itself; it helps both gentlemen are otherwise very funny).

Add to this the problem that for years, it at least seemed that if you wanted to do humor in science fiction/fantasy, the type of humor you had to do was *Hitchhikers*-like, because it had sold millions and was the most obvious example of what humor in the genre was. If you have as the most prominent example of humor in the genre a variant of humor that is particularly hard to do, it's not entirely surprising to discover that even many years on, there are very few valid pretenders to the throne. This one reason why I'm fond of saying that the success of *Hitchhiker's* was an extinction-level event for any other sorts of humor in written science fiction, just like *Star Wars* was an extinction-level event for the type of science fiction that was being made in Hollywood before it: It was so clearly, obviously, blindingly popular that it just obliterated everything else in the field.

To be clear, this is not saying this is the *fault* of Douglas Adams, who did nothing wrong; quite the opposite, of course—he was delightfully and blazingly funny in a way few have been before or since. He earned his spot on that throne. He just happened to get there via a path that's hard for anyone else to follow.

I am certainly not attempting British-style farce. I love the stuff, but writing-wise it's not my natural humorous tradition. Nor am I particularly concerned about taking science fiction's humor crown from Adams; that's like trying to take the melodic pop crown from Lennon/McCartney. You can try, but they're just going to call you "Beatlesque."

What I would like to do instead is continue to expand the *sorts* of humor that work in science fiction. Because as much as I love Adams' British farce—and I *do*—we're long past the time where other sorts of humor should be commercially successful in science fiction, and for humor to come in through the genre's front door, rather than being snuck through the side as it often is now. Instead of guessing who will be the *next* Douglas Adams, let's get to work on the *first* whomevers, doing humor in science fiction and fantasy in their own way.

And in fact that's the thing I am proudest of regarding *Redshirts*: It's funny and it's even absurd, and it's unapologetically so—we didn't have to pretend it was an action-y novel that *just happened* to be funny. We sold it as humor, and people bought it as humor, and generally speaking, they seem to like it as humor. It's not the next *Hitchhiker*. It's just *Redshirts*, and that's enough. In a post-*Hitchhiker* world that was not insignificant. And I like to think King Douglas, long may he reign, would be just fine with that.

Don't Type Angry, Well, Okay, Fine, Go Right Ahead, or, Writing Controversies and Other Such Nonsense

Hey, Looks Like It's Time Once Again For Me to Talk About Writing On Politics

Dec
1
2016

(Note: This one was written after the 2016 election, but I've written several variations of this piece over time. This one has the virtue of being the most recent and also the most on point (and, the most fun to read, I think).)

Because of the election and all, I've gotten a few people griping to me about the fact I write about politics here and in other places. It's been a while since I talked extensively about me writing about politics, and also, about the more general topic of entertainers and creative people who talk about politics, and the people who tell them to shut up about it. So let's talk about these things, shall we.

For ease of discussion, I've broken this up into ten points. The first five are about me specifically, and are short. The second five are more general, and rather longer. Ready? Let's get to it.

I. The Short Points About Me Writing On Politics

1. If you tell me you're tired of me talking about politics, or tell me to shut up about them, I'll tell you to kiss my ass. I'll write about what I want, when I want, where I want, which in this case happens to be about politics, now, here.

2. If you don't want to read me opining on politics, you are pre-sumably a grown human being with free will and the ability *not* to read things. Skip over the piece or stop reading the site entirely.

3. If you complain to me about my expressing political opinions in areas under my own control that you are not actually being forced to read, there's a very good chance I'm going to be rude to you.

4. I don't give a shit if you become unhappy with me for being rude to you.

5. Likewise, I don't care if your dislike of my writing about politics and/or your being upset that I was rude to you when you complained about it means you no longer choose to read my books. Stop reading my books, then.

II. The Longer Points About Creators and Entertainers, Including Me, Opining On Politics

6. For the occasional jackass who opines that entertainers like myself should stick to entertaining and not write about politics or anything else that might possibly offend someone, **a)** fuck you, **b)** you're wrong, **c)** independent of either of those points, long before I was an author I got paid to write about politics, and still do from time to time (as recently as last month, in fact, in one of the largest newspapers in the nation). So, yeah, actually, writing about politics *is* a thing I do professionally, thanks so much for asking.

Now, here's a hot take for you: "Entertainers" are fully-dimensional human beings who don't exist solely to entertain you, writers in particular write professionally and/or critically about many things over the course of their career, and *you* suggesting that people not express themselves about politics (or anything else) because they are an "entertainer" makes you the asshole in that scenario, not them. So maybe don't be shocked when they tell you to sod off.

7. Likewise, this blog existed before I was a published author, and before I was a published novelist. I've been writing about politics here literally since the very first week it was up (that week I also wrote about baseball, journalism, my pets, tech stuff and sending out invoices. The site lived up to its name even then). The blog isn't here to sell my books, although it's done that incidentally, which makes me happy. It's here for me to write about whatever I want to write about, when I feel like writing about it, and has been since 1998. Sometimes I will write about politics! And sometimes I won't—there are entire years (see: 2014) where I pretty much didn't, because I didn't want to.

Which again is the point of the blog: It's about me, writing about what interests me, when it interests me. It's *not* about *you*, or what *you* want me to write about, or to *not* write about. Likewise, my Twitter feed, or anything else I control that I put my words out on. If you're confused about the vector of impetus and control regarding these outlets, for any reason, you're likely to have a bad time. Especially if you complain to me about it. Other entertainers and creative people may feel similarly about their own spaces, which is a thing you should consider as well.

8. With that said, if my politics make you itchy, then actually, you *should* probably consider skipping out on the next four years here. I can't imagine I'm *not* going to write about politics on a regular basis. I mean, come on: whatever one thinks about Trump, that asshole isn't *boring*. Nor are American politics or social issues going to be anything but a bumpy ride the next few years. I'm not going to say it's going to be *fun*. But it's not going to be something I'm likely to take a pass on as a writing topic. If you want a spoiler alert on the matter, this is it. Don't expect me *not* to go off on politics, folks. And don't expect other creative/entertaining folks to be quiet about politics either, the next four years. That's just not gonna happen.

9. Why, yes, I'm cranky on the subject of people trying to tell me—or other writers, creators and entertainers—to stop expressing opinions on politics and other social issues. People have been trying to do this for my entire professional writing life, which is twenty-six years now, and much of which has consisted of me *being paid to have a goddamned opinion on things*. I imagine it will continue, as people with fragile worldviews and/or monstrous senses of entitlement and/or a wildly misplaced sense of my desire for their input and/or simple, virulent passive-aggressiveness decide they need to tell me what and how and when to write, or not write.

And, folks. One: Are you my spouse or my editor? No? Then feel free to fuck right off. Two: You may have noticed I'm doing pretty well for myself with this whole writing thing. One secret to that is *not* listening to various randos telling me what to do, or what not to do, with my writing career. Three: Do you understand how *boring and exasperating* it is for me—or any writer, creator or entertainer—to have to deal with various randos telling us what to do or not to do? It's really goddamn boring and exasperating! And maybe other folks who have to deal with this bullshit choose to be patient or quiet about this because they're earlier along in their career, or they're still under the impression that their career can be hurt by some rando telling them to shut up *or else*, or because they're nicer than me, or because they're not, like me, a well-off straight white dude so they actually *have* to worry about *their* randos being terrifying stalkery bigot assholes, especially now, when actual fucking Nazis are cracking off salutes like it's 1933. All of those are fine reasons for them to be quiet about this shit.

But *I* am not *them*, so I'm pretty comfortable saying the following: Piss off, rando yutz, *you're boring me*. After twenty-six years, you're not going to find a way to tell me to shut up that I haven't heard before and haven't already offered a middle finger to. And after twenty-six years, I've run out of fucks to give on the matter. Tell me to stop writing about politics? Fuck you. *Suggest* that I shouldn't write about politics? Fuck you again. Whine to me that you're *tired* about me writing about politics? Fuck you a third time. There's the door. Go.

10. Seriously, people, what do you think you're *doing* when you tell a writer (or musician, or actor, or whomever) that they shouldn't talk about politics, or social issues, or whatever? Do you believe they will genuinely think, "My god, this random person I don't know has entirely changed my mind about expressing an opinion in public! I am so grateful"? I can't speak for all creators everywhere, but anecdotally speaking, I can tell you that most of the creators I know do not think *oh wow, this random person is so right*. They think, *what an asshole*.

And maybe you are an asshole! Certainly there are any number of people who send me notes along the line *lol shut up dude no one cares what you think*, which aren't meant to persuade, but just to try to insult or belittle me, and, well. That's adorable. But if you didn't *intend* to be an asshole, maybe consider a different strategy.

For example, a couple of years ago there was a Scottish entertainer I admired, so I followed their Twitter account, which turned out to be nothing but blathering about Scottish independence. Did I tell this entertainer to *oh my God will you just stop talking about Scottish independence I don't even care?* No, I just stopped following their Twitter account. Because you can do that! There are whole *swaths* of creators and entertainers whose work I admire who I don't follow on social media, or read their blogs, or otherwise track their lives because I know they care about things I don't, or that I disagree with. There are other swaths of entertainers who I *do* follow, but when they get a bug up their ass about something I don't care about, I skip over those topics. A writer I admire has gone on for years about vaping. I couldn't give a shit about vaping; I think it's a dumb thing to invest any brain cycles on. But they disagree! Good for them. I skip over the vaping rants. It's really just that simple.

It's okay to disagree, sometimes vehemently, with people whose work you admire. It's all right to think they spend too much time on things you don't care about. It's fine to think to yourself or to tell others *ugh why can't they just get over that dumb thing I don't care about*. But the minute you go out of your way to tell them to shut up, no matter how "politely" you put it, you're the asshole. Yes you are. And some of the people you've told to shut up will treat you like the asshole you've become.

I will, in any event. Fair warning.

Amazon, Local Bookstores, Me

Dec

13

2011

The *New York Times* has a piece today by author Richard Russo about the recent Amazon stunt of encouraging people to go into bookstores, using their cell phones to read the prices of items for sale and then for their efforts receive up to $5 off things they buy at Amazon. Russo and the authors he talked to in his piece (which included Stephen King, Scott Turow and Ann Patchett) were generally not pleased with this antic.

Nor am I, since it seems like an entirely unnecessary dick move. Yes, Amazon, you have lower prices. Point taken. But even in recessionary times such as these, not everything is about the absolute lowest price. I pay slightly higher prices for books at my local bookstore, but then I also help a local business, keep people in my community employed and make the place I live a nicer place to be. These are warm, fuzzy, altruistic things that are mockable if one lives by the creed that in business it's not enough to win, everyone else must lose. But, you know, the hell with that. I can afford an extra couple of bucks on each book, and the return I get is worth it. Mind you, it's not just a soft-hearted choice; it's also a practical investment in the local economy and in a store where people can find *my* work.

This isn't a reflexive hate-on for Amazon, incidentally. Amazon sells a lot of my books for me, including through their Kindle program, from which I've bought more than a few books myself (generally books I own but am too lazy to fish out of basement storage. Yeah, I know). I am appropriately grateful. Likewise, Amazon is, among other things, one of my publishers through its Audible Books division, and they have done an excellent job with the books I've done with them. I have an Amazon Prime account and I get lots of use from it, because where I live often the alternative to buying from Amazon is buying from Wal-Mart, and on that strata of retailing, I'm happy to let them go after each other, with knives and bludgeons. If there's a locally-owned alternative, however, then I generally go there. I pay extra for what amount to intangibles for me, but what's intangible to me means a job and a business to someone else. That matters, especially these days.

Jeff Bezos is doing fine, and lord knows he gets enough of my money. I like giving my book money to my local guys. I think they probably appreciate it more, right about now.

Aspiring Writer Stockholm Syndrome

(Note: In late 2009, I wrote a series of posts decrying a publisher called Black Matrix for offering a fifth of a cent per word for the stories it purchases. This rate is, in a word, outrageous, and I went to town on these people. As always happens in cases like this, some folks came out of the woodwork to defend Black Matrix and its appalling per-word rate. I was not, shall we say, sympathetic.)

One of the things I'm finding interesting—and by interesting, I mean *appalling*—about my recent thumping upon Black Matrix Publishing for paying an insultingly low fifth a cent a word for its stories is that there's a category of aspiring writer who appears genuinely offended that I would call out this company for paying its authors so very poorly. The complaint goes a bit like this, and you'll understand that I'm excerpting from various sources:

> *It's not really fair that Scalzi is singling out Black Matrix Publishing when so many others are doing the same thing. Doesn't he remember what it was like to be a new writer? We can't all make what the pros make. A market like this gives me hope. It's not Scalzi's business anyway.*

Allow me to address each of these in turn.

"It's not fair Scalzi is singling out Black Matrix Publishing"—This is an "if lots of people are cheapskates, you shouldn't call out just *one* of the cheapskates" argument, which as you may expect is not an argument I have much time for. Sure, lots of *other* publishers might have business plans predicated on screwing the writer, but this is the one I was looking at that particular day, and its payment scale richly deserved comment and derision. Is this fair? Of course it is: Calling out ridiculously poor payment rates is always fair. One is not required to make a list of all known poorly-paying publishers in order to justly and fairly criticize one of them. If and when I call out another publisher for equally ridiculous payment levels, that'll be fair too.

I do notice Black Matrix Publishing is currently wrapping itself in the "we're just simple fans doing a hobby, here, we never intended to be a pro market" justification for paying writers badly. Really? Planning to publish four magazines and two separate book lines is a hobby? Does one generally create an LLC for one's hobby? Call me skeptical. This is a business.

"Doesn't he remember what it was like to be a new writer?"—Sure I do. And when I made my first science fiction sale, it was to Strange Horizons, because it was a market which made a point of paying what's regarded as a pro rate in science fiction (and still does). Because even as a new writer, I felt very strongly that I deserved fair payment for my work, and, separately but equally importantly, I placed *value* on my work. Even as a newbie writer, I wouldn't have sent a damn thing to a publisher like Black Matrix, because I assume my work deserves better than a market that values it that poorly.

Mind you, this isn't limited to fiction, either—when I was starting out as freelance writer back in college and then again after I left AOL, I also didn't write for markets which didn't value my work; I wrote for the ones that paid me what I felt should be paid. It's worked pretty well for me, and trust me, I am not *so very special* as a writer that this is not replicable for others.

"We can't all make what the pros make"—Why not? All it takes is the decision not to take less than that for your work, and patience until you get to that point. This is why I advise writers to keep their day jobs. If you can't or won't wait, pick a lower amount you're happy with, below which you do not go. Allow me to suggest that amount be a positive integer when it comes to pennies per word.

"A market like this gives me hope"—A market that thinks so little of you that it takes five words to get to a penny gives you hope? You need better hope standards, my friends.

Look, this is pretty simple: Black Matrix Publishing pays crap rates because it *can*. The people running it appear to be running it on a shoe string, if the proprietor's lament about paying a few thousand dollars to date into it is correct, and they're likely well aware that none of the other vendors providing elements for their little operation are so fungible in their costs as writers. The people who print their magazines will not be pleased to make 4% of their generally accepted "pro rates" for their printing services; the Staples down the street is not going to give them a 96% discount on pens and printer cartridges. The only group of people so willing to offer such a steep discount on services rendered are writers. Why? "Because at least they pay *something*." "Because I'm working my way up." "Because no one writes this stuff to make money." "Because it gives me *hope*."

Bullshit. Someone intending to make a profit off your words offering you a fifth of a penny per word isn't giving you hope, he's giving you the shaft—and he's banking on your psychological need for approval and recognition in a field you want to be a part of to make you grab your ankles and sings his praises while he reams you. This isn't hope, it's Aspiring Writer Stockholm Syndrome. Snap out of it.

"It's not Scalzi's business anyway"—Sure it is. I'm a writer. It's in my interest to call out markets that in my opinion are taking advantage of writers, because I prefer a marketplace filled with markets that value the work I provide, not filled with markets that take as read that writers will be pathetically grateful just to be published not matter how badly you pay them. How would I feel if Black Matrix Publishing folded its tent? *Delighted.* Good riddance to publishers who value writers so poorly. But what would make me *even more delighted* is if the proprietors stopped saying they were committed to writers and actually *showed* some commitment by paying something more than a fraction of a cent per word. I think it's not too much to ask. I also think it's my business to say so.

BAD REVIEWS: I CAN HANDLE THEM, AND SO SHOULD YOU

Jul

17

2012

n Twitter, a hopeful request:

> Paige Vest @paigevest
> I, for one, am srsly hoping to see an article by @scalzi about this #StopTheGRBullies nonsense. If he writes it, the 'net may 'splode again!
> 10:15 PM– 17 Jul 2012

Oh, well, okay. Since you *asked*.

For those who don't know, "Stop the GR Bullies" relates to a Web site created by some folks to go after people on Goodreads who write reviews that the people who founded the GR Bullies site find to be "bullying" in some way or another. It appears that the plan the GR Bullies folks have to deal with this issue is to be bullies themselves to the people they've decided they don't like. This is the sort of recursive stupidity that makes you wonder how self-aware people actually are on a day-to-day basis.

So, some brief thoughts on the matter, in handy numbered form. First, for those folks who are fans of a particular writer and his or her work:

1. Everyone is entitled to their opinion about the things they read (or watch, or listen to, or taste, or whatever). They're also entitled to express them online.

2. Sometimes those opinions will be ones you don't like.

3. Sometimes those opinions won't be very nice.

4. The people expressing those may be (but are not always) assholes.

5. However, if your solution to this "problem" is to vex, annoy, threaten or harass them, you are *almost certainly* a bigger asshole.

6. You may also be twelve.

7. You are not responsible for anyone else's actions or karma, but you are responsible for your own.

8. So leave them alone and go about your own life.

Speaking for myself as an author, I am a big boy and can handle criticism just fine. I can't imagine most people I know going frothy on someone who doesn't like my writing, because I'm not the sort of people who inspires Justin Bieber-like foamyness in my fans, and anyway I assume most people who read my work are emotionally developed to the point of recognizing inappropriate behavior. But just in case some of you *aren't* one of those people, a handy guide:

When I need your help with a negative review, I will ask for it.

If I don't ask for it, I don't need your help.

If I *do* ask for it, you should consider me temporarily out of my head and ignore me.

If you decide to attack someone in my name without consulting me, you make me look bad. That will annoy me, and I may take it out on you, possibly publicly. It will also make me wonder what the deal is that kept you from learning impulse control.

Consider the above in effect for all eternity.

Finally, if you're an author who thinks it's peachy for folks who post negative reviews of your work to be harassed by vengeful mental infants for the dubious crime of expressing an opinion, please grow the fuck up and stop embarrassing the rest of us. Thank you.

I trust this makes my position on this matter sufficiently clear.

A Boy's Own Genre, or Not

A nother thing for people to please stop sending to me: a recent and fairly random blog post in a purported online magazine, the premise of which essentially boils down to: "Science Fiction is by boys and for boys and now girls are ruining it for anyone with testicles, except the gays, who are just like girls anyway (and whose testicles frighten me)." I'm not going to link to it, as abject misogynist stupidity should not be rewarded with links. You can track it down on your own if you like.

Nevertheless, two general points to make here.

1. Verily I say unto thee that science fiction is *founded on girl cooties*, what with Mary Shelley and *Frankenstein*, so anyone dumb enough to whine about those awful women ruining SF for boys really does need to STFU and take his ignorant ass back to his snug little wank hole;

2. What? An insecure male nerd threatened by the idea that women exist for reasons other than the dispensing of sandwiches and topical applications of boobilies, mewling on the Internet about how girls are *icky?* That's unpossible!

At this late date, when one of these quailing wonders appears, stuttering petulantly that women are unfit to touch the genre he's already claimed with his smudgy, sticky fingerprints, the thing to do is not to solemnly intone about how far science fiction has yet to go. Science fiction *does* have a distance to go, but these fellows aren't interested in taking the journey, and I don't want to have to rideshare with them anyway. So the thing to do is to *point and laugh*.

Well, *actually*, the thing to do is trap such creatures in a dork snare (cunningly baited with Cool Ranch Doritos, Diet Ultra Violet Mountain Dew and a dual monitor rig open to Drunken Stepfather on one screen and Duke Nukem 3D on the other), and then cart them to a special preserve somewhere in Idaho for such as their kind. We'll tell them it's a "freehold"—they'll like that—and that they will be with others of a like mind, and there they will live as *men*, free from the horrible feminizing effects of women and their gonad shriveling *girl rays*. And then we'll tag them with GPS and if they ever try to leave the freehold, we'll have them hunted down by *roller derby teams with spears*. That's really the optimal solution.

But since we can't do *that*, then pointing and laughing will suffice. So, yes: let's all point and laugh at these funny little terrified stupid men, and then ignore them. Because that's what they rate.

THE BRAIN EATER

<table>
<tr><td>May</td></tr>
<tr><td>3</td></tr>
<tr><td>2017</td></tr>
</table>

(Note: The context for this is that it seems an unusually high number of science fiction and fantasy writers get into middle age and apparently just plain lose their shit and become real schmucks. This is my attempt to explain it. Please be aware there may be other factors, too.)

So, let's say, there's this writer.

(It doesn't have to be a writer. It could be a musician, or painter, or actor, any aspirant in any creative or indeed *competitive* field, in which there will be many who participate but few who will end up on top, commercially or critically.)

Let's also posit this writer is probably white and straight and male. Mind you, for this exercise, one doesn't *have* to be white and/or straight and/or male—it's possible that others could be slotted into this exercise—but let's also allow that this exercise requires a certain amount of expectation, whether consciously acknowledged or not, that there is a path, and the path is achievable; and indeed not only achievable but achievable by *them*; and one might say, not only achievable, but *expected*.

So, again: This writer. He starts in his twenties in his field, writing short stories and perhaps working on a novel. And things start to happen for this writer. He gets work accepted by magazines and publishers. People start to talk about his work. He starts getting good notices and acceptance in his field. He begins to see his name pop up in conversations about the best work of the year, and selected for anthologies with the word "best" somewhere in the title. He has peers coming up with him. They hang out at conventions and book fairs.

One day, to his delight, as he edges into his thirties, he discovers some of his work has been nominated for an award, or possibly even two. Now when he goes to conventions and book fairs, his peers high-five him. When he sits on a panel, he no longer modestly suggests that he doesn't know why he's there when everyone else on the panel is so better known than he is. An agent at a convention asks him if he's working on a novel (and of course he *is*, even if he wasn't two seconds previously) and gives him a card and tells him they'd love to see it. Magazine editors invite him to submit. Anthology editors do the same, hinting that his name might even make it onto the cover.

The writer goes home and starts work on a novel. The agent likes the work and takes him on. When the novel is finished, the agent shops it—and it finds a home. The writer announces the deal on social media to the acclaim of peers and fans. The books goes out to reviewers and the first reviews are kind. The book hits stores and the sales are good! For a debut.

Our writer smiles to himself and says, *now I am on my way.* The path so far has been an unbroken upward road—not without challenges but one still clear and tractable—and from his vantage point he can see everything that lies on that upward path: More award nominations, this time for his novel(s), and then award wins. Then bestsellers status and with it attention from film and TV producers. A novel is adapted into a film and launches the book into the stratosphere of general public consciousness. He's liked, and admired, and in appropriate time new writers speak of him as a signal influence on their own work. From there, he garners his career awards—a Grand Master accolade, maybe a National Book Award or even a Pulitzer—and is comfortable in the knowledge that his work, his legacy, his part in the national conversation—is assured, even when he's gone. This continuing upward path is not without its challenges, of course. Of course! But again, the path so far has been clear and tractable. There's no reason for him not to be able to continue on it, predictably, inevitably.

And, then, one day, our writer looks around and he's fifty. And he realizes that the book awards and the bestsellers and the movie deals haven't come. He's still publishing his novels (or maybe he isn't), but he and his peers not part of the conversation like they used to be (well, one or two of them are. Just not *him*). His sales are slowly declining and some of his previous work is out of print. His agent admits that it's harder to sell his work than it used to be. New writers—who *are* these kids?—are coming up and winning the awards, hitting the best seller lists, getting those TV and movie deals.

Our writer's body is thicker than it used to be, and slower, and creaks. He's not young anymore nor ever will be again. He's not one of the Young Turks; he senses he's barely part of the establishment. The new writers coming up treat him like just another writer; he's not an influence, he's just another jobber in the word mines. His upward path—that clear and tractable path, the expected and one would dare to say *entitled* path—is not the path he's on. He's on a path that has plateaued and indeed may be starting to run downhill, getting steeper as it goes.

How did this happen?

Well, our writer thinks, it can't be because of *him*; he's done the work, put in the words, is writing at the same level he always has. He'd been up for awards, back in the day, and doesn't know why he shouldn't still be. And it can't be just be because sometimes, despite your best efforts, things don't happen for you—that you could have been in the right place at the right time but weren't, and someone else was, and they got a boost and you didn't because on occasion that's the way it goes. No, things don't *just* happen, things happen for a *reason*.

And things, in particular, are happening to our writer—or more accurately, *aren't* happening, because someone or a group of someones, are actively making it *not* happen. Our writer looks around at who is new, who is hot, who is making it in the field and who isn't, adds up the anecdotal evidence that doesn't involve the impossible factors of himself or just plain bad luck. And then he thinks to himself:

You know, maybe it really is *the Jews keeping me down.*

Or the blacks. Or the gays. Or the liberals! Or the Millennials! The lousy SJWs and the feminists! Or all of them! All at once! For starters!

And that's when our writer looks up from the path, and in front of him stands the Brain Eater.

Who pulls out a spoon, cracks open our writer's skull, and starts feasting, while our writer goes onto the Internet and talks angrily and at length about who it is that is keeping him from what he *deserves*.

Please note that this is just one representative example. Not every path to the Brain Eater is traced into the dirt like this particular one. Some come to the Brain Eater sooner; some come later. Some get further along in their career before they arrive at the Brain Eater, having won accolades and fame (but just not *enough*); some leap into its arms at the first available opportunity. What's important is the *gap*, that wide space between where they think they should have been and where they are now—and the "fact" that someone *else*, not them and not chance, is solely responsible for their failure to be who they are *supposed* to be, and their failure to achieve what they were *entitled* to achieve.

Please also note that no one has to come to the Brain Eater at all. Even folks statistically most susceptible to the Brain Eater can realize how much luck, circumstance and timing plays a part in one's career, and resist the temptation to ascribe their own situation to a shadowy cabal out to defeat them personally. They might also realize that the "expected" path *isn't and never was real*, and that nothing in one's career or even life is ever a given.

They might also recognize that in writing, at least, it is never *too late*—as long as you're writing and submitting and putting your work out there, there's always another chance for you and your work. There are writers who failed and failed and failed and failed and hit. There are writers who hit, hit bottom, and hit again. There are writers who didn't start publishing until they were in their fifties, or beyond. There are writers who started early, kept at it, never "hit," but nevertheless loved the life that being a writer gave them.

There is no expected path. Believing that there is will only make you unhappy, and from there, bitter, and from there, blame-seeking. There is only the path you make for yourself and where it takes you, however long you choose to be on it.

Or, you can let the Brain Eater feast. It might make you feel better temporarily. But then you might find that what you've long suspected is actually true: People *don't* want to work with you. Not because of some shadowy cabal directive but simply because people are reluctant to work with someone who descends into blame-seeking and bigotry when things don't go their way. It's unpleasant to watch and deal with, and people will suspect that if everything doesn't go your way, sooner or later that your impulse to blame will be directed at *them*.

And thus the irony of the Brain Eater: It makes you become, by your own hand, the thing you suspect others were working so hard to make you be: A failure.

CORRELATION IS NOT CAUSATION, HUGO DIVISION

Mar
23
2009

(Note: Every year when the Hugo Awards are announced, speculation abounds as to why those particular works and people were nominated and what it means and (if one is feeling cranky about the nominees) who is to blame. This piece was written in the wake of the announcement of the 2009 nominees, of which I was one, for my book Zoe's Tale.

This was well before the "Sad/Rabid Puppies" jammed up the Hugo nomination process for ideological reasons, I would add.)

The entrail reading around the Hugo selections has begun, notably regarding the Best Novel candidates. One of the leading memes about this year's batch of nominees is how the Internet is a prohibitively influential factor on the ballot. It goes a bit like this: "Look! Four of the five authors on the Best Novel ballot have *significant Internet presences*. Therefore, the Internet is fiddling the Hugos, and all you need to do to get on the Best Novel ballot is be a big shot on the Internet."

Perhaps. On the other hand:

• Four out of the five authors on the Best Novel ballot have been on the Best Novel ballot before. Therefore the Hugos are fiddling with the Hugos and all you need to do to get on the Best Novel ballot is to have been on the ballot before.

• Four out of the five authors on the Best Novel ballot have won a Hugo before. Therefore the Hugos are fiddling with the Hugos (again!), and all you need to do to get on the Best Novel ballot is to have won a

Hugo before.

- Four out of the five authors on the Best Novel ballot have been on a *New York Times* bestseller list within the last year. Therefore the *New York Times* is fiddling with the Hugos and all you need to do to get on the Best Novel ballot is be on the *New York Times* bestseller list.

- At least four of the five books on the Best Novel ballot were "lead titles" from their publishers in the months they were published; i.e., they got a significant publicity and media push by their houses. Therefore the publishers are fiddling with the Hugos, and all you need to do to get on the Best Novel ballot is to have your publisher buy you a slot.

- Four of the five books on the Best Novel ballot have teenagers as their main protagonists. Therefore teenagers and their inexplicable fondness *for hanging out on my lawn* are fiddling with the Hugos, and all you need to do to get on the Best Novel ballot is to have your lead character be a teenager.

- All of the books on the Best Novel ballot are from white, male authors within fifteen years of age of each other. Therefore the white male extended generational cohort is fiddling with the Hugos, and all you need to do to get on the Best Novel ballot is be a white male within fifteen years of age of the other nominees on the ballot.

- At least four of the five authors on the Best Novel ballot have been known to rock the facial hair. Therefore scruffy hirsuteness is fiddling with the Hugos, and all you need to do to get on the Best Novel ballot is to wear more facial hair than John Waters, but less than Billy Gibbons.

- Four of the five authors on the Best Novel ballot are known to have provided genetic material in the furtherance of the species, i.e., are parents. Therefore parenthood is fiddling with the Hugos, and all you need to do to get on the Best Novel ballot is procreate successfully.

- Four of the five authors on the Best Novel ballot have last names two syllables in length or longer. Therefore multisyllabism is fiddling with the Hugos, and all you need to do to get on the Best Novel ballot is to have ancestors who identified their clan or profession with more than one syllable.

- At least four of the five authors on the Best Novel ballot have been (or will be) Guests of Honor at a science fiction convention in the last year. Therefore convention attendees are fiddling with the Hugos, and all you need to do to get on the Best Novel ballot is be a GoH and charm the pants off those easily impressionable fans.

What do we learn from the above list? Well, mostly, if you're looking for patterns of commonality in a grouping, you will find them. Whether those patterns of commonality are significantly *causative* of that commonality is another matter entirely.

The Internet thing is a fine example of this. Is an author's internet presence a factor in the presence of a book on the Best Novel ballot? It's possible, and even probable, I would say (and I *am* in a position to say). But is it *more* significant than other factors? I think not, otherwise Cory Doctorow, with easily the largest Internet footprint of any of the Best Novel authors via his participation in Boing Boing, would be on his third Best Novel appearance rather than his first, while Neal Stephenson, whose Internet presence has been bare bones for a decade, wouldn't be on the ballot at all, despite his previous two appearances (one of which resulted in a win). Likewise, an author's Web site is not necessarily causative in their popularity; Neil Gaiman, as an example, was wildly popular long before he thought to put up his shingle on the Internet; one rather strongly suspects he would continue to be popular without it.

In point of fact, there is only one specific and verifiable reason that these five authors and their books made the Hugo Best Novel ballot this year: that out of the 639 ballots cast in the category by members of last year's Worldcon and this year's Worldcon, these were the five that garnered the most nominations. I suspect that if you were to ask the people who cast those 639 ballots why they chose the books they chose, the answer would not be because they were influenced by the Internet, or because the author made a bestseller list, or because the publisher had it as a lead title, or because the author had a snazzy goatee or whatever. The answer would be because the voter read that book, and liked it enough to say that it was one of the best science fiction novels they read this year.

Which is a point of some significance, and which appears often overlooked in the reading of the Hugo nomination entrails. The Internet might help an author get known, a publisher will strive mightily to get a book into a reader's consciousness, fans might have favorite authors to read. All of these as well as other factors might put a book into the hands of someone who will nominate for a Hugo. But at the end of the day, it's that book that has to perform; it has to be good enough relative to everything else that voter reads—and one suspects that Hugo voters, as a class, are heavy readers of the genre—to recommend itself for the ballot. Internet fame, publisher marketing, author popularity, etc may still have some effect, of course. But not nearly as much as the book itself. Suggesting otherwise is to suggest the Hugo voters are easily mislead by inessential trivia. Which, while possible, doesn't sound much like the people I know who nominate and vote for the Hugos.

None of this is an exact process, and no matter what gets on the ballot, in the Best Novel category or elsewhere, someone somewhere will sigh heavily and complain about the state of science fiction, or at least the state of the fans who nominate for Hugos, and will then search for patterns that explain their dissatisfaction (alternately, someone somewhere will squee happily, exult at the nominations and then search for patterns that explain why their vision of SF/F is now suddenly ascendant). But ultimately it really is simple: certain people make the effort to nominate. They nominate works they like. If enough people who nominate like a work, it gets on the ballot. That's what's causative.

A Creator's Note to "Gatekeepers"

Aug

5

2013

Which is to say, a note to those (mostly) dudes in geek circles, who decide it's their job to determine who is geeky enough to enjoy the same entertainments and recreations that they do (hint: If you're a woman, you start off with a failing grade).

So, let me talk to these dudes from the point of view of being a creator, i.e., one of the people who creates the stuff these (mostly) dudes spend their time defending from the horrible encroaching interest of others (mostly women).

Dudes: Cut that shit out. You're fucking with my livelihood.

Let's break this down a bit.

First: I didn't ask you to be a gatekeeper. Did I, John Scalzi, come up to you and say, "Dude. I am *so* worried that the wrong people will like my stuff, and by 'wrong,' I mean 'teh womans,' so if you're not too busy I totally want to deputize you into the Society of Dudes Keeping Scalzi's Stuff Safe From Teh Womans"?

No? Then it's not your job. Quit pretending that it is. When I want your help, I will ask for it. *Directly* to you. Until then, back off.

Second: I don't *need* you to be a gatekeeper. You dudes understand this is my job, right? As in, this is what I do for a living. As in, if I don't sell what I produce, I don't pay my mortgage, my kid doesn't go to college, and my pets start evaluating me for my protein content. Books, which are what I produce, aren't terribly expensive, and I don't get to keep every penny of their sale price—I get a percentage. So in order to make money from these books, I have to sell a lot of them. Some of them get sold to geeky dudes. But a lot of them get sold to *other* people, who aren't necessarily geeky, or dudes.

When you attempt to gatekeep my work, you're trying to wave off people *I want to have buy my work*. If you manage to do this, then congratulations, you've made it more difficult for me to be successful with my work, and thus, make more of the work *which you also like*. Well done you. I'm curious how you think I should feel about people who make it more difficult for me to make a living. Do you think I should feel grateful? Because of the many words I would use to describe how I would feel, "grateful" isn't one of them.

I write books geek dudes like. But I don't write books for *only* geek dudes to like. The difference there is subtle but real. Which brings me to my next point:

Third: Gatekeeping runs entirely counter to my intent as a writer. I've always been very clear that I write science fiction that's meant to be readable to people who aren't science fiction fans—or as I prefer to think of them, people who don't know yet that they might like science fiction. *Old Man's War, Redshirts, Fuzzy Nation*—all of these books were written with the intent of being readable to outsiders to the genre. To people who are willing to take a chance on trying something other than what they already know they like. I write gateway science fiction—science fiction designed to make the reader want to read *more* science fiction.

So, when I take the time and effort to create a gateway, to invite people into the genre, and then some dude shows up at that gateway, unasked, telling people they can't come through unless they can name every Heinlein book in reverse chronological order (or whatever), I am, shall we say, less than pleased. One, demanding that people new to something be versed in all its trivia is stupid (it's also stupid when they have liked it for some time). Two, assuming that one's own interests are the *only* interests that define real geekdom is also stupid.

Three, get the fuck out of my gateway, asshole, *I'm working here*. Working to expand not only *my* audience, but the audience for written science fiction and science fiction in general. *You are not helping*. Go find someone one who really wants to you to gatekeep their work.

But here's the thing about that:

Fourth: Almost no one wants you to be a gatekeeper. Geek dudes: Do you honestly think Marvel comics, owned by Disney, wants you to harass women away from enjoying the X-Men? Do you think DC Comics, owned by Time Warner, appreciates when you demand a woman present you with a list of every Green Lantern in order to be worthy of "true geekdom"? Do you think Paramount Pictures, owned by Viacom, is grateful that some dude has appointed himself Arbiter of Star Trek Fandom? Do you believe that Tor Books, owned by Macmillan, one of the world's largest publishers, will pat you on the head for judging any potential customers of their books, including mine? Do you actually understand what it is these corporations *do?* They produce *commercial art.* To be widely *enjoyed.* By as many people as *possible.*

Moving away from corporations, do you think individual writers and creators really want you to wave away potential fans from their work? Almost all of them are in the same boat as I am, either directly or indirectly dependent on volume of sales for income. They are happy you like their stuff. They would be even happier if *not only you* liked their stuff. When you attack other people who like their stuff, you're potentially cutting into their livelihood. You're not making friends with the people whose work you're making a centerpiece of your life. You're hurting them.

Do you think the staff of the conventions you attend are in any way *happy* when you troll the other attendees? Those attendees go on Twitter and Facebook and blogs and talk about how unfriendly or even dangerous that convention is. Others pick up on that and amplify the complaints. The people who are trying to run the convention have to deal with it and have to apologize for the fact that *you* are being an asshole, because *they* are getting some of the blame for it. Who do you think the convention staff would *prefer* to have as an attendee? The cosplaying woman who is excited to be there and is enthusiastic about the convention, or the geek dude who spends his time shitting all over other people's enjoyment of a convention, which the staff has invested so much time in to make work?

Nearly every creator wants you to enjoy what they create. Almost none of them want you to *police* it.

Now, bear in mind that I understand that when you're off haranguing a woman (or anyone else) on the subject of geek worthiness, you're not actually thinking of me or any other person or company who makes the work you enjoy and have made a focus of your life. You are effectively working under the assumption that all this stuff just magically appears out of nowhere, a golden store of treasure, of which there is a limited supply, and thus must be defended at all costs against the unworthy, which in this case are usually Teh Womans.

Well, surprise. It doesn't come out of nowhere; we creators make it. It isn't a limited resource; we can make enough for anyone who wants it. It doesn't need to be defended from anybody; we like it when it's shared as widely as possible, including to Teh Womans.

And as for who is unworthy of it: Well. It's not the women or anyone else who wants to try it, or who has tried it, liked it, and wants in to get more. It's the people who are trying their hardest to keep them out.

Dear Consumers Who Apparently Think the Current Drama Surrounding eBooks is Like a Football Game

Apr
12
2012

(Note: This is commenting on a 2012 event where Amazon and Macmillan had a go-around with eBook pricing. Macmillan prevailed in the short run, although later it and the other "big five" publishers settled with the US government on price-fixing allegations. Amazon and the "Big Five" publishers would do another go-round later with book prices, and I imagine will do so again in the future.)

Please stop, seriously. You're driving me a little bit nuts.

Amazon is not on your side. Neither is Apple, or Barnes & Noble, or Google, or Penguin or Macmillan. These are all corporations, not sports teams, and with the exception of Macmillan, they are publicly owned. They have a fiduciary duty to their shareholders to maximize value. You are the means to that, not the end. The side these companies are on is their own side, and the side of their shareholders. This self-interest doesn't make them evil. It makes them corporations.

Amazon wants you to stay in their electronic ecosystem for buying ebooks (and music, and movies, and apps and games). So does Apple, Barnes & Noble and Google. None of them are interested in sharing you with anyone else, ever. Publishers, alternately, are interested in having as many online retailers as possible, each doing business with them on terms as advantageous to the publishers as possible. All of them will work for their own ends to achieve their goals. Sometimes, their corporate goals will work in your immediate personal interest. Sometimes they will not.

At all times, the public-facing goals of these corporations are only a small number of their total goals. It's the goals that don't affect you (or don't *obviously* affect you) that will often have the most significant long-term implications.

Each of these companies are interested in making it appear that they are on your side, or at the very least, will wish to validate your choice to be on their side. Please be smarter than that. Recognize that they love you for your money. Recognize that they have entire corporate departments at their disposal to distract you from the fact that they love you for your money. Recognize that they are happy to use your desire for affiliation to help further goals that not only are you not necessarily aware of, but ultimately may not be in your interest. Recognize that things these corporations do that you see as immediate gains can lead to long-term losses, and vice versa.

In other words, ditch the simplistic binary framing. You're not watching a sporting event, with simple rules and clear-cut goals. It really is more complicated than that, and your understanding of it should reflect that. When you reduce the players and tactics down to a simple "us vs. them" framing, you lose a lot of the reality of the situation. You also look like you're not actually following what's really going on.

(**Disclosures:** I publish with Macmillan and with Penguin and with Amazon. I am sold by Amazon and Apple and Barnes & Noble and Google and Macmillan and Penguin, the latter two of which have retail fulfillment through their company Web sites. I own a Nook, an Android Phone, an iPod and an iPad. All of these disclosures may indicate why I have increasingly little patience for binary framing.)

Dear Writer: I'm Sorry, I Don't Have Time to Crush You

Holly Black—who is *awesome*—has a post on her LiveJournal concerning a recent shibboleth floating about regarding a cabal of young adult authors ("the YA Mafia") who some writers in the field apparently believe will go out of their way to crush under their Doc Martens those writers who would do anything untoward to a member of the YA Mafia, like, say, write something negative about one of their books.

Holly for her part denies the existence of a YA Mafia—but then she would, *wouldn't she*—and also points out that even if such a cabal of writers *did* exist, sniggering nefariously in the shadows, the chance of them actually being able to crush someone else's career is nil, because, honestly, that's not how it works in the real world—not in the least because, as Holly notes: "writers are basically lazy and impractical people. We live in our heads a lot and we can barely get it together to do anything. Seriously, it took me until after 3pm yesterday to get myself a *sandwich*."

First, I want to agree with her wholeheartedly on the lazy thing, because for the last week I've been subsisting on Nature Valley Fruit and Nut Bars, not because I'm in love with their sticky, graintastic goodness but because at this point, the thought of having to shove something into the microwave to *cook* it fills me with such a sense of ennui even just typing those words *makes me tired*.

Second, this wave of anxiety is part of a recurring theme in the writeosphere, in which it is posited that those people with some measure of

297

success actively and jealously guard their perks and privileges against the smudgy others mewling on the other side of the gate, and collude to maintain the status quo, and so on and so forth, back, *back* you mangy animals! Right now this fear is erupting in YA circles, but it's been everywhere else, too. It's not new, and it's not news.

So in the interest of explaining why it's unlikely that any group of successful writers is colluding to keep you down, let me offer up an example of just the sort obnoxious bastard writer who would want to keep the rabble at bay, namely me.

So, hi, I'm your basic reasonably successful author type, and despite being lazy enough to grumble how how *awful* it is that I have to *unwrap* my granola bar before I can *eat* it, my daily schedule is not unpacked. On a daily basis I write a couple thousand words on whatever novel I'm writing, crank out two or three blog posts, check in with SFWA in my capacity as the organization's president and take care of what needs to be addressed that day, do other paid copy not related to novels, take the dog out on at least two walks, answer e-mail and other correspondence, make business-related phone calls to agents, editors and such, spend time with wife, child and pets, occasionally leave the house for errands, read the entire Internet, maybe also some portion of a book, update Livejournal and Twitter, kill me some zombies, eat, ablute and sleep. That's not on days when I'm traveling, mind you, during which I often do many of these things and also hurl myself across the country at several hundred miles an hour.

That being my schedule, let me ask you: Where do you propose I slide in *fucking with your career?*

Because, I gotta tell you, after everything *else* I do on a daily basis, I don't have a lot of *time* left over to take your dreams, lovingly cradle them in my arms and then just when they feel safe fling them into a pit filled with gasoline and napalm and laugh boisterously while they shrivel and burn. I mean, sure, I *suppose* I could cut back on reading the Internet or headshooting the undead and pencil you in there, but you know, I really do love reading Gizmodo, and those pesky zombies won't kill themselves (again). If I have to choose, I'm going with tech blog reading and Left 4 Dead.

It's nothing personal. It's not like I'm saying that thwarting your career *isn't* important. Indeed, that's just the thing: If I *have* decided that what I really need to do is to block your every entryway into the world of publishing, you better believe *I'm gonna focus.* It's going to be my new hobby to make every single day of your life a *miserable cesspool of unremitting woe.* And that's not something you can just do in five minutes a day, or whatever. No, that shit's hand-crafted and detailed-oriented, and that takes *time.* Lots and lots and lots of time. Nor am I going to farm it out to a posse of lackeys; no, when I come for you and your career, you're going to see me coming from a long way off, and you're going to have lots of time to think about just what I'm going to do to you before I stand in front of you. Giving you lots of time to think about what I'm going to do to you is what makes it *fun.*

But I have to say: unless I've decided to give you that level of personal, *absolutely terrifyingly psychotic* attention, eh, I'm just not going to bother messing with your career. Because, again: who has the time? *I* don't. No one does, except for people who are, in fact, absolutely and terrifyingly psychotic, and very few of them are successful enough at publishing that they are the people these other folks are paranoid about. Even if they were, they wouldn't start a cabal. Terrifying psychotics get along with each other about as well as cats in a bag. It's well-nigh part of the definition of "terrifying psychotics."

Yes: There is the occasional writer who gets their undies all bunched up about a review and then goes on a passive-aggressive public rampage about it. Authors are often neurotic. This should not be news. But what can they really do to you or your career? Short of doing something that will get them rightfully thrown into jail, pretty much not a damn thing. Because you know what? *It's not the way it works in the real world.*

Let's go back a couple of paragraphs to where I got all steroid-y about the level of woe I would rain down upon you if I decided to make you my personal project. Sure, I talk a good game up there—I've got a way with words, you know—but in the real world, how would that play out? Let's whip up scenarios, here:

STEROID SCALZI MEETS WITH HIS EDITOR:

Me: There's this writer who I hate with the white-hot intensity of a thousand suns. Never ever publish her. I am Scalzi. You must heed my words.

Editor: Well, I will take that under consideration (makes mental note that I have finally crossed the line from "reasonable human" to "text-extruding asshole who must be managed").

STEROID SCALZI MEETS WITH OTHER WRITERS:

Me: There is a writer whom I wish to destroy. Join me in my quest to smoosh his career like a grape caught under a high school cafeteria table wheel.

Other writers: Send us an e-mail about that (make mental notes to avoid me in the future, because I am clearly a mean drunk).

STEROID SCALZI MEETS WITH A REVIEWER:

Me: If you do not give this writer whom I despise a soul-shriveling review, then never again will I have my publicist send you advance copies of my work. EVER.

Reviewer: I'll remember that (crosses me off the list of people he reviews, reviews someone who is not a dick instead).

STEROID SCALZI COMMUNICATES WITH THE INTERNET:

Me: ARRRGH MINIONS MUST SMASH POOPY WRITER WHO POOPS DO MY BIDDING YOU DARK LOVELIES

Internet: Dude, you're kind of a prick.

And so on. Look, when you're an asshole to people, then other people know it. And while people generally will not stop you from being an asshole, if such is your joy, they're also not going to go out of their way to help you. Humans see assholes as damage and route around them. So much for mafias and cabals.

One final thing to remember is every presumed cabal member is someone who was outside looking in, and probably not as far back as you think. I do like reminding people that my first novel was published in 2005, which was six years ago. Six years is not a lot of time to go from schmoozing one's face against the glass of the cabal HQ to being well into the cabal itself. Perhaps it's more accurate to note instead that the idea of a cabal or a mafia is a little silly, and in fact there are just writers. Some of them are nice, some of them are neurotic jackasses, and in all cases the influence they can have on one's career is exponentially smaller than the influence one has on one's own.

DRINKING POISON AND EXPECTING THE OTHER PERSON TO DIE

(Note: So, the nonsense surrounding "Sad/Rabid Puppies" and the Hugo Awards is hard to explain to people who aren't in science fiction and fantasy, or who simply find internecine squabbles stupid and pointless. Nevertheless, here is my quick take on it, which to be clear would be angrily refuted by those identifying as "Puppies":

An author who happened to be conservative really wanted a Hugo Award and also felt aggrieved he did not win another award and openly campaigned for a nomination on the grounds it would annoy liberals. This was not successful. The next year he did it again and teamed up with an actual racist to get a bunch of stuff on the ballot, with more blather about politics. That worked but nothing they nominated won. The next year a different aggrieved writer who was conservative teamed up with the racist and swamped the nominations, plus more political blather, but voters once again punted their nominations. The next year it was mostly just the racist fielding nominations, and more failure. It's settled down since then because the Hugo instituted new guidelines to keep people from pulling the sort of nonsense the "Puppies" had been pulling, and also, I suspect, it's hard to keep up the outrage, especially when you have to pay money to vote.

During the Puppies nonsense, I was a frequent target of their ire, both because of my politics (which in the US track liberal) and because I had won Hugos before and they steadfastly maintained it was because I was "politically correct" rather than the merit of the work. I was a convenient whipping boy, in other words. Nothing came of it as *relates to me because at the end of the day very few people outside of core science fiction fandom cared about this stuff, and core fandom is a relatively small slice of the book-buying public. There are likely people who won't buy what I write because of this nonsense, but they're swamped by the people who have no idea or simply found it silly.*

This entry comes in the wake of various fulminations about me by some of the Puppies, and whether their venting about me made me wish them ill.)

A question in email about a recent post, asking whether when I said, of one of the head Puppies, "So well done him, and I wish him all the best in his career," if I was saying it with the same tone and meaning that a US Southerner might say "Well, bless his heart," about someone they dislike, or see doing something irretrievably stupid.

Short answer: No.

Longer answer: No, and why would I? As a *practical* matter, and as hard as it might be for some to believe, publishing is not a zero-sum game; the success of other authors doesn't have a direct or material effect on my success, except with regard to the small, indirect benefit that a genre that sells well has more readers overall, and those readers are unlikely to read only one author, and thus might read my stuff, too (if you think there's no overlap in my readership or the readership of any Puppy author you might care to name, you are, to put it politely, very likely to be wrong). So, again, as a practical matter, wishing any other author a lack of success would have no benefit to me, while wishing them the best of success might accrue some small and indirect benefit. So there's that.

As a moral and ethical matter, I do take to heart the adage, usually attributed to Buddha, but reasonable no matter who said it first, that hating someone is like drinking poison and expecting the other person to die. I don't hate any of the Puppies; I have cause to personally dislike a couple of them, but even then I try not to get to that point of things, either. I posit that the large majority of them are or at least have the capacity to be, decent humans. I disagree with them on many points, and think their current course of action is stupid, wrong, detrimental and childish; I think many of them have behaved poorly, selfishly and in a way that highlights their own insecurities and personal issues; I think it's sad they try to project those same insecurities and issues on others and use them to justify their own bad actions.

But that doesn't rise to the level of hate, or actively wishing misfortune on them. I'm mostly sad for them, and occasionally irritated, the latter of which is my problem. And while I'm fine pointing out their bad actions and snarking on their bad logic, what I genuinely *hope* for them is that they might find a level of success that makes them happy, *without* the need to view their success through the prism of how their successes stack up to anyone else's. This whole Puppy mess is because some of them *weren't* happy, and were searching externally for that happiness, either by seeking a validation in outside rewards, or by punishing people they saw (erroneously and/or conspiratorially) blocking the path to that validation. Envy and revenge, basically. They're drinking poison and hoping others die, or at the very least, suffer. It's why they called themselves "Sad Puppies" in the first place: it was about what they thought their Hugo nominations would make people they decided they didn't like feel.

Which is their karma. It doesn't have to be mine (or yours).

So, no. I wish the Puppies success in their publishing endeavors, and I wish them happiness—*genuine* happiness, not contingent on comparison to, or the suffering of, others. I also wish for them the capacity to recognize success, and to be happy. It doesn't seem they're there yet. I hope they get there, and will cheer them if and when they do.

HUGOS AND CLASS

Apr

23

2015

(Note: More on the Hugo and the Puppies. 2015 was the peak Puppy year, when their nominees dominated the Hugo categories, winning none (and most finishing behind "No Award," i.e., the voters would choose to give no award in the category than award it to those nominees.)

I'm musing on class today, so I'd like to take a moment to address something I see being attempted by the Puppies, which is to cast the current Hugo contretemps as something akin to a class war, with the scrappy diverse underdogs (the Puppy slates) arrayed against "powerful, wealthy white men" such as myself, Patrick Nielsen Hayden and George R. R. Martin, the latter being a late addition to the non-existent SJW cabal; apparently we are now a cackling, finger-steepling triumvirate of conspiracy.

So, let's unpack this a bit.

One, I'm not entirely sure how much credit the Puppy slates should get for "diversity" when their most notable accomplishments are reducing the overall demographic diversity of the Hugo slate from the past few years, locking up five (previously six!) slots on the final ballot for the same straight, white, male author, and getting much of their "diversity" from conscripts to the slates, at least some of whom did not appear to have foreknowledge of their appearance there, and some of whom have since declined their nominations. Basically, if you're going to argue diversity, you should probably not make the assertion so easily refutable by actual fact (it also helps not to have one of the primary movers behind the slates be an actual, contemptible racist and sexist).

Two, with regard to me, George and Patrick being "powerful, wealthy white men": okay, sure, why not (I suspect Patrick, earning an editor's salary in New York, might snort derisively that the idea that he is actually *wealthy*), *but* it's interesting for any of the three of us to be criticized for these things by a partisan of slates whose dominance on the final Hugo ballot was accomplished substantially through the machinations of a fellow who is himself a scion of wealth and power, with enough dosh on hand to have his own publishing house (for which he is using the current Hugo contretemps as very cheap advertising), and, to a rather lesser extent, by a fellow who has many of the same advantages I or George do: Bestselling status, award nominations and, at least from public statements I can recall, a rather comfortable income from his work, largely from a company that shares at least one parent in common with one that publishes me, is a major house in the field, and is distributed by a major publishing conglomerate. Indeed, as it is an article of faith among the Puppies that I don't actually sell all that many books, I suppose the argument could be made that he is *more* wealthy and powerful than I am! So well done him, and I wish him all the best in his career. But between these fellows and their circumstances, it's difficult to cast this as a battle of underdogs versus wealth and privilege. There's quite enough wealth and privilege to go around.

(There *is* at least one salient difference between me, Patrick and George, and the fellows I've mentioned, who share so many of the advantages that we three do. What that difference is I will leave as an exercise for the reader.)

Three, the Puppies drama isn't about class, or privilege. It's about envy and opportunism, and it's also, somewhat pathetically, apparently about the heads of the Puppy slates being upset that once upon a time, they felt people in fandom were mean to them. As if they were the only people in the world that folks in science fiction fandom had ever been *mean* to. True fact: There is almost no one in science fiction and fantasy that someone else in fandom hasn't been mean to at one time or the other. Science fiction fandom contains many people, including quite a few with questionable social skills. Not all of them are going to like you. Not all of them are going to like what you do. That's not a conspiracy; that's just a basic fact.

Here's a thing: Look back in time to when I was nominated for Best Fan Writer. There was a whole lot of mean going on there; there are still fans who are righteously upset with me about it. Look at what people have said about each of the books of mine that have been nominated for Best Novel (look at what was said after I won it!). Look what people in fandom say about me on the Internet *all the damn time*. Hell, I remember rather vividly being at the Montreal Worldcon during my autograph session and this dude coming up, handing me *Zoe's Tale*, and saying "It's not really a good book and I don't think it should be on the ballot and I don't know why it is, but I guess since you're here you might as well sign it for me." Which I thought was really kind of amazing, in its own obnoxious way.

You know what I did? I signed his book. Because **a)** apparently he *bought* it and **b)** I'm not emotionally twelve years old. I can handle people being thoughtless and stupid and even occasionally intentionally mean in my direction, without deciding the the correct response is to burn down the Hugos, screaming *I'll show you! I'll show you all!* Which is, as it happens, seems to be another salient difference between me, Patrick and George, and these fellows. Unless you're under the impression Patrick and George haven't got their fair share of people disliking *them,* or saying mean things about them. They have; they've just decided to deal with it like the grown up humans they are.

So, no. This Hugo contretemps isn't about class. But it might be, a little bit, about who *has* class, and how that affects what they do with their wealth and power.

IN WHICH A COVER STRAPLINE DOES NOT, ALAS, REVEAL A VAST CONSPIRACY FOR MY BENEFIT

Feb

1

2017

I was pointed this morning to a blog post by an author not previously of my acquaintance who was making a bit of noise about the UK cover of *The Collapsing Empire*; the June 2016 cover reveal of the UK cover featured the strapline "The *New York Times* Bestselling Series," and the author was questioning how Tor (he was apparently not aware that Tor and Tor UK are separate companies under the overall Macmillan umbrella) could make such a statement. He also then suggested that "after noise was made," a new cover was created, i.e., the US cover for the book, which in point of fact was publicly debuted before the UK cover.

A little further digging revealed that this author almost certainly got this idea from one of my usual suspects, who trumpeted the strapline as evidence that Tor is planning to fake a position for me and TCE on the *New York Times* bestseller list. As apparently they have done with *all* my work, because as you know I don't actually *sell* books; Tor and Tor UK and Audible and a couple dozen publishers across the planet give me lots of money strictly because I am the world's best virtue signaller, and therefore worth propping up with byzantine schemes to fake my standing on bestseller lists, because who doesn't like *virtue*.

Well, it *could* be that! Alternately, here's *another* theory, which is that the UK cover reveal last June featured a mock-up cover with text from other Tor UK covers standing in for straplines and blurbs to come. Like, say, the Tor UK version of *The Ghost Brigades,* which had the same strapline and blurb as the cover reveal for *The Collapsing Empire.*

This sort of thing, as it happens, is not entirely unusual; lots of cover reveals happen before covers are finalized for printing. Why? Well, because of marketing, of course—the publisher wants to generate excitement for an upcoming book. Covers are good for that, and cover art is also often done and completed long before the book is in—as it was in the case of both the UK and US versions of *The Collapsing Empire.*

Covers are tweaked constantly prior to publication; I know of one recent cover that was changed literally as it was about to get printed, because of a late-coming blurb for the book. Nor are the cover tweaks finished when the book is printed: if a book wins an award or shows up on a bestseller list, for example, the cover will often reflect those things in subsequent printings. So long as a book is in print and being reprinted, a cover is never final; it's always subject to tweaking.

Now, as it happens, I have seen the final pre-pub cover of the UK edition of *The Collapsing Empire.* The strapline has changed; it now says "The *New York Times* Bestselling Author." You might also notice the cover blurb has changed, from one from the *Wall Street Journal* to one from Joe Hill.

I'll also note this is not the first time for me where there's been a difference between a cover reveal and a final cover. Usually the changes are on the level of what we're seeing here—verbiage tweaked and blurbs replaced—but sometimes the changes are more dramatic. Some of you might remember that between cover reveal and publication, *The God Engines* cover was completely swapped out: new art, new typeface, new *everything.* As noted, tweaking happens sometimes literally right to the moment of printing, and then beyond, when appropriate.

So, while it's *possible* the Tor UK cover reveal accidentally let slip the vast and complex conspiracy on the part of several multinational corporations to falsely position me as a bestselling author, for *reasons,* the rather less exciting but, alas, more *likely* explanation is that in June Tor UK just put up placeholder text to be swapped out later (as indeed, it was). You can believe what you like!

For the record, the wee little racist almost certainly knows there's no vast conspiracy on my behalf, he just likes to lie about me. The other author in question here I don't suspect of willful obtuseness; he appears to be self-published and may just not know how all of this stuff works, because this stuff is pretty opaque until you're doing it, or have it explained, and he has the misfortune of believing this other fellow is giving him information that's anywhere near accurate.

Also for the record, I wish I *did* have a vast conspiracy on my behalf! My life would be easier then. Heck, if I had a conspiracy working for me, I probably wouldn't even have to actually *write* books. I could just sit back while minions did everything and I drank Coke Zeros on the beach. Sadly, I actually have to do the work myself. It's *so* unfair.

The silver lining to not having a vast conspiracy on my side, however, is that I do get to geek out about things like covers and the mechanics of how they come together. The reality of how covers get made and tweaked and sent out into the world is all kinds of good, nerdy fun. I like it, and it's fun to share it with you. I mean, I think it's silly these folks think there's something nefarious about it, but it's given me a chance to go "okay, so here's how this *really* works." And now you know!

(P.S.: If you would actually *like* to see me get on the *New York Times* bestseller list with *The Collapsing Empire*—or in the UK, the *Times* bestseller list (that's the *Times* in the UK, that is, these newspapers with the same names are confusing)—then be part of the *vast conspiracy* of people who pre-order the book, either from your local bookseller, or via your favorite online retailer. Sadly, my publishers don't actually prop me up. I really do have to sell books for a living. Again: *Soooooooooo* unfair!)

ON THE CLAIM THAT HEINLEIN COULDN'T WIN A HUGO TODAY

May
9
2014

(*Note: This involves an argument among some conservative-leaning science fiction writers, regarding political bias in science fiction awards. Note that since this was originally published, Heinlein's won two "retro" Hugos, awarded for years there were no Hugos given, for his 1940 short "The Roads Must Roll" and the novella "If This Goes On..." So, that answers that.*)

I t's in fashion at the moment to argue that Robert Heinlein, multiple Hugo Award-winner, could not win one those famed rockets today. The "Heinlein couldn't win a Hugo today" argument is predicated on the idea that Robert Heinlein, a man who rather famously *and successfully* tuned his career to escape the poorly-paid ghetto of pulps by tuning his works to "the slicks"—magazines like *Collier's* and *The Saturday Evening Post*—would be writing *the same books today* as he did in the 40s, 50s and 60s. Which is, in my not uninformed opinion, a fat lot of nonsense. A great portion of Heinlein's success was that he was tuned into his time, and well aware of where the money was. The suggestion that he would not do the same today, is specious at best. Heinlein did a lot of work to make science fiction an explicitly commercial genre, rather than merely a niche one.

If we grant that a resurrected Heinlein would read the lay of the land, commerce-wise, could he win a Hugo today? Sure he could—or at the very least could get nominated. Charlie Stross wrote a homage to late Heinlein called *Saturn's Children* which was nominated for a Hugo in 2009; its sequel *Neptune's Brood* is on the ballot this year. Robert J. Sawyer, who writes in a clear, Campbellian style, is a frequent Best Novel nominee, most recently for *Wake,* which has a clear antecedent in *The Moon is a Harsh Mistress.* James S. A. Corey rolled onto the Hugo Novel list in 2012 with *Leviathan Wakes,* which is solidly in the Golden Age tradition, updated for today's audiences. And I can think of at least one recent Hugo award winner who has a thrice-Hugo-nominated military science fiction series, who has been explicitly compared to Heinlein all through his career. So could Heinlein win a Hugo? Hell yeah, he could—and if he were as commercially smart today as he was back in the day, it wouldn't even be question of *if,* but when.

When people say "Heinlein couldn't win a Hugo today," what they're really saying is "The fetish object that I have constructed using the bits of Heinlein that I agree with could not win a Hugo today." Robert Heinlein—or a limited version of him that only wrote *Starship Troopers, The Moon is a Harsh Mistress* and maybe *Farnham's Freehold* or *Sixth Column*—is to a certain brand of conservative science fiction writer what Ronald Reagan is to a certain brand of conservative in general: A plaster idol whose utility at this point is as a vessel for a certain worldview, regardless of whether or not Heinlein (or Reagan, for that matter) would subscribe to that worldview himself.

They don't *want* Heinlein to be able to win a Hugo today. Because if Heinlein *could* win a Hugo today, it means that their *cri de coeur* about how the Hugos are really all about fandom politics/who you know/ unfairly biased *against them* because of *political correctness* would be wrong, and they might have to entertain the notion that Heinlein, the man, is not the platonic ideal of *them,* no matter how much they have held up a plaster version of the man to be just that very thing.

I imagine that if Heinlein (or his quietly cultivated and therefore relatively youthful clone) were alive and writing today, his response to this sort of thinking would be, "The hell with you lot. I have a career I'm working on." And then he'd write a 2014 version of a Heinlein book that would knock a bunch of readers on their asses, and then, sooner rather than later, he'd walk off with a rocketship.

PROFESSIONAL JEALOUSY

Apr

1

2008

Brendan wants to know about:

Dealing with professional jealousy.

I'm not talking about nasty, stalking vendettas or anything, but comparing of yourself to others in your field to an unhealthy degree. Seeing someone else succeed can be a personal motivator, especially if you can learn how they did it, but it can cross the line into harmful obsession when a lot of your emotional well-being gets wrapped up into it. I'd love to be the sort of person who never experiences pangs of real jealousy, but mea culpa, mea culpa, mea maxima culpa.

So:

Topic #1: Dealing with your own jealousy of a colleague's success.

Topic #2: Dealing with a colleague's jealousy of your success.

Idon't engage much in professional jealousy. The closest I ever came to it was in 2001, when Dave Auburn, with whom I went to college, won the Pulitzer Prize for writing the play *Proof*. I was at my computer, writing a video game review and feeling pretty smug that I was getting paid to play video games, and then I clicked over to CNN and saw what Dave had been doing with his morning. And in sequence, these were my thoughts:

1. Dude, I know Dave Auburn!
2. Aw, man, *I* want a Pulitzer, too.

3. But writing video game reviews, while fun, is not the path to Pulitzer goodness.

4. Oh, well.

5. I ought to write Dave an e-mail and congratulate him.

Which is what I did.

At no time during this was I actually jealous of Dave. Partly because, you know, Dave put in the *time*—he supported himself writing pharmaceutical copy while he learned his craft, if I remember, and then wrote an excellent play (he also won a Tony Award for it). It's hard to be jealous of people who deserve the acclaim they get. Partly because knowing someone who is being successful is *cool*; it's nice to see people I was friendly with at one point in my life doing well. And then partly because, while I didn't get a Pulitzer (and still haven't, nor am likely to in the near future), I was still playing video games and getting paid to write about them, and on balance that continued to be a pretty sweet deal. I couldn't really be jealous if I was actually *happy* with my life, and I was (and still am). So when I wrote Dave that congratulatory e-mail, I was able to be genuine and genuinely happy for him.

Personally I find being happy with one's life takes care of nearly all jealousy issues. Jealousy is a cocktail of envy and covetousness and neurosis, but if you have a life in which you are happy, it's difficult to be either envious or covetous, since that would imply dissatisfaction with your own life (I'm still neurotic from time to time). People sometimes ask me if there were something I could change about my past, what it would be, and I tell them honestly that there's nothing in my past I'd change, because I wouldn't want to risk not getting to my present. Jealousy works the same way; being jealous, professionally or otherwise, would suggest I think someone else's life would be better for me than the one I have. And, well. Just not seeing that.

The other thing about jealousy, particularly of the professional sort, is that I think it's ultimately predicated on the idea that life is somehow zero-sum: that someone else's success takes away from whatever success you might have, either in the short term or, if you're feeling particularly apocalyptic, ever. And I think that's kind of silly. Lots of people are wildly more successful than I am, and perhaps are more successful than I will ever be; it hasn't stopped me from being pretty happily successful in my own way. I'm likewise sure that my being successful, to the extent that I am, doesn't impede the success of anyone else.

(Indeed, I think it's the opposite. A fellow writer of mine likes to joke that my job is to be successful enough that our mutual publisher can afford to publish someone like him. I don't suspect I'm anywhere near that successful at the moment (or that this author needs *my* help), but I *like* the idea; I would love to be someone who, like Robert Jordan did, helps pour enough money into a publishing house that the house was able to publish a few more authors every year than it would have been able to otherwise.)

As for how do I deal with other folks being jealous of me in a professional sense? Well, mostly, I don't. The type of people who are jealous of me don't appear to put themselves in my path with any regularity, so I don't have to deal with them on a daily basis. Also, you know, what *should* I do? It's their karma, not mine. I'm not going to *change* what I do to make them feel a little less jealous; it's not my responsibility, and at the end of the day, I still have a mortgage to pay for. So I'll keep doing what I do. If it makes someone upset or jealous, they'll just have to live with it.

But I hope for their sake they'll let it go. Any amount of time and energy they spend on being jealous of me (or anyone else) is less time and energy they have to spend on building success for themselves. In that respect, jealousy really is about a zero-sum game. But they are the person who inevitably loses.

REASONABLY
UNSCREWED-UP
CHARACTER ≠
MARY SUE

Mary Robinette Kowal and I did an event at Borderlands Books in San Francisco, and during the Q&A portion of the evening, I went off the ranch a bit and kvetched about one of my pet peeves concerning science fiction reviewers: the assumption that any main character who is not screwed-up is somehow automatically a Mary Sue wish fulfillment character for the writer…or perhaps more accurately that *my* main characters are Mary Sues for *me*. Here's the kvetch:

Forgive me father, for I have sinned, I have been reading my reviews. And there's one thing that just always pisses me off, and that it is that when they mention characters, they say, well his main character is fine and blah blah blah but it's really just a Mary Sue character. And it just drives me insane because it's in all my reviews: "The main character's a Mary Sue." Well, no, the main character is not a Mary Sue, he's just not incredibly fucked up to begin with!

There's a difference between having a character that's, you know, fairly on beam, and having a Mary Sue. Having a Mary Sue would be like, 'Harry Creek, five foot eight, a little more portly than average but still devastatingly handsome and sexy, stepped in. And they said "Thank God, Harry, you're here!" And he said, "Why yes, I am, and I will solve that problem for you. Now, now, don't thank me—this is what I do. I will now go retire and have sex with many people."'

So all these things…they're like John Perry is a Mary Sue, and my immediate response was just because the dude lives in my little town, in my house, and is a writer, doesn't mean he's my Mary Sue. Which I understand is unconvincing. But then there's Harry Creek, he's a Mary Sue. I wrote something for METAtroplis, and the review was "this is yet another Mary Sue character." That Mary Sue character was the nineteen-year-old screw-up who gets a job as a pig farmer and on his first day on the job gets enveloped in shit. I'm like, yeah, I want to be that character! When I was right out of college, which is the equivalent of what this character is, my first job was as a movie critic at a newspaper—I watched movies for a living, and I got to tell people about it. For an egotistical twenty-two-year-old man, it doesn't get any better than that. This guy is not my Mary Sue, I'm his!

So just because a character is not immediately in pain doesn't mean he's not a Mary Sue. He's just not in pain.

Bear in mind that as I was saying this all, I was in ranty hyperactive mode, playing to an audience, who was laughing with me (as opposed to *at* me, you can be sure), so I'm a little more strident here than I might be otherwise. On the other hand, I do have a point here, which is I think SF reviewers have gotten into the lazy assumption that any character that's not immediately laden down with problems and/or is meant to be more competent than usual in a particular skill or skills is a Mary Sue for the author.

Now, maybe that's the way it works for other authors, but for me, not so much. I make some of my characters more competent than usual because **a)** non-competent people don't generally interest me as primary characters and **b)** from the standpoint of story mechanics, unless the journey to competence is the point of the story, the less time you have spend getting your character up to competence, the more time you have to deal with the story itself. None of this has to do with me having any wish fulfillment, other than the practical wish of keeping my story bubbling along. As for why I don't make my main characters all fucked-up, well, I suppose it's because the stories I've written so far don't need them to be. When I need one, I'll write one. But I'm not going to make a character all fucked-up just *because.* Seems a mean thing to do to a character, and possibly a bad thing to do to a story.

Again, this is less about my own wish fulfillment than practical issues of story construction.

(And as for John Perry, as I've noted before, the reason he lives in my town and in my house and is a writer is because I'm *lazy*, not because he's *me*. In the OMW universe, the character most like me is Harry Wilson, who doesn't get his own star turn in the universe until the short story "After the Coup." And even then (spoilers!) he gets the crap beat out of him, which doesn't seem like something you'd let happen to your Mary Sue on a regular basis.)

I'm aware that the term "Mary Sue" is experiencing some definition creep so that aside from meaning "author wish fulfillment character" it's also come to mean "supercompetent, non-screwed-up main character." But this seems like critical and linguistic laziness to me—Let "Mary Sue" mean what it's supposed to mean, and let something else mean that other thing; I vote for "Campbellian Competent," myself. I think it's perfectly legitimate to criticize writers on both counts—Campbellian Competent characters can be lazily constructed and boring as hell, just as Mary Sues are painful to read in their own way. I'd just suggest critics actually try to parse the difference. It'd be more useful to readers, and I know it would annoy *me* less.

SF YA These Days

Keith asks:

I have to preface my question with a story. Recently, I met and spent some time talking to a middle school librarian from Des Moines, IA. Naturally, conversation turned to what books we read when we were that age, as opposed to what 'tweens are reading now.

I mentioned that I cut my teeth on the juveniles (now called Young Adult!) of Robert Heinlein, and asked if many kids still ask for those. I got a blank look in response. She didn't know who I was talking about, and was sure that her library contained no books by said author. Asimov, Clarke, Pohl—same thing. She thought she might have heard of Asimov...I thought I might cry.

So, John, my question for you is, WTF?

Do middle school kids not read science fiction anymore? Does (this) science fiction have an expiration date? Is it because they're in a middle school in Des Moines (no offense intended to Midwesterners in general...)? Am I hopelessly out of touch with the youth of today, and should just start yelling at them to get off my lawn?

The answer: Yes, Keith, you *are* in fact hopelessly out of touch with the youth of today. Here's your cane; remember to shake it vigorously (or at least as vigorously as you can manage) as those Youth of Today™ scramble off your Kentucky Bluegrass. And be thankful, because think about it: Do you really want to have the same tastes as a bunch of thir-teen- and fourteen-year-olds? Wouldn't that be weird? Wouldn't that be, well, *creepy?* Like, *restraining order* creepy? You know it would be. So be proud of your old man crankiness.

But more to the point, one has to ask why one should be so sur-prised that the Youth of Today™ have not necessarily read the juveniles of Heinlein, or Asimov (the "Lucky Starr" series, writing as Paul French) or whomever. Dude, those books are all more than fifty years old. You might as well be shocked, shocked that the YoT™ aren't listening to the Flamingos or the Drifters or the Isley Brothers, each of whom had one of the top ten songs of 1959, or are torrenting videos of *Darby O'Gill and the Little People* or *The Hound of the Baskervilles,* to name but two of the top ten movies of that same year.

But, you say, *The Star Beast* is excellent in ways that *Darby O'Gill* is not. And maybe you're correct about that, but it doesn't really matter, for reasons both social and practical. On the social front, if you spend any amount of time with kids (it helps to have one in the house, as I do, if you don't want that wacky restraining order action going on), you know that they have a strange allergic reaction to anything that's not explic-itly created for them, and specifically a reaction to anything you, as an adult/parent, might like. This reaction starts as soon as they're able to be judged by other kids on their aesthetic choices and continues until they realize (usually around thirty) that a whole other generation of kids think they are now completely out of touch, so they can relax and just enjoy what they like. When my then ten-year-old niece commented a few years ago that No Doubt sounded like something her *mother* might like, I realized that no amount of pushing and prodding would ever get her to listen to Gwen Stefani and pals thrash about, even if soni-cally it was right in line with what she was listening to otherwise. I have no doubt (no pun intended) that it works the same way if an adult drops *Star Beast* on a kid these days.

On the practical front, the future of fifty years ago is not the future of today, both for social and technological reasons, and kids today know it. Hell, when I read *The Star Beast* as a kid in the early 80s, it already felt a bit quaint, and that was more than a quarter century ago. Writers are writing for their day and age, and their day and age passes. That Heinlein's juvies kept selling for so many years is a testament to his readability (and to the relative dearth of passible new SF for younger readers for a number of years as well), but sooner or later readability alone isn't going to compensate for a world that doesn't feel right anymore to contemporary readers, and science fiction doesn't have the ability that some other books have in being a snapshot of their current time. It's supposed to be the future. The only way you get to the future of *Star Beast* or *Red Planet* or *Citizen of the Galaxy* is by going backwards first.

But just because kids aren't reading what we read when we were kids doesn't mean they're not reading science fiction. My daughter is currently sucking down Margaret Peterson Haddix's "Shadow Children" sequence of books like there's no tomorrow, the latest of which was written only three years back. One might roll one's eyes at James Patterson's "Maximum Ride" series of YA SF novels, but they are seriously popular; each of them hit #1 on the NYT Young Adult bestseller list. Suzanne Collins' *The Hunger Games* has been making quite a stir recently, and of course let's not forget Scott Westerfeld, whose *Uglies* series is legitimately a watermark in modern YA science fiction. Finally, let's not forget that on the Hugo ballot this year there's also *Little Brother*, which has done very well both in sales and in critical acclaim. These are the YA SF books I can reel off of the top of my head; there are quite a few more I can't.

Which is to say: Don't panic. The kids are reading science fiction just fine, even if they're not reading what you did, back in the day. And here's the good news: If they get hooked on science fiction, eventually they probably will read the Heinlein juvies. Probably in college, as part of a survey course, to be sure. But, hey. That's something. This is your cue, incidentally, to start shaking your cane again.

TARGETS OF
OPPORTUNISM

(Note: In 2012 I announced I wouldn't be a Guest of Honor at any convention without a harassment policy, and I regularly write about politics, mostly but not always from a stereotypically (US) liberal point of view. Why? Because I write about things of interest to me. Do I do it for the "cookies"—i.e., to win points with other liberals? Read on.)

Out there in the stupidosphere comes the suggestion that the reason that I write articles about my privilege as a white dude, or ask conventions who want me as a guest to have robust anti-harassment policies, is because I am a stone-cold opportunist who doesn't really believe in these things, but says and does them to get ahead in science fiction, a genre apparently positively overrun by feminists and cowering males. My master plan is apparently to get in good with all the wimmins, reap all the awardz, and then profit! Or *something*.

(No, I'm not going to link to the blog post in question, because it is in the stupidosphere. You can probably find it if you make the effort. But why would you? Now, then—)

Points:

1. Well, you heard it here first, straight white gentlemen: The way to *win all the things* and *sell all the books* in science fiction and fantasy is to acknowledge your own stacked set of privilege conditions and to publicly sign on to the idea that all people regardless of race, sex, gender identification or physical ability should be able to enjoy a convention or gathering without fear of harassment or marginalization. Yes, with those *two simple steps,* a Hugo and a *New York Times* best seller slot will be yours. Who knew it would be *so simple?* Besides *me,* apparently?

2. Mind you, if the Feminist Diversity Cabal™ were *actually* running all the skiffy things, there would be the question of why it would need (or reward) me for anything at all. I think the answer, implicit in the assumption that I'm am doing and saying these things for coldly opportunistic reasons, is that I have craftily realized one of two things: One, the Feminist Diversity Cabal™ secretly craves recognition from straight white men and wishes to reward them for even the slightest of notice; Two, the Feminist Diversity Cabal™ needs a willing patsy to lull the Straight White Men of science fiction and fantasy into a state of complacent quiescence until The Night Of The Castrating Knives (i.e., The Hugo Awards Ceremony, 2014).

Or, hell, Three: Both! Then I will be king! Of the Feminist Diversity Cabal™! Insert maniacal laugh here!

Truly, I have been playing *a very long game* with this insidious, opportunistic plan of mine.

3. And, you know, it's worked! For I now have a Hugo! And best sellers! And such! Thus, having achieved *all the things* I can finally TOSS OFF MY CLOAK OF LATTER DAY ALAN ALDA-NESS AND REVEAL MYSELF AS WHO I TRULY AM, THE ALPHA OF ALL ALPHAS. COMMENCE WITH THE SANDWICHINATION ALL YOU LESSER BEINGS—

Oh, wait, I haven't won a Nebula yet.

4. So, *uuuuuuuh,* forget point three.

Go diversity!

5. Now, there *is* an alternate theory for why I do what I do. It involves a scenario in which I actually believe in what I do and say rather than being a Cat-Stroking Bond Villain for Feminism. But that's not *fun,* nor does it feed into the "I am a complete asshole and therefore cannot conceive of others *not* being a complete asshole, especially people I don't like" mindset of the stupidosphere. So never mind *that.*

6. Here is the one thing this dipshit in the stupidosphere was correct about: I am, in fact, *all about* taking advantage of opportunities. As it happens, I have *many* opportunities, due to my place in the world, to speak and act on things that are important to me. I also have the will to take the opportunities when they come up. And in the last year, events have conspired to give me *even more* opportunities to do so. So, guess what? I'm going to take them.

What will I do with those opportunities? Well, I will say this: I can pretty much guarantee the stupidosphere won't like it.

Insert maniacal laugh here.

Today's Grammar Gripe, Seemingly Out of Nowhere

Aug

24

2009

People:

It's "centers on," *not* "centers around." If you give it some thought, you'll figure out why. If you can't figure out why, your nearest mathematician specializing in topology will be happy to explain it to you.

If you must use "around" in a phrase, try "revolves around." That will work, and will keep me from wanting to *beat you to death with a hammer*.

Thank you, that is all, for now.

WHEN GUARDIAN
COLUMNISTS SAY
DUMB THINGS

Jul

14

2009

Several e-mails today from people who want me to put a hammer to the *Guardian's* Stuart Jeffries for this statement yesterday:

> *This is a golden age for British science fiction, chiefly thanks to a wave of writers who are tackling an area their American rivals tend to leave well alone—far-future set, space-operatic, hard sci-fi. Americans tend to set their sci-fi in soft (ie, scientifically unsupported) near futures. Wimps.*

Leaving aside whether this is a golden age for British science fiction (which as it happens is a statement I tend to agree with), this is in fact a fairly ignorant statement by Jeffries. Dear Mr. Jeffries: Meet Elizabeth Moon. Meet David Weber. Meet Jack Campbell. Meet Robert Buettner. Meet Sandra McDonald. And unless memory fails me, there might be at least one other American writer out there who has written a series of best-selling, award-nominated, highly-acclaimed books generally considered space-operatic, not to mention scientifically supported. His name escapes me at the moment. Perhaps it will come to me.

The point, however, is that none of these writers are exactly toiling under a *rock;* nearly all of these authors has at least flirting acquaintance with best seller lists and some measure of acclaim. They're not difficult to find. Some of them might even be sold in the UK. Yes, I'm aware that military science fiction (which most of the above write) is not synony- mous with Space Opera. But the two sub-genres overlap rather a bit, and these writers write in the overlap (also, not everything written by the above is straight on MilSF, Drake's recent trilogy being an example).

Also, I really would like Stuart Jeffries to go up to Elizabeth Moon and call her a wimp. I like imagining all the things Moon, a former lieutenant in the US Marines, a sometime paramedic and a woman who raised a child with autism, could oh-so-easily do to him. When she's done with him, maybe he can say the same thing to McDonald, eight years in the Navy, or Buettner, who was in military intelligence, or Hemry, who also spent years in the Navy.

Mind you, I'm well aware Jeffries was trying for a bit of snark, and of course I love me some snark. But snark works better when it's not completely couched in ignorance. Try again, Mr. Jeffries; try better.

WRITERS AND FINANCIAL WOES: WHAT'S GOING ON

Nov

9

2009

(Note: Written in the grips of the great recession. I should mention I was between book contracts at this time.)

An e-mail:

You talk about money and writing a lot, so let me ask you: What is it with writers and money? Lots of them seem to be in financial hot water these days.

Hmmmm. Well, let's start by pointing out two rather salient points (note this discussion is primarily US-centric, but may have application elsewhere):

1. Things are tough all over. "These days" includes a profound recession, for which employment is a lagging factor, so let's make sure we factor that not-trivial datum into our mindview. On top of this general employment malaise, writers of all sorts are taking an extra set of lumps: Journalism is losing thousands of full-time writers out of newspapers and magazines, writers in corporate settings are no safer than any other white-collar worker and publishing companies are actively trimming their author rosters and slicing advances. I'd hesitate to suggest that writers are having it worst of all recently, but you know what, they're not just skating through this recession, either. They've got it middlin' bad.

On top of this:

2. It's not just writers who make lousy financial choices. There aren't enough writers in the United States to cover all the bad mortgages out there right now, to make one obvious point. It's not just writers who push the average consumer debt above $7,000 per card holder. It's not just writers who save almost none of their income, leaving them vulnerable to sudden, unexpected changes in personal fortune. Writers are often bad with money, but then so are secretaries, and doctors, and teachers, and plumbers, and members of the military and any other group of people you might care to imagine, excepting possibly accountants, and honestly I wouldn't even put it past *them*. So when we're singling out writers for discussion, let's remember they are not alone out there on the far end of the "wow, we really *suck* at finances" spectrum.

Having noted the above, here are some additional reasons why writers seem to so often fall face first, financially. Note that not all of these apply equally to every writer; we're talking in vast generalities, here.

First, some practical issues:

3. Writer pay is generally low and generally inconsistent. And if one writes fiction for some/all of one's writing output, especially so. I've written in detail about writing rates and payment before so it's not necessary to go into detail again right at the moment. But what it means is that if one is a writer, one does a fair amount of work for not a whole lot of money, and then has to wait for that payment to arrive more or less at the pleasure of the person sending the check. Unfortunately, writers like pretty much everyone else have fixed expenses (mortgage/rent, bills etc), and *those* people generally do not wait to be paid at the pleasure of the writer; you pay your electric bill regularly or you don't get electricity. This means writers are often in a situation where despite working prodigiously, they don't have money in hand to pay regular, fixed monthly expenses.

4. Writers often lack what meager social net actually exists in corporate America. Writers are often self-employed, which means they bear the full brunt of the cost of health insurance or go without, and when they do pay for health insurance, they pay a lot because their individual plans don't spread out risk like corporate plans do. Since per point three writers don't get paid a lot (or regularly), very often they go without—as often do their spouses and children, if the spouse does not work for someone who provides health insurance. Which means they are quite susceptible to even incidental medical costs wreaking holy hell with their finances, and my own anecdotal experience with writers is that they are not exactly a hale and hearty group to start.

Self-employed writers don't get 401(k)s and often don't get around to funding IRAs, so their ability to save for retirement is made that much more challenging. They are on the hook for their full amount of Social Security taxes and also have to file taxes quarterly, and the IRS keeps a close eye on them (and all self-employed folks) for fraud and so on. Add it all up, and not being formally on the corporate teat makes it easier for writers to find themselves in a compromised financial situation.

5. Writers, like many people (even presumably educated folks), often have rudimentary financial skills. Which means even when they do have money and a desire to save it intelligently, they often don't know how or have already gotten themselves into a compromised financial situation which makes smart and sane financial practices more difficult. Now, for writers, to some extent we can blame them and their arty-farty educations for this lack. I'm not sure how many MFA or undergrad writing programs out there require a "real world basic finance" class for a degree, but I'm guessing I can count them on one hand and have up to five fingers left over. Likewise, my anecdotal experience with writers suggests that not a whole lot of them have a vibrant love affair with mathematics, even the relatively basic sort that underpins day-to-day financial planning. So there are two strikes against them right there.

But to be fair to writers, once again, it's not just them. I have a philosophy degree; it didn't require a real world financial management class either. I don't believe I actually ever took a class in basic financial planning and management, *ever*, and I'm guessing I'm not the only one there. This leaves basically everyone to get their financial educations from rah-rah financial bestsellers, fatuous talking heads on CNBC and folks like the sort who recently suckered millions of Americans into buying far more home than they could rationally afford on the basis that hey, the real estate market will never ever go down. This is, basically, an appalling state of affairs, and not just for writers.

Having enumerated some practical issues, here are some (for lack of a better term) "lifestyle" reasons why writers often have money problems:

6. Writers are often flaky. Which can mean (pick one or more) that they have short attentions spans, which penalize them for things like finances; they get bored quickly and therefore make bad economic decisions because they want to stop thinking about them and get on to interesting stuff; because they are clever with words they think that means that they are smart outside of their specific field (and particularly with money), which is a common mistake people good in one intellectual area make; they trust people they should not with their money and/or their life situations; they go with their guts rather than with their brains; they prioritize immediate wants over long-term needs; and so on.

We could have a nice fun argument about whether flaky people become writers or whether being a writer makes one flaky, but it's a discussion that's not relevant at the moment; the point here is that many authors by their personal nature are not well-composed for the sober, staid and completely *boring* task of dealing with money.

(Note I'm not simply running down other writers here; ask my wife why it was when we met I had all my utilities on third notice, despite the fact I could afford to pay the bills. It will confirm my own "flaky like a pie crust" nature.)

Related to this:

7. Writers are often irrational risk-takers. Because how can you *write* about life without *experiencing* it, etc, which is a convenient rationale for doing stupid things and getting caught in bad situations, up to and including terrible relationships, addictions, impulsive life-changing decisions and so on, all of which end up having a (not in the least) surprising impact on one's financial life. Hell, even a bog-standard nicotine addiction will set you back $9 per pack in NYC and $5 everywhere else (not counting the cost of one's lung cancer treatments later). Whether these sorts of irrational risks actually *do* make one a better writer is of course deeply open to debate, but again, it's a rationale as opposed to a reason.

Note that in the cases of 6 and 7 above, there's another potential correlating issue, which is that writers like many creative types appear to have higher incidence of mental illness than your random sample of, say, grocery store managers or bus drivers. Mental illness—particularly illness that goes untreated/undertreated due to financial constraints—will have corresponding effects on one's financial situation.

8. Writers are often attracted to other creative folks, including other writers. Nothing wrong with this in a general sense, mind you. We all love who we love, and what's not to love about another witty, smart and talented person? The problem *financially speaking*, however, is that other writers very often have the same basic financial issues: low, irregular pay, no benefits, poor finance skills, tendencies toward flakiness and risk-taking, and such. Two incomes are theoretically better than one, but two sporadic incomes accompanied by everything else that comes attached to the writing life isn't necessarily as much better than one would expect. And don't forget: Kids may happen. They often do.

9. Writing can be expensive. The actual *act* of writing is not expensive, mind you—if one had to one could do it for free off a library computer, although few do—but everything around it adds up. Typewriters, paper, ribbons and correcting fluid have been replaced by computers, printers, printer ink and internet access, so the sunk cost there is roughly the same as it ever was, as are the costs of sending manuscripts and correspondence, at least to the markets which still require paper submissions. Writers who write in coffee shops and cafes pay "rent" in coffee and pastries; it sounds silly, but those things ain't cheap when you check the tab. Writers are gregarious and go to things like workshops and conventions and writers' nights at the local bar; these aren't required costs but they are desirable activities and they cost money to attend (even if it's just to get an overpriced beer).

Do all these things mean writers are more susceptible than other trades/professions to encounter serious financial issues? Not necessarily; folks in other creative fields (acting, music, art, dance) have the same set of practical and lifestyle challenges, and while the challenges of other lines of work will vary, they're still there—hell, even doctors and lawyers find themselves saddled first with huge amounts of debt and then with some impressive overhead to keep their practices going. Pick a profession—there's lots of ways to get yourself in financial hot water doing it.

However, there is one thing that can make it appear that writers as a class are in more financial trouble than other folks, regardless of whether or not it's true:

10. Writers write about their situations. Because they're *writers*, you see. Writing is what they *do*. And lots of writers feel the need to share their financial situations with an audience, to a greater or lesser degree. Why? Because (again, pick one or more) writing helps writers think through their situation; writing is therapy; writers feel an obligation to share; writers are hoping for sympathy, encouragement and possibly solutions or even help. Whatever their reasons, it shouldn't be very surprising that you'll more than occasionally read an author lay out his or her financial woes, and (yes) do it in an interesting and engaging style that sticks in your head more than, say, a similar blog post by a janitor might. It's an interesting curse, you might say.

So those are some reasons writers might be having a hard time of it right now—and why it might seem they're having a harder time than some others.

YOU CAN'T TAKE
BACK WHAT YOU
ALREADY HAVE

O ut on the Internet, I see, yet another rant about how science fiction is being taken over by the politically correct. This is only one dude ranting, to be clear, but his defensive, angry and *utterly terrified* lament is part and parcel with a chunk of science fiction and fantasy fandom and authors who want to position themselves as a last redoubt against...well, *something*, anyway. It essentially boils down to "The wrong people are in control of things! We must take it back! *Attaaaaaaaaack!*" It's almost endearing in its foot-stompy-ness; I'd love to give this fellow a hug and tell him everything will be all right, but I'm sure that would be an affront to his concept of What Is Allowed, so I won't.

Instead let me make a few comments about the argument, such as it is.

1. The fellow above asserts that fans of his particular ilk must "take back" conventions and awards from all the awful, nasty people who currently infest them, as if this requires some great, heroic effort. In fact "taking back" a convention goes a little something like this:

Scene: CONVENTION REGISTRATION. ANGRY DUDE goes up to CON STAFFER at the registration desk.

Angry Dude: I AM HERE TO TAKE BACK THIS CONVENTION AND THE CULTURE THAT SO DESPERATELY CRIES OUT FOR MY INTERVENTION

Con Staffer: Okay, that'll be $50 for the convention membership.

(Angry Dude pays his money)

Con Staffer: Great, here's your program and badge. Have a great con!

Angry Dude: ...

I mean, everyone gets this, right? That conventions, generally speaking, are open to anyone who *pays to attend?* That the convention will be delighted to take your money? And that so long as one does not go out of one's way to be a complete assbag to other convention goers, the convention staff or the hotel employees, one will be completely welcome as part of the convention membership? That being the case, it's difficult to see why conventions need to be "taken back"—they were never actually taken *away.*

But the conventions are *run* by awful, nasty people! Well, no, the small local conventions (and some of the midsized ones, like Worldcon) are run by volunteers, i.e., people willing to show up on a regular basis and do the work of running a convention, in participation with others. These volunteers, at least in my experience, which at this point is considerable, are not awful, nasty people—they're regular folks who enjoy putting on a convention. The thing is, it's work; people who are into conrunning to make, say, a political statement, won't last long, because their political points are swamped by practical considerations like, oh, arguing with a hotel about room blocks and whether or not any other groups will be taking up meeting rooms.

(Larger cons, like Comic-cons, are increasingly run by professional organizations, which are another kettle of fish—but even at that level there are volunteers, and they are *also* not awful, nasty people. They're people who like participating.)

But the participants are awful, nasty people with *agendas!* That "problem" is solved by going to the convention programming people and both volunteering to be on panels and offering suggestions for programming topics. Hard as it may be to believe, programming staffers actually do want a range of topics that will appeal to a diverse audience, so that everyone who attends has something they'd be interested in. Try it!

Speaking as someone who once was in charge of a small convention open to the public, i.e., the Nebula Awards Weekend (I would note I was only nominally in charge—in fact the convention was run and staffed by super-competent volunteers), my position to *anyone* who wanted to come and experience our convention was: Awesome! See you there. Because why *wouldn't* it be?

Again, science fiction and fantasy conventions can't be "taken back"—they were, and are, open to everyone. I understand the "take back" rhetoric appeals to the "Aaaaugh! Our way of life is *under attack*" crowd, but the separation between the rhetoric and reality of things is pretty wide. Anyone who really believes conventions will be shocked and dismayed to get *more paying members and attendees* fundamentally does not grasp how conventions, you know, actually *work*.

2. Likewise, the "taking back" of awards, which in this case is understood to mean the Hugo Awards almost exclusively—I don't often hear of anyone complaining that, say, the Prometheus Award has been hijacked by awful, nasty people, despite the fact that this most libertarian of all science fiction and fantasy awards is regularly won by people who are not even remotely libertarian; shit, Cory Doctorow's won it three times and he's as pinko as they come.

But yet again, you can't "take back" the Hugos because they were never taken away. If you pay your membership fee to the Worldcon, you can nominate for the award and vote for which works and people you want to see recognized. All it takes is money and an interest; if you follow the rules for nominating and voting, then everything is fine and dandy. Thus voting for the Hugo is neither complicated, nor a revolutionary act.

Bear in mind that the Hugo voting set-up is fairly robust; the preferential ballot means it's difficult for something that's been nominated for reasons other than actual admiration of the work (including to stick a thumb into the eyes of people you don't like) to then walk away with an award. People have tested this principle over the years; they tended to come away from the process with their work listed below "no award." Which is as it should be. This also makes the Hugos hard to "take back." It doesn't matter how well a work (or its author) conforms to one's political inclinations; if the work itself simply isn't that good, the award will go to a different nominee that is better, at least in the minds of the majority of those who are voting.

The fellow above says if his little partisan group can't "take back" the awards, then they should destroy them. Well, certainly there is a way to do that, and indeed here's the *only* way to do that: by nominating, and then somehow forcing a win by, works that are manifestly sub-par, simply to make a political (or whatever) point. This is the suicide bomber approach: You're willing to go up in flames as long as you get to do a bit of collateral damage as you go. The problem with this approach is that, one, it shows that you're actually just an asshole, and two, it doesn't actively improve the position of your little partisan group, *vis a vis* recognition other than the very limited "oh, those are the childish foot-stompers who had a temper tantrum over the Hugos." Which is a dubious distinction.

With that said: Providing reading lists of excellent works with a particular social or political slant? Sure, why not? Speaking as someone who has been both a nominee and a winner of various genre awards, I am *utterly unafraid* of the competition for eyeballs and votes—which is why, moons ago, I created the modern version of the Hugo Voter's Packet, so that there would be a better chance of voters making an informed choice. Speaking as someone who nominates and votes for awards, I'm happy to be pointed in the direction of works I might not otherwise have known about. So this is all good, in my view. And should a worthy work by someone whose personal politics are not mine win a Hugo? Groovy by me. It's happened before. It's likely to happen again. I may have even nominated or voted for the work.

But to repeat: None of this constitutes "taking back" anything—it merely means you are participating in a process *that was always open to you*. And, I don't know. Do you want a *participation medal* or something? A pat on the head? It seems to me that most of the people nominating and voting for the Hugos are doing it with a minimum of fuss. If it makes you feel *important* by making a big deal out of doing a thing you've always been able to do—and that *anyone* with an interest and $50 has been able to do—then shine on, you crazy diamonds. But don't be surprised if no one else is really that impressed. Seriously: join the club, we've been doing this for a while now.

3. Also a bit of paranoid fantasy: The idea that because the *wrong* people are somehow in charge of publishing and the avenues of distribution, this is keeping authors (and fans, I suppose) of a certain political inclination down. This has always been a bit of a confusing point to me—how this little partisan group can both claim to be victimized by the publishing machine and yet still crow incessantly about the bestsellers in their midst. Pick a *narrative*, dudes, internal consistency is a thing.

Better yet, clue into reality, which is: The marketplace is diverse and can (and does!) support all sorts of flavors of science fiction and fantasy. In this (actually real) narrative, authors of all political and social stripes are bestsellers, because they are addressing slightly different (and possibly overlapping) audience sets. Likewise, there are authors of all political and social stripes who sell less well, or not at all. Because in the real world, the politics and social positions of an author don't correlate to units sold.

With the exception of publishing houses that specifically have a political/cultural slant baked into their mission statements, publishing houses are pretty damn agnostic about the politics of their authors. The same publishing house that publishes me publishes John C. Wright; the same publishing house that publishes John Ringo publishes Eric Flint. What do publishing houses like? Authors who sell. Because selling is the name of the game.

Here's a true fact for you: When I turn in *The End of All Things*, I will be out of contract with Tor Books; I owe them no more books at this point. What do you think would happen if I walked over to Baen Books and said, *hey, I wanna work with you?* Here's what would happen: The sound of *a flurry of contract pages* being shipped overnight to my agent. And do you know what would happen if John Ringo went out of contract with Baen and decided to take a walk to Tor? The *same damn noise*. And in both cases, who would argue, financially, with the publishers' actions? John Ringo would make a nice chunk of change for Tor; I'm pretty sure I could do the same for Baen. Don't kid yourself; this is not an ideologically pure business we're in.

(And yes, in fact, I would entertain an offer from Baen, if it came. It would need *many zeros* in it, mind you. But that would be the case with any publisher at this point.)

Likewise, I don't care how supposedly ideologically in sync you are with your publisher; if you're not selling, sooner or later, out you go. These are businesses, not charities.

But let's say, just for shits and giggles, that one ideologically pure faction somehow seized control of all the traditional means of publishing science fiction and fantasy, freezing out everyone they deemed impure. What then? One, some other traditional publisher, not previously into science fiction, would see all the money left on the table and start up a science fiction line to address the unsated audience. Two, you would see the emergence of at least a couple of smaller publishing houses to fill the market. Three, some of the more successful writers who were frozen out, the ones with established fan bases, could very easily set up shop on their own and self-publish, either permanently or until the traditional publishing situation got itself sorted out.

All of which is to say: Yeah, the paranoid fantasy of awful, nasty people controlling the genre is just that: Paranoid fantasy. Now, I understand that if you're an author of a certain political stripe who is not selling well, or a fan who doesn't like the types of science fiction and fantasy that other people who are not you seem to like, this paranoid fantasy has its appeal, especially if you're feeling beset politically/socially in other areas of your life as well. And that's too bad for you, and maybe you'd like a hearty fist-bump and an assurance that all will be well. But it doesn't change the fact that at the end of the day, no matter who you are, there will always be the sort of science fiction and fantasy you like available to you. Because—no offense—you are not unique. What you like is probably liked by other people, too. There are enough of you to make a market. That market will be addressed.

Again, I am genuinely flummoxed why so many people who are ostensibly so in love with the concept of free markets appear to have a *genuinely difficult time* with this. It's not *all* illuminati, people. It never was.

4. And this is why, fundamentally, the whole "take back the genre" bit is just complete nonsense. It *can* never be "taken back," it *will* never be "taken back," and it's doubtful there was ever a "back" to go to. The genre product market is resistant to ideological culling, and the social fabric of science fiction fandom is designed at its root to accommodate rather than exclude. No one can exclude anyone else from science fiction and fantasy fandom when the entrance requirement is, literally, an interest in the genre, or some particular aspect of it. You can't exclude people from conventions that require only a membership fee to attend. Even SFWA has opened up to self-publishing professional authors now, because it recognized that the professional market has changed. To suggest that the genre contract to fit the demands of any one segment of it doesn't make sense, commercially or socially. It won't be done. It would be foolish to do so.

The most this little partisan group (or those who identify with it) can do is assert that *they* are the true fans of the genre, not anyone else. To which the best and most correct response is: Whatever, dude. Shout it all you like. But you're wrong, and at the end of the day, you're not even a *side* of the genre, you're just a part. And either you're participating with everyone else in what the genre is today, or you're off to the side wailing like a toddler who has been told he can't have a lollipop. If you want to participate, come on in. If you think you're going to swamp the conversation, you're likely in for a surprise. But if you want to be part of it, then be a part of it. The secret is, you already are, and always have been.

If you don't want to participate, well. Wail for your lolly all you like, then, if it makes you happy. The rest of us can get along without you just fine.

JEEZ, SCALZI, DOES IT ALWAYS HAVE TO BE ABOUT YOU? WHY YES, YES IT DOES, OR, NOTES FROM MY CAREER

HOW TO HAVE A WRITING CAREER LIKE MINE

Jun

15

2011

You can't.

Which is not to say you can't have a career as a writer; maybe you can. But you can't have a career like mine. Because here's what you would have to do:

1. Start writing freelance in college.
2. Get a movie critic gig right out of school.
3. Have your second job be for the largest online service on the planet.
4. Get laid off and go solo.
5. Start a blog and have it become very popular.
6. Sell four non-fiction books before you sell your first novel.
7. Sell your first novel off your Web site.
8. Have that novel be an award-nominated breakout success.
9. Etc.

Each of these steps is actually important to having a career like mine; each step informs the steps after it. Skip a step and suddenly your career isn't like mine anymore; it's something else entirely, and the map I used to get where I am is no longer useful to you. You can't have a career like mine. The only one who gets a career like mine is me.

Other careers you can't have: Neil Gaiman's, Ursula Le Guin's, Robert Heinlein's, Cherie Priest's, Nalo Hopkinson's, Toby Buckell's, Pat Rothfuss', Mary Robinette Kowal's, Cassandra Clare's or Robert Silverberg's, to name just a few people off the top of my head. Their careers are not replicable, because they are to a very large extent the product of time and personal circumstance—and in many if not most cases a healthy helping of luck, which matters, too. Learning how each of them reached their successes can be interesting, and may yield some general ideas that you might apply to your own career-building. But if you look at their careers with an eye to ape particular moves, you're likely to be disappointed by the results.

If you feel you must look at other writers' careers, a suggestion: Look at more than one, and see what they have in common. What did Neil do that Ursula also did that Robert did too that Cherie is now doing? Look at the things that consistently appear in the careers of multiple authors, and you'll find the things that might be worth incorporating into your own. As a warning, they are likely to be *boring* things like "write regularly," or "minimize distractions" or some such, which are the "eat less, exercise more" of the writing career world. But that's life for you.

I can guarantee you this: If you try to have a writing career like mine, you won't have a career like mine—and more to the point, you won't be having the career you could have had. And that will happen no matter whose career you try to make yours like. So don't try to have a writing career like mine or anyone else's. Have *your* writing career. You'll be happier.

THE 10 SF/F WORKS
THAT MEANT THE
MOST TO ME

For no particular reason other than I want to, and because tomorrow marks the 12th anniversary of my very first pro publication in science fiction, here's a list of the ten science fiction and fantasy works that meant the most to me before I was professionally published as a science fiction writer—with additional Honorable Mentions following.

What does "meant the most to me" mean? Pretty much what it says—that these works are the works I returned to again and again as pieces of writing, as stories, and as experiences. I'm not interested in arguing whether these books and works are the "best"; I couldn't possibly care about that. I am interested in explaining why they mean as much as they do to me.

The list is arranged alphabetically rather than by rank, because, honestly, I really wouldn't know how to rank them.

1. *Always Coming Home,* **Ursula Le Guin:** From what I can tell, this is not one of Le Guin's best-regarded books, in part, I would assume, due to its unconventional structure; only about a third of it is tied into a narrative, while the rest of it is basically worldbuilding background and fragments. But it's these very fragments that made it so hugely important to me as a teenager. I'd always been the sort of kid who could stare at maps for hours, or read books of trivia about ancient civilizations—and fantasy ones too, since in junior high I read the Dungeons & Dragons bestiaries not to run a campaign but simply to enjoy the fiddly details of the D&D world.

Always Coming Home was like that...except that it was written by Le Guin, which meant that there was a true structure behind all the fragments of worldbuilding, and art to the manner in which it was all written. I didn't read the book in one go, all the way through—I would read a little bit, flip forward to another section, go back further to another part, and so on. There was more there than I could absorb in one sitting, which to me was part of the point of the book. I was always coming back to it, and in doing so, letting the world of the book grow on me organically, until it became as real as I believe Le Guin would hope it would become for her readers.

2. *The Dark is Rising Sequence*, by Susan Cooper: By today's standards the installments of Cooper's series are laughably slim—all five of its books could fit comfortably within one of the later books of the Harry Potter series, with room left over. But volume isn't power, and in particular the second book, from which the entire series takes its name, is a masterclass in how to vividly draw characters, setting, and stakes in remarkably few, well-considered words and story choices. I read *The Dark is Rising* just as I was about to have my eleventh birthday, the same birthday on which series hero Will Stanton learns of his new, mystical powers as well as his calling to save the world. I was as disappointed not to become an Old One as children a generation later would be to discover that an owl was not coming to invite them to Hogwarts.

One other thing that I appreciated about Cooper's work, even as a child, was that she was canny in understanding how even good people can be thoughtless or even heartless. There's a genuinely tragic betrayal in the course of *The Dark is Rising* that's brought about because one of the ostensibly good characters risks the life of another character in a way that seems almost trivial. Cooper's writing makes even a child feel the slighted character's confusion and pain, so when temptation comes to him, you understood why he turned away from the light... and why it wasn't mere weakness of character (or plot convenience) that he did.

3. Dune, by Frank Herbert: *Dune* is so well-known in science fiction circles that I feel I can probably be brief about it here and simply note that it's a highwater mark of massive-scale science fiction world-building for a reason.

Mind you, *Dune* also absorbs its fair share of potshots as well— the characters are humorlessly heroic, and its plotting and pacing can accurately be described as both epic and turgid. For me, that works here. *Dune* is very clearly mythology, and mythology has (for me, anyway) its own sort of ridiculous stateliness about it. Indeed, when the Dune series downshifts into more intimate stories (as it does in *Children of Dune* and *Dune Messiah*; the additional books in the series are unread by me), it rapidly loses its appeal. For *Dune*, it really is go big or go home.

4. *Fall of Hyperion*, by Dan Simmons: This book is the sequel to *Hyperion*, which won the 1989 Hugo Award for Best Novel in part because Simmons, that rat bastard, showed off how easily he could write in several different styles and off several different discrete stories, and still tie them all together into a single narrative whole. It's a well-deserved Hugo win.

But for all that *Hyperion* exists for me largely to set the scene for *Fall of Hyperion*. *Hyperion*, for all its immense technical skill, is all origin stories, all the time. In *Fall*, we don't have to waste time setting up characters, we just chuck them headlong into the story—and Simmons has got one hell of a story here. It's propulsive, it's dramatic, and it's the end of the world, in more than one sense. And it's every damn thing happening at once, with Simmons following several different plot lines, keeping them all sorted and switching between them with the sort of fluidity that you usually only get by hiring Thelma Schoonmaker.

Hyperion is the flashier of the two works, but *Fall of Hyperion* is to me just as technically impressive in its story telling—and even better in paying off the trials of its characters. *Hyperion* impresses me. *Fall of Hyperion* speaks to me.

5. *Grass*, by Sheri S. Tepper: In my mind, *Grass* is in many substantial ways the worldbuilding equal and counterpoint to *Dune*—each essay a unique global ecosystem with very specific creatures and cultures that exist only in them, and introduce an outsider (Paul Atriedes in *Dune*, Marjorie Westriding-Yrarier in *Grass*) who massively disrupts the equilibrium. And both touch more than a little on religion as a political system.

What Tepper manages that Herbert could never could in the *Dune* series is to make her characters recognizably examples of humanity—flawed and frustrated people, not always likable, and often in over their heads. This gives *Grass* the best of both worlds: epic scale and down-to-earth, relatable characters. It also makes *Grass* in many ways one of the most *complete* science fiction books I know of, functioning on every scale it works in.

(I'll also note that in many ways, *Raising the Stones*, *Grass*' very loose sequel, is even better—and more subversive. Honestly, I don't know why Tepper is not better known and better honored in science fiction than she is.)

6. *Perdido Street Station*, by China Miéville: As I've explained elsewhere, *Perdido Street Station* gets my vote for the best science fiction/fantasy novel of the 21st Century to date, and, to quote myself, "to be clear, I don't think the vote is even close":

> *Bas-Lag in itself is a monumental achievement in world-building, a place Miéville so cannily describes that I can picture it in my head better than I can imagine some places here on my own planet. I love re-reading Perdido simply to go walking the streets of New Crobuzon once more. The novel's story is less of a direct narrative than it is following around people too wrapped up into their own concerns to realize just how much they're pushing their world toward oblivion, but this is a feature, not a bug, in my opinion. And then there's the fact that as a formal exercise in genre, it's a bomb lobbed into the intersection of science fiction and fantasy—Perdido is neither, it just is and is enough so that the term "New Weird" was either created or retconned into service to accommodate it.*

The way I would explain Perdido, *in reference to* Old Man's War, *is as follows:* Old Man's War *is a thick, juicy steak that when you put it in your mouth you go, "Damn, I forget how much I love steak."* Perdido Street Station, *on the other hand, is* molecular gastronomy: *a whole new way of looking at cooking, which when the results are put in front of you, you go, "Wait. Is that food?" Both are good, and depending on your taste, one may suit you more than the other. But at the end of the day, one is a truly excellent steak, and one is an invention. And that matters.*

Yup, that still works for me.

7. *Snow Crash,* **by Neal Stephenson:** There are many reasons to love *Snow Crash,* among them the fact that Stephenson seems to be pegging the 21st century decline of Western civilization in it rather depressingly accurately. But the reason I love it is that it still has the best first chapter in all of science fiction, one that not only reads like effortlessly cool beat poetry, is funnier than 99.9% of science fiction ever was and has the sort of propulsive rhythm to it that dares you to blink, but it also, compactly and elegantly, sets you in the world of novel and makes it make sense without making you aware that it's doing so.

In short, *Snow Crash's* first chapter is a perfect miniature of worldbuilding, so successful that you never doubt anything else that Stephenson tells you about the world he's built—you just go along for the ride. I would *teach* that first chapter, people. I would teach a whole *class* on it.

8. *Speaker For the Dead,* **by Orson Scott Card:** Another second book I consider better than its more famous predecessor, in this case *Ender's Game.* Why do I like *Speaker* better than *Ender?* Well, for one thing, in this book, Ender has agency—he's not a child manipulated by adults desperate for a solution to their problem and willing to destroy an innocent (actually, many innocents) in order to achieve their goals. Rather, he's an adult who has chosen to put himself on a path of atonement, despite the loneliness and isolation that path requires of him.

Which is to say that Ender is more relatable and sympathetic here than he is in *Ender's Game,* and also more realistic, in the sense that rather than being a preternaturally precocious child, he's a grown man who has had time to experience life, deal with actual humans and temper his own self. He's a major science fiction figure with a recognizable second act—that thing that F. Scott Fitzgerald (in an entirely different context, to be sure) denied it was possible to have. For me, it's the far more interesting act.

9. *Time Enough For Love*, by Robert Heinlein: *Like Always Coming Home*, this is a sort of off-brand choice for this particular writer; it's not the best known or best loved of Heinlein's books, and indeed it's problematic in a number of ways, not the least is that it's recognizably the start of Heinlein's later phase, in which his urge to tie together all his works in a sexy, polyamorous bow degrades the actual storytelling that's going on. Not to mention Lazarus Long having sex with his mom, which despite all attempts to normalize it is still pretty damn squicky.

But, *eh*, I don't care. I love the character of Lazarus Long, a man who has lived for so long that he's forgotten how to die, not that anyone around him is interested in helping him remember. He's cantankerous, sentimental, blustery, full of great dialogue and, for better or worse, the apotheosis of the Heinlein/Campbell "competent man"—someone so many science fiction readers and writers want to be, despite the fact that Heinlein built his universes around Lazarus, an advantage normal humans don't have, with regard to the universe in which they exist.

I'm pretty sure growing up that I didn't fall into the trap of wanting to be Lazarus Long, or Jubal Harshaw, or any of the other stock Heinlein wise men one could name, but I did learn to appreciate what they do in science fiction, and when they're valuable—and what their pitfalls are. To that end, I think Lazarus Long might recognize John Perry as a distant relation: Competent and sentimental, to be sure. Maybe a little less crankily judgmental.

10. *Winter's Tale*, by Mark Helprin: One of the most gorgeously written books in the English language in the last quarter century of the 20th Century. You can argue with me about that if you like. I will just smile and nod politely and ignore you. This is one of the few books of fantasy or science fiction where I literally do not care whether the book pays attention to its plot, because the writing is so lovely that it is its own reward.

This is also a book that I can love unreservedly without any authorial jealousy, because it is so far removed from my own skills and interests as a writer that there's almost no intersection between its strengths as a book and my own talents as a storyteller. It's nice to read a book without having an urge to pick it apart to reverse engineer it.

This is also, incidentally, one of those books that some people will tell you is not actually a fantasy book, because Helprin is otherwise known as a literary writer, and the book itself is highly regarded by people who care about serious literature and blah blah blah. My response to this: Whatever. It's fantasy and anyone who would deny it, either in genre or out of it, is foolish.

Honorable Mentions:

Ariel by Steve Boyett and **Emergence** by David R. Palmer, both of which have the light hand with dialogue and exposition that I love to read and very definitely cribbed from when I became a writer. **The Wrinkle in Time** series by Madeleine L'Engle because of its lovely characters, including Charles Wallace, still the best-drawn example of the "young genius" archetype. **The Sandman** by Neil Gaiman and **The Watchmen** by Alan Moore, which broke me of my (totally unconscious) snobbery regarding visual storytelling. **Bridge of Birds** by Barry Hughart, which hit me sideways with its gentle humor and inspired me to learn more about a culture unknown to me. **The Martian Chronicles** by Ray Bradbury, which offered empathy and anger, and showed that single stories could add up to a larger whole. And **The Hitchhiker's Guide to the Galaxy** by Douglas Adams, because it showed humor could happen in science fiction. Which ultimately turned out to be a good thing for me, I would say.

10 NON-SF/F BOOKS THAT MEANT THE MOST TO ME (AS A WRITER)

Jan

12

2014

A few months back I wrote about The 10 SF/F Books That Meant the Most to Me in the days before I was a published science fiction author. It's worth noting, however, that I didn't only read science fiction and fantasy growing up, nor were the writers and books I admired—and which I think eventually helped shape me as a writer—confined only to those genres. Indeed, how much poorer my life would have been, both as a reader and a writer, if I had read only in one thin slice of the literary world.

So, for your interest and delight, I present ten non-SF/F books that meant the most to me as a growing writer. Again, this list is confined to the time prior to me writing books of my own; the latest I encountered one of them was when I was in college. Likewise, as with the earlier list, this is not a list of "best" or "most important" works in a general or competitive sense—just the ones that had an impact on me, and with particular regard to the sort of writer I would eventually become. This list is in alphabetical order, by author.

J.L. Austin: *How to Do Things With Words*: I have a degree in philosophy and the focus of that degree is language and all the things we do with it. Of all the books and philosophers that I read in the course of obtaining that degree, this book, and Austin, stand out. For one thing, *Words* is a surprisingly enjoyable read—it's taken from a series of lectures, and Austin was apparently aware that speeches work better if you're not falling asleep at them. For another thing, Austin put into words a thing I had always believed but (appropriately) wasn't able to express: That language itself could *do* things, not just *say* to do things—that it wasn't just a vehicle for intention, but could be used for action. Whether Austin intended it this way or not, this said to me that language has its own native powers, and got me to think about what I and everyone else was doing, intentionally or not, when we used the words we used. That's been useful for both my fiction and non-fiction.

Truman Capote: *In Cold Blood:* I read this in middle school, for my own curiosity rather than a book assignment (I don't imagine the book, then or now, would be assigned in most middle schools). I can't remember specifically why I picked up the book, but I remember being sucked into it by the way Capote told the story, setting the scene and chronicling the events in a way that read halfway between journalism and fiction. I'd learn later that people called it (both positively and negatively) a "non-fiction novel," which I think very accurately represents the feel of the book. There is some question as to whether all the details of the book are accurate to true life (it seems not), but for me it was captivating to read it and know that this—or something very like it— happened in the real world.

Louise Fitzhugh: *Harriet the Spy:* I read this, I think, in fifth grade, and there was a massive disconnect between the late 70s poverty-ridden suburban California boy I was and the mid-60s privileged New York girl that Harriet was, and yet I felt a very real connection to her. We were both smart, observant, stubborn and more than occasionally jerks, as much out of the principle of the thing as anything else. Fitzhugh did two important things in *Harriet*: One, she didn't make Harriet any more likable than she should have been, and that was a revelation in itself. Two, she told an unvarnished truth about human relationships (through the character of Ole Golly) and trusted Harriet— and by extension the reader—to understand the subtleties at play there. It was a book for kids that took the kids seriously, as characters and readers both.

Stephen King: *Christine*: *Christine* was not the first Stephen King book I read (that would be *The Stand*, which I read at ten years old, which is, uh, an *interesting* age to read that particular book), but it was the first Stephen King book I read where I got what it was that King was doing—making a normal world with normal people in it and have everything progressively go further and further into hell. King doesn't write like someone who condescends to the Great American Middle, or tries to explain the people in it to readers on the outside, staring in like they were at the zoo (which is among other things why he was underappreciated for as long as he was by literary critics). He just shoves those people into the crucible and waits for the heat and pressure to kill them or make them heroes, and writes interestingly about what happens to them either way. This is hugely important stuff. *Christine* isn't King's best, but it's the one that I first took an important writing lesson from, and for the purposes of this list, that's good enough.

Gregory Mcdonald: *Fletch*: Fletch and Mcdonald are important to me for one word: Dialogue. As in, Mcdonald was a master of it, and it was absolutely essential to *Fletch* (and its many sequels). How important? Important enough that the book's dialogue was a featured graphic element on the book covers of the entire series. That's a genuinely remarkable thing. And it's correct; the dialogue is incredibly important in establishing characters, setting scene and telling large chunks of the story. Mcdonald was not big on description; it was hardly there and when it was, it was the bare minimum required for the story. It's not a stretch to suggest that of all genre writers, the one that my writing style is closest to is Mcdonald. It's also worth noting that when I first set down to see if I could write a novel, I more or less flipped a coin to see if I would write one in science fiction or one in the crime genre. In another, slightly different universe, it's entirely possible that the reviews for first novel I had published have me hailed as "the next Mcdonald" rather than "the next Heinlein." I would have been okay with that.

H.L. Mencken: *A Mencken Chrestomathy*: In my freshman year of high school I was reading from a book of quotations and noticed that many of the best quotes—the ones that were really punchy—were from some dude named Mencken. I went to my school library, which had the *Chrestomathy*, checked it out and started reading. By the time I was done with the book two things had happened. One, I had fallen in love with the 1920s (a fact which will be important later in the list). Two, I wanted to be a newspaper columnist *really really* badly. It's not at all incorrect to suggest that for the first portion of my writing life, the part where I wrote columns and reviews for a living, Mencken was arguably the most significant influence. Nor is it incorrect to suggest that he continues to be important, since you may note that I've been writing columns here for more than fifteen years, and have no intention of stopping.

Dorothy Parker: *The Portable Dorothy Parker*: As noted above, HL Mencken was my entrance into the world of 1920s literati, and it wasn't long until I made the acquaintance of the members of the Algonquin Round Table. They were funny and witty and, from across the gulf of six decades, the possessors of the sort of deeply romanticized writing life I wanted to have one day when I grew up. Pre-eminent among them for her wit, her quippiness and general smarts, was Parker. The *Portable* has many of the good bits I first enjoyed from her, as well as the bits that I enjoyed the older I got and the more I learned about Parker and her compatriots, and realized that the quippy glamour of their lives was not all there was to it, and the rest of their lives were as muddled and occasionally unhappy as anyone else's (she did end up attempting suicide, after all). For all that, if one has to have an early idol of humor and wit, one could have done far worse than Ms. Parker.

Carl Sagan: *Cosmos*: The companion book to the TV series was given to me as a birthday gift, I think for my eleventh or twelfth birthday. The big, beautiful, full-color hardcover, I would note, which to me seemed like the most amazing thing humanity had created to that point. I spent about a month just looking at pictures and captions before diving in and reading the actual text—which of course was another treat in itself. Sagan's obvious love of science and the universe, and his desire to share that love in a way that was accessible to all but the most truculent of others, is something that I took to heart when I was writing my own non-fiction and even in my science fiction: That most things can be explained to most people, in a way that didn't talk down or condescend but instead lets people in on the secret and makes them want to know more. That's a gift I can't thank the man enough for.

George Bernard Shaw: *Saint Joan***:** In high school I had a class called Individual Humanities, the idea being that the whole point of civilization was the development of "independently acting and thinking individuals who saw as their highest life crisis service to their community." Which is a hell of an idea if you think about it. One of the readings for the class was *Saint Joan,* and along with the play itself, we read the prefatory material (which with many of Shaw's works was often longer than the play itself) in which Shaw discussed the "evolutionary appetite": the idea that some people, against all personal benefit or gain, are compelled to act in a way that pulls humanity forward (often with kicking and screaming on humanity's part). It's a heady idea, and whether it has a rational basis in fact, it's something that's embedded in my head when I write characters who are facing crises of their own.

David Wallechinsky and Irving Wallace: *The People's Almanac***:** I *ate* this book and its two sequels when I was a kid. It was random and yet so densely packed with digestible information that it seemed likely that everything it was possible to know was in the book. For a six-year-old with a voracious reading appetite, which I certainly was, it was godsend. My mom thought the same thing, since she could give it to me and I would squirrel up in a corner with it for hours at a time. From these books I learned that everything *could* be interesting, and since everything *could* be interesting, that it was interesting to learn about everything. This is an idea and ethos that have served me well as a writer: Since I know a little about a lot of things, it's convinced people to pay me to write on those subjects (which has given me a reason to learn more about them and get paid while doing it). It also makes me excited to tell other people about what I've learned. If you want to know where it all began for me, in terms of writing, this really is the place to start.

Not noted here: A number of works for stage and screen, and other non-literary media which still require writing, and the brains that create that writing. I'll talk about those, possibly, some other time.

BEING FICTIONAL

Jan

30

2011

Threeother day I linked to author Elizabeth Bear's discussion about being fictional—or, less pithily, her dealing with that fact that lots of people who read her books and/or her blog have an image of her in her head which is a construct, based on that writing, which may or may not have much to do with who she actually is. The number of people carrying a fictional version of her around in their head is smaller than the number of people who have a fictional version of, say, Angelina Jolie or Barack Obama in their head, but it's a large enough number of people that she does have to deal with it.

And it's a weird thing to deal with. As eBear notes:

> *Sometimes, it's a little like dealing with 5,000 high school crushes. Sometimes it's like dealing with 5,000 high school enemies. Sometimes, I learn things about myself I did not know from my Wikipedia page.*

I understand where eBear's coming from, because she and I have essentially the same level of micro-celebrity, and with the same subset of people—which is to say it's difficult to imagine people who know of me not knowing who she is, and vice-versa. And I think she's essentially correct when she notes that the fictional version people have of you in their heads in more about them than it is about you; everything gets filtered through their brain and how people fill in the blanks is by sticking in bits based on their own experiences, sometimes from others but mostly from themselves.

This fictional version of you is additionally compounded by the fact that, if you're a writer, the version of you they're building from isn't the *experience* of you (as in, you're someone they know in real life), but from the fiction you write and/or the public persona you project, either in writing (in blogs and articles) or in public events, such as conventions or other appearances. The fiction one writes may or may not track at all to one's real-world personality or inclinations, and while one's public persona probably does have something to do with the private person, it's very likely to be a distorted version, with some aspects of one's personality amped up for public consumption and other aspects tamped down or possibly even hidden completely.

All of which is to say these fictional versions of one's self are to one's actual self as grape soda is to a grape—artificial and often so completely different that it's often difficult to see the straight-line connection between the two.

And this is why I personally find them fascinating, especially—since I am both an egotist *and* a narcissist—when they involve me. I like going out onto the Web and discovering these strange, doppelganger versions of me, and also the people who speak so authoritatively about the sort of person these doppelgangers are. Occasionally those doppelgangers are better, more clever people that I am in real life, and occasionally they're complete jackasses. Sometimes they're people I'd like to meet; often they're people I would avoid at parties. Their life and career details are generally similar but not precisely my own, and it's interesting to see how those variations have spun their lives off of mine, and what conclusions people have made about them based on those variations.

What do I do about these fictional versions of me out there? Generally speaking, nothing, because there's nothing to be done about them. When one is in the (mostly) happy position of having more people know of you than you can personally know, an abundance of fictional versions of you is part of the territory. I can't make a deep and personal two-way connection with everyone who reads my books or this blog, and I can't demand that people don't make assumptions about who I am from what they read or hear (well, I *could*, but then part of their data set when they think about me would be that I was both paranoid and completely unrealistic). Generally I try not to do things in public which would encourage people to think I'm a unremitting prick, but I would try to do that even if I didn't have the level of micro-fame I have. And of course some people think I'm an unremitting prick *anyway*.

But you do try not to worry about it. Teresa Nielsen Hayden, who is often a font of wisdom on many fronts, has a useful standard response for dealing with people who confuse their fictional construct of someone with that actual person, which I will paraphrase thusly: "I am not responsible for actions of the imaginary version of me you have inside your head." This is an important thing for people to remember, when they get to the point where more people know them than they know.

Personally, I'm less interested in the fictional versions of me that are out there than I am about the moment where people first ever meet me—either in my real-life "I'm actually standing in front of you" version or the first time they read one of my books or come to this site. I always wonder what that's like for people, and what impression they come away with. There's no way to ask them as they're having it, and I always wonder about it (I could when they were *actually* meeting me, I suppose, but it would be both meta and obnoxious: "Hey! You're meeting me now! How is it for you?"). I'm not worried about the fictional versions they construct from that point, but I always hope the first time they "meet" me it goes well.

THE CUBS, THE 108-YEAR-LONG STREAK, AND OLD MAN'S WAR

This year, as the Chicago Cubs came closer and closer to winning a World Series, people wondered what that might mean for the Old Man's War series of books. After all, in several places I had people in the books discussing the Chicago Cubs and their inability to win a World Series, and in *The Human Division*, it's actually a plot point. So what happens to those books, now that the Cubs, after 108 years, have won a World Series?

Well, you know. In one sense, nothing. The books are fiction, take place in the "future" and in a multiverse where space travel isn't actually traveling in space, it's traveling from one universe to another, where things are (usually) just one electron position different. So now either the events of the Old Man's War series have been pushed further out in the timestream, for at least another 108 years (or so), or we've just become a universe *so improbable* that it's unlikely the events of the Old Man's War book will ever happen in it, but those events continue, about a billion universes to our left.

Which is it? You choose, either is valid.

As a *practical* matter, mind you, I think the plot points still work, they just got more meta. Now readers in North America, at least, are aware that the long suffering of Cubs fans has come to a close, and will enjoy the presence of the plot point on that grounds (or if they're Cleveland fans, not). Readers will hit those points in the books, enjoy the slight bit of cognitive dissonance, and then move on.

But of course, with all those assertions above, it's *possible* I might be rationalizing just a tiny bit. In which case, yup, it's time to come right out and admit it: Now the Old Man's War books suffer from the same problem as all the science fiction stories before 1969 that named a first man on the moon, or the ones that imagined canals on Mars. The real world caught up to them and passed them by, waving as it did so.

And that's okay. This is the risk you take when you put a plot point in your books that's contingent on the real world. It is the fate of science fiction books and other media to be continually invalidated by real-world events, or at least, to have the real world catch up to it and then have the work, by necessity, consigned to a nearby but undeniably alternate universe. This had already happened to the Old Man's War series in a small ways (no one calls hand-held computers "PDAs" anymore, but the folks in the OMW series do, because that's what they called them in 2001, when I wrote the first book), and in larger ways for other books of mine. *Agent to the Stars*, for example, has a plot point involving an elderly Holocaust survivor. In 1997, when I wrote that book, that was still a reasonable thing. Today in 2016, it's a pretty long stretch. In another ten years, *Agent to the Stars* will undeniably take place in the past, in an alternate universe.

The real world catches up to science fiction. It always does.

But it doesn't *always* kill the book (or film, or whatever), thankfully. *1984* is still read despite the titular year now being more than thirty years in the past; we watch *2001* despite us not having moon bases or monoliths at the moment; people still enjoy the various Star Trek television series despite the fact the communicators in each iteration are laughably less complex than a smart phone today. People seem to get that science fiction stories have plot points and details that expire, or, at the most charitable, "go meta."

I suspect that will be the fate of the Old Man's War books. The Chicago Cubs in that universe are a plot point, but a minor one overall. I don't expect that many people will decide that the Cubs continuing to be lovable losers there will be the thing that throws them entirely out of suspension of disbelief. And if it does, I mean, okay? Their life. Everyone else will either push out the timeline, enjoy the meta moment, or, alternately (and especially if they're not baseball fans), not care. I think the books will survive, is what I'm saying.

In the meantime, congratulations to the Cubs and all their fans. As someone who attended college in Chicago, this is lovely moment; as someone who now lives in Ohio, this is a disappointment; and as someone who grew up in Los Angeles, I stopped caring one series back. No matter what, however, having the Chicago-Cleveland series decided in the tenth inning of a game seven is just about perfect. It could not have been written better.

I've gone on the record in years past saying it's more existentially satisfying for the Cubs to keep losing than to ever win the World Series—they crown a World Series winner every year, after all, but no one else has a 108-year-long streak of futility to their name, with the potential to add to it every season. Streaks like that don't come around every year, or even every century. Seems a shame to throw something like that away on mere winning. But, you know what? Right now, there's not a single Cubs fan in the world, living or dead, who agrees with me, if indeed there ever was. That's fair enough. I hope they all enjoy their moment of winning, and the end of the long, long, *long* losing streak. The Cubs earned it.

And, also, if they ever make a TV series or a movie series out of the Old Man's War books, Chicago in the text will be replaced by Cleveland, and it will still work. Sorry, Cleveland. You know I love you.

DIMINISHING
RETURNS

M
ike Lyon is concerned about:

> *The Law of Diminishing Returns in Series Science Fiction &*
> *Fantasy.*
>
> *Don't tell me it hasn't come up before. And no disrespect to you,*
> *Scalzi, since thus far the three Old Man's War novels have been of*
> *a uniformly excellent quality, but everyone from Orson Scott Card*
> *to Frank Herbert have suffered from the endless serialization of their*
> *greatest successes.*
>
> *How far can a high concept and beloved characters be taken before*
> *they descend into fan-service for a paycheck?*

I don't know, Mike. Let me write six other "Old Man's War" books
and get back to you on that.

Having just written a fourth book in the OMW universe (which,
depending on how you want to slice it, is the fourth book of a quartet,
the second book of the second of two duologies (OMW and TGB being
one, about military life in that universe, with TLC and ZT being the
other, about colonial life) or just a simple stand-alone, with the possibility of being the first book in a sub-series; really, take your pick, and the
answer could very well be "all of the above"), this is something that I
do think about. As most of you know, after *The Last Colony* I said I was
probably going to take a step back from the Old Man's War series and

do some other stuff—and yet the next novel to come out will be a OMW series book. Was it because I suddenly had a good idea I just *had* to do in the universe, involving a character there? Or was it to cash in on an increasingly successful series, and strike while the iron was hot?

The answer, as you might expect, is: Yes.

Which is to say they are both correct. After I finishing TLC, I developed an interest in Zoe as a character, and thought it would be a worthy skill challenge both to try to credibly write a 16-year-old female protagonist and to write a book in parallel time to another story in the universe. But *also*, I know what my sales and royalties are, and I know that the OMW series is selling at a very nice clip, and I knew that Tor would be very happy to have an OMW-universe hardcover to put out when *The Last Colony* was slated to go into mass market paperback, so that each could build sales for the other.

So I talked to Patrick, my editor, about this, and the conversation went a little like this:

Me: I know I'm supposed to be writing something else, but I have an idea for another OMW book and I was wondering if you'd like me to go ahead with that one first.

Patrick: You're kidding, right?

And here we are.

It's pretty obvious that publishers like series, since they put out a whole lot of them; it's hard to think of a science fiction/fantasy author who gets by only on standalone books. But publishers like them because *people* like them, and the reason people like them, as I said to another writer friend recently, is because when they read them, they know when to stand and when to sit. Which is to say, they know the players, they know the rituals and they know the lay of the land. Even when the series takes place in world that's aggressively fantastical, once you're in, you're in.

It works the same way with the writers, too—

\<cranky writer hat\>

—because, look, people: World building is *hard*. You want us to have to build an entire universe from scratch every single time we write a book? Well, okay. You want us to have to run a marathon every time we walk down to the corner store to get some milk, too? Or maybe assemble a car from the wheels up, every time we want to drive to the mall? We spend all this time building this ginchy universe and its rules, and then you say "Oh, *that* world again?" No one ever pulls that shit with other genres. People don't go up to Carl Hiaasen and say "What? Another book on *Earth?*" And he didn't even make up that planet! It's an *open source* planet! Damn *slacker*.

</cranky writer hat>

So that's why it's nice to have a series, and why so many of us write them.

How far can you take a series before it turns into hackery? It really depends on the writer, doesn't it? I'm reading Iain Banks' Culture series at the moment, in a backwards way—I read *Matter*, the latest, before reading *Consider Phlebas*, the first, and if there's a descent into hackery from first to last, I'm missing it. On the other hand, without naming names, I can think of plenty of series which should have been strangled in the womb, preferably by going back in time, sneaking over to the author's computer, and replacing the very first as-yet-unsubmitted manuscript in the series with the sentence "GET A DAY JOB" repeated out to novel length. Lesson: Authors are important.

I don't think series decay is inevitable, but I do think you have to work at it to make sure it doesn't happen. One thing working against that, from a practical point of view, is that publishers want books on a regular schedule—Tor would have rather have had *Zoe's Tale* ready a year after the release of *The Last Colony*, and if given their druthers, I'm sure they'd want another OMW universe follow-up roughly a year after *Zoe's Tale* goes out the door, too. And that can be a real challenge in maintaining really high quality. To come back to Banks, *Matter* is high-quality stuff (I wouldn't at all be surprised to see it as a Hugo contender next year), but it's also been eight years since the release of the last Culture novel. And maybe that's made a difference; sometimes letting the field lie fallow works.

As for me, well. I don't ever deny that I keep an eye on my financial bottom line when I write—I'm an unapologetically commercial writer, both stylistically and as a matter of personal philosophy—but I also know myself well enough to know that writing novels in a series just for the paycheck would bore the ever-living *crap* out of me. Which would mean books that suck, which is not something I want. I'm fine with people not liking my work for whatever reason, but what I don't want is to have people get the impression that I don't *care* about what I'm writing, quality-wise. I write books for money, but if I was *just* writing books for money, I can make *more* money writing other things that take a lot less effort. I did very well financially as a writer before I started writing novels; I could do just fine financially without them. This is actually a positive thing for you guys, because it means that I don't actually *have* to stoop to mere hackery to pay my bills. There has to be something *else* going on there, some element that makes the writing of the book in itself interesting to me, or else it's not worth my time.

This is something I've talked to the Tor folks about as well. I don't think it's any secret that Tor would like more OMW books, because, to be blunt about it, they sell great and two of the three titles in the series to date have gotten Best Novel Hugo nods. If Tor didn't want more of 'em, they'd be dumb. They're not, so they do, and this has been communicated to me—which I appreciate; it's nice to feel wanted. But to Tor's additional credit, it's also been communicated to me that their quality control concerns mirror mine. We've both got a good thing going here, and it would be dumb for either of us, writer or publisher, to let the series descend into mere hackery. So we do work hand-in-hand to make sure **a)** individual books don't suck, and **b)** that I have enough opportunity to other stuff so that when I come back to the OMW universe, it's fun for me and not a drag, which is key to making sure the rest of you enjoy those books too. It's a nice partnership so far.

I think maybe the answer to your question, Mike, is that the distance you can take a series until it descends into hackery is the distance after which neither the writer or publisher sees the novels as *work*, but simply as *product*. I'm happy to say we're not there yet with the Old Man's War series. And we're working to stay off that particular road.

FURTHER THOUGHTS ON FAME AND SUCCESS

To questions today. The first, from Chris Salter:

> In 2008 you wrote about your level of fame. Has that changed in any meaningful way? And as a follow-up: You seem to be friends with a number of semi-famous (or actually famous) people. Does it ever feel weird to see your friends being chronic topics of discussion on the Internet, on TV, etc?

The second, from **Frankly**:

> If it is not too personal I'd like to hear a bit about how your life has changed given the success you have had as a novelist. You went from newspapers to online 'reportage' (for lack of a more accurate description) to novelist and from populated sections of California to much more rural Ohio. That is a heck of a range. To say nothing of starting off in a low income family to what has to be a bit more comfortable even if it is not 'Vanderbilt-esk'. I'd love to hear your musing about that you miss, what you don't miss, what you enjoy now that you didn't imagine and how you think those experiences have changed you.

On a professional level as a writer, I've often had a (usually very minor) level of fame. My first job out of college was as a movie critic for a newspaper, and the paper promoted me as a personality, so I was a local celebrity, not unlike a TV weatherman or a radio deejay. Later on

I experienced more minor fame as part of the first generation of blog-gers (or online diarists, as we called ourselves). So when I experienced my first taste of (again minor) fame as a novelist, it was an experience that was not entirely unknown to me. I think that prior experience was ultimately beneficial, because it gave me a roadmap for how to deal with it.

Also useful: The fact that I had spent years meeting and inter-viewing film makers and movie stars, which is to say, people who had *actual* undeniable fame in our culture. That was helpful because I had something to compare my own little slice of fame to. This was key in allowing me to keep perspective on what my "fame" was and how far it went in the world: rather little and not very far, respectively. This has been useful in keeping me from becoming too much of an asshole, or at the very least, from using fame as an excuse for being an asshole.

Which brings us to the question of how my own fame has changed over the last five years. There are two ways to answer this. In the field of science fiction and fantasy, certainly, I am more famous than I was in 2008. This is the aftereffect of having a few bestselling novels, win-ning a couple of Hugos and other awards (and being nominated for several others), being the president of SFWA for three years, and (duh) having a Web site that is a hub for science fiction and fantasy readers, pros and fans. Note this is not a discussion as to whether I *deserve* to be famous, *should* be famous, will *continue* to be famous, or if fame has made me a *dick* or whatever. Simply that I am famous in my field right now.

Outside of the field of science fiction and fantasy, my fame is about the same as it was in 2008: Close enough to zero as to not make any real difference. I am slightly more *notable* outside SF/F than I was five years ago—if you say my name in room of writers outside the SF/F genre there's at least a small possibility they have heard of me as a writer and/ or someone who talks about writing/publishing online. But *notability* is not the same as *fame*. What's the difference? If you are *notable*, people say "oh, I know who he is." If you are *famous*, people say "oh, shit, is he here? I'd love to *meet* him." If you're notable, people won't think you're out of place at the party. If you're famous, people came to the party because you're there.

As I've noted before here on Whatever, I think that the sort of highly limited fame I have suits me. I have enough of an ego that I think it's neat to go to a convention or book fair and have people squee in my general direction for a day or three, and I'm not going to deny I dig on the other perks, like travel and money and the ability to meet on a more or less equal footing talented people whose work I admire. But I also have enough of a desire to have a life that I am glad I don't get recognized in restaurants and supermarkets. I have friends who do; their general consensus on it is that it is less fun than people imagine. I am willing to believe them, especially because they've been dealing with it for years. When your desire to go out in the world is constrained by your need to be let alone, fame stops being fun and becomes a burden. And yes, it's a high class burden to have. But famous humans remain human, and stress works on them like anyone else.

I do have a number of notable and/or famous friends at this point. Some of them came up with me in the genre or were within a couple of years of me on either side; some of them I got introduced to through mutual acquaintances and sometimes some of them wanted to meet me, because they were fans of my work (which was—and remains— *totally cool*). And as noted above, sometimes I get to use my own limited fame to get to meet people I admire, and then I become friends with them from there. My famous friends and I are friends because we like each other as people. As a bonus, we have a common pool of relatively unusual experiences that we can talk to each other about without feeling weird about it, which turns out to be really important for one's sanity. It's nice to be able to talk to people about a topic, positive or negative, and to have them know from their own lives what you're dealing with.

Having friends who are famous can be a lot of fun: It's a kick to watch a television show or open up a magazine or go to a bookstore and say, *oh, look, there she is*. It's even occasionally fun to brag about knowing these folks to someone I know likes or admires them. I'm not generally envious or jealous of their fame/notability because I'm happy with my own level and in any event I think envy and jealousy are stupid things.

If you're not happy for your friends when they do well, then you should question if you are really their friend.

On the flip side, however, when I see someone take a whack at them, online or elsewhere, yeah, it annoys the crap out of me. It annoys me because frequently these whacks are gratuitous or based out of ignorance or stupidity or actual malice, brought on by prejudice or envy or whatever. I also think there are some people who have a hard time recognizing that people who are famous are also real live humans, and like other real live humans are nowhere close to perfect, nor are they meant to be your dancing monkey on a leash. To be clear, there are some friends who stake intellectual, social or policy opinions out in public, and it's perfectly valid for people to disagree with those—vehemently, even. I don't like it when they unfairly cross the line into personal attack, any more than any person likes it when their friends are attacked.

(I will note that the large majority of my friends are not famous in any significant way, which should not be entirely surprising if only because, again, outside of my field, *I* am not famous in any significant way. I am lucky to know all the friends I know, and am glad that any of them choose to be friends with me.)

To move away from the topic of famous friends and to address another aspect of Frankly's question, being a novelist has not materially affected my life in a way I think people might assume. For example, my transition from being poor to being well-off, and from living in a (sub)urban California environment to a rural Ohio one, all happened well before I was ever published as a novelist. To be blunt about about it, when I sold *Old Man's War* to Tor, I wasn't expecting it to change my life in any significant way—I was paid $6,500 for the book and assumed that's all I would ever see from it, and mostly intended for fiction to be a sideline to my then-happily profitable career as a non-fiction writer and corporate consultant.

It turns out I was wrong (funny about that), but when everything hit for me in fiction, most of the most dramatic changes in my life circumstances were already behind me: I was in my mid-thirties, I was happily married with a kid, and I was well into a financially successful writing career. My success as a novelist was a bonus on top of that. I do tend to think it was a good thing that I was, in many ways, already squared away before I hit as a novelist. It meant I wasn't overwhelmed either by the money or attention, and that I had a reasonably good idea who I was and what I wanted.

In fact, I think it's fair to say that all my life experience to that point helped me *not* to change my life dramatically. And I think that's been to my benefit in the long run.

HAVING FANS

'm writing you today from Toronto, where I am because a bunch of very nice Canadians decided it would be a groovy thing to pay for my plane ticket, put me up in a hotel, and fete me for a weekend as one of their guests of honor at the SFContario science fiction convention. Tonight, I'll do a reading, and people who like my books will show up and listen to me preview an upcoming book and then blather on about my life. Over the next few days, while I'm at the convention, I'll get to do even more of that. Usually when you go on and on about yourself for *days*, you're labeled—not without *reason*—as an insufferable jackass blowhard. But not only am I encouraged to do this, indeed, this is part of why I'm *here*.

Having fans is *awesome*.

It's also dangerous, of course, for the sort of attention-seeking monkey I and many other creative types are. Jamming this sort of appreciation into our brains is likely to encourage a positive feedback loop of personal entitlement and self-regard wildly out of proportion to our actual worth as human beings. And then we become *assholes*. That is in fact the precise, technical term. You can look it up. But that's very definitely more about that person than it is about the people who appreciate his or her work. Fans don't make people assholes, people become assholes when they misinterpret enthusiasm for them and their work to mean that the normal strictures of being a decent human being don't apply to them anymore. All fans do is say "That thing? That you do? I *like* it."

This is nice, and can lead to nice things. When people like the things you do, they very often support them, often by buying the things you create (or otherwise putting money into things involving you), and encouraging others to do the same. This can lead to bills being paid, a mortgage being topped off, groceries being put in the pantry, and children getting things like shoes and a college education. It can also lead to you being able to keep doing that thing that makes the fans happy, whether it be books or music or TV shows or whatever it is they like. And since you were probably originally doing that thing because it made *you* happy to do it, this is typically not a bad thing at all. If in life people want to pay you to do the thing you always wanted to do, and want you to keep doing it, you should probably be appreciative of that.

But wait, I hear you say, you're the same person who's thumped on fans for being out of line with writers. Doesn't this make you a hypocrite, or at least not able to keep track of what you've said before? I don't think so. Like authors, fans are people too, and just as the objects of fans' affections can get sucked up into their own sphincters regarding their importance to the world, so may some fans occasionally transmute their enthusiasm into "I *made* you; you *owe* me." Some people, creators and consumers alike, struggle with being jerks. It doesn't mean that as a class, fans are not important to a creative person's career, or that they shouldn't be thankful for them.

Personally speaking I think I've been very lucky. My fans don't typically seem to be the problematic sort. In meeting them, here and out in the real world, they usually seem like what they are: People who like my work and appreciate what I do and hope I keep doing it. I make an active attempt to return the favor by not letting my own personal ego monster out of the box too often. I'm genuinely happy and honored that people like my work and that in one way or another it has meant something to them, and I don't want them to think that I take that lightly. It helps that I'm a fan too—I have my own list of writers, musicians, actors and other creative folk whose work has made my life better. I've even gotten to meet some of them and say "thanks." It made me happy to see that they were happy I liked what they did. I want to be able to express that too, to the people who like what I do.

(It also helps a lot that in science fiction and fantasy, the fan-creator line is highly permeable and always has been. So many fans have become friends, and some of my fans have become pros who I in turn have become fans of, and some of the pros who I have admired for years have become friends and even fans as well (at least, that's what they tell me). This community has been one of the great joys for me in becoming a science fiction writer; I hope writers in other genres get the same sort of dynamic, and if they don't, well, that's a shame.)

I'm fortunate to get fan letters from time to time, so consider this me returning the appreciation. Dear fans: Most sincerely, I thank you and am thankful for you. Thank you for reading, and thank you for letting me and my work be a part of your life. I hope I get to keep doing it. It's my plan, in any event.

How I Sold
My Books

(Note: As an addendum to the information here, in 2015 I signed a 13-book contract with Tor, which should keep me busy until, uh, 2027 or so.)

Over on Twitter, author Wesley Chu has been leading a discussion on how authors sell their books—whether by submitting the full manuscript, by submitting a partial, or by proposal. This lead me to think about how I sold my own books. So, for informational and educational purposes, this is how I've sold each of my books to their respective publishers. I'm going to divide these up into fiction and non-fiction categories, and list them (mostly) in order of publication.

Non-Fiction:
1. The Rough Guide to Money Online: Sold by my agent selling me to Rough Guides as a suitable author, them telling me what they wanted from the book, and me writing an outline that satisfied their needs.

2. The Rough Guide to the Universe: Sold via outline.

3. Book of the Dumb: Publisher wanted this particular book and wanted me to write it; we discussed what should be in it and I went off to write it. Note the publisher did not come to me out of the blue; I had contributed dozens of pieces for their "Uncle John's" series of books by that point.

4. Book of the Dumb 2: Publisher: "Hey, let's do a sequel." Me: "Okay."

5. The Rough Guide to Sci-Fi Movies: Sold via outline.

6. Your Hate Mail Will Be Graded: Brief proposal (the material already existed).

7. You're Not Fooling Anyone When You Take Your Laptop Into a Coffee Shop: Book specifically of pieces on writing, spun off from *Hate Mail* and actually published first. I basically said, "Hey, would you like these as a separate book?" and Subterranean Press said yes.

8. 24 Frames Into the Future: I was the Guest of Honor at Boskone and NESFA, the organization that runs the con, likes to published a limited edition book from their guests. I pitched a book of my film columns; they said yes.

9. The Mallet of Loving Correction: Me, to Subterranean Press: "Hey, wanna do another Whatever collection?" SubPress: "Yup." This proposal-to-acceptance process took roughly fifteen minutes, making it the quickest I ever sold a book.

Fiction:

1. Old Man's War: Wrote it, put it up on Web site, it was discovered by Patrick Nielsen Hayden of Tor, who made on offer on it.

2. Agent to the Stars: Wrote it, put it up on Web site, it was discovered by Bill Schafer of Subterranean Press, who made an offer on it.

3. The Ghost Brigades: Patrick Nielsen Hayden: "So, you should write a sequel to *Old Man's War*." Me: "Okay."

4. The Android's Dream: Part of a two-book deal I signed when I signed with Tor for *Old Man's War*. Pitched it on the sentence "man solves diplomatic crises through the use of action scenes and snappy dialogue." Patrick Nielsen Hayden said, more or less, "Sounds good, go write it."

5. The Last Colony: Patrick Nielsen Hayden: "So, you should write a third book in the Old Man's War series." Me: "Okay."

6. Zoe's Tale: Me, to Patrick Nielsen Hayden: "This sequel I'm writing to *The Android's Dream* isn't working and I'm shelving it. Would you take another Old Man's War book as compensation?" Patrick: "Why, yes. Could you write it kinda as a YA?" Me: "Sure."

7. METAtropolis: Audible director Steve Feldberg wanted me to do an anthology; I fleshed out an idea with him, recruited the other authors, and acted as editor. Originally published in audio; Subterranean Press expressed interest in the limited hardcover rights; Tor asked for the paperback rights.

8. The God Engines: Me: "I want to write a dark fantasy in which really terrible things happen." Bill Schafer: "Dude, sold."

9. Fuzzy Nation: Wrote for my own amusement with no intention of selling it; my agent Ethan Ellenberg declared he could sell it and did, to Tor.

10. Redshirts: Me, to Patrick Nielsen Hayden: "Hey, I wrote this thing. Want it?" Patrick: "Why, yes."

11. The Human Division: Tor wanted to experiment with online distribution; I'd been wanting to go back into the Old Man's War universe. We agreed the two aims could work together. There was no proposal in terms of the content, but there was definitely a roadmap created by all the interested parties in terms of how the thing should work, theoretically. THD was in fact probably the most intentional and built-out, in term of design and distribution, of all the fiction books I've written to date.

12. Lock In: Brief proposal to Patrick Nielsen Hayden.

13. The End of All Things: I think we all just assumed this would happen; I don't recall directly pitching it or being directly asked for it. Both *Lock In* and TEoAT were part of a two book deal with Tor.

There's additionally the novella I wrote earlier in the year which I've sold to Tor (e-book), SubPress (limited hardcover) and Audible (audio), the details of which I will announce a bit later. That one I wrote up and then offered up to each publisher; each then accepted it for publication.

In addition to all the books I have published (and THD2, which is not written but will be, soon), there are three projects I specced out to a greater or lesser extent but didn't write. One was the sequel to *The Android's Dream*, which I sold after the first book came out; that contract is unfulfilled to date. I plan to get around to it again at some point. Another was a two-book series which I sold on proposal; it was shelved when another very similar book became a bestseller and I didn't want to appear to be cashing in on that book. The contracts in question were applied to *Zoe's Tale* and *Redshirts*. The third was a YA proposal that I wrote at the request of the publisher; the proposal was accepted but we couldn't come to terms financially, so there are no contracts to fulfill.

Looking at all the projects to date it's clear I sell either on full manuscript or on proposal (with or without an outline). I have never sold a book on a partial manuscript, and it seems to me anecdotally that selling on a partial is an unusual circumstance, although I could be wrong on that (see the word "anecdotally").

If I were advising someone on selling a first novel, I would suggest—and I believe most editors would back me up here—that you have the full manuscript in hand before you go shopping. Having a partial in hand when you are an unpublished author doesn't suggest you know how to finish a novel, and for a publisher, having a finished novel is actually key. Yes, this means doing work without a guarantee of a sale, but, well. If publishers want to buy from partials, there are a lot of already-pubbed authors who they know can produce that they can worth with. So I would have the whole thing ready to go. It's what I did, in any event.

IMPOSTOR SYNDROME, OR NOT

Jan

30

2016

Att ConFusion science fiction convention last week, I had a great many conversations with a great many folks on a large number of topics, but there was one topic that seemed to pop up more than usual: Impostor Syndrome.

Impostor Syndrome, briefly put, is the feeling that one's achievements and status are a fluke, and that sooner or later one will be revealed as a fraud. Anecdotally speaking, it seems, Imposter Syndrome affects a lot of writers, editors and other folks in the publishing life. I think this is in part because the writing life is a precarious one, financially and otherwise, and also in part because people in publishing seem to be a generally neurotic lot anyway. Imposter Syndrome is just another log on that particular fire.

Imposter Syndrome is a real thing and it's not something I'd want to make light of because I think it has harmful effects. I think it can make people cautious in the exercise of their art and their career when they could be (and *want* to be) taking chances, and I think it can make people vulnerable to being taken advantage of by people/organizations who intentionally or otherwise leverage those feelings for their own advantage.

It's pernicious, basically, and it frustrates me that so many talented people who have earned their places in the field with their work battle with it. I think it's good that people are talking about it, however. It means that they are aware that it's a thing and that it's a lie. Naming it and describing it and knowing of it goes a long way in fighting it.

The discussions over the weekend also made me reflect on the issue of Impostor Syndrome and me, and the fact that as far as I know I have never had it, particularly in regard to being a writer. This isn't an *accomplishment*, mind you, or something to brag on. It's just an observation; at no point in my writing career did I ever feel like I didn't deserve to be where I was, doing what I was doing. I've always been, *yup, this is who I am and what I do.*

Which is nice for me, you know, but also prompted me to think about *why* it was that I felt that way. I mean, it could be the Dunning-Kruger effect, in which incompetent people don't believe they're incompetent. Certainly I have enough detractors who would be happy to suggest that this is *exactly* the case, when it comes to me. Which, okay, sure. Maybe. Why not.

But if it's *not* that, and I'm *pretty* sure it's not, then what explains my lack of Impostor Syndrome?

Here's what I think.

One, I knew fairly early that I wanted to be a writer and worked toward it directly. I knew at age fourteen that I wanted to be a writer. Having decided that, I was done seriously considering any other career choice. I didn't have a back-up or fallback plan.

It helped, I suspect, that the type of writing I wanted to do back then was journalism, which was at the time both a practical and achievable goal—there were newspapers in the 80s! And they *hired* people to write in them!—rather than to be a novelist or fiction writer, which was (and is) a more amorphous thing.

But basically, having decided in my early teens that I was going to be a writer, I did not doubt I would ever become a writer. So when I became a professional writer I didn't question how I got there. I got there because I had planned it all along. That said,

Two, no one ever questioned my intent *or ability* to be a writer. Which is to say that, particularly in high school, no one ever pulled me aside and said to me either "hey, you know, writing is a tough gig, maybe you should plan to do something else with your life," or "you idiot, what makes you think *you* can be a writer?" Not my mom, or any of my teachers, or any of my schoolmates.

Indeed, quite the opposite: At every step in the early years of my ambition I was encouraged. My mom encouraged me because among other things that's what parents should do at that point. My teachers were more grounded about it but did the same—they gave me tips on how to write, and pushed back at me when I got lazy (which was often), and otherwise were very much like, *this is what you want to do? Okay, let us help.* And as far as my schoolmates were concerned, they very quickly accepted my persona as That Dude Who Wants to Be a Writer (plus I wrote stories where many of them were characters, and they were all very clever in the stories, and who doesn't like that).

So: I knew I wanted to be a writer early on, and early on everyone I knew—really, *everyone*—accepted that I was going to be a writer. That early determination and reinforcement went a long way.

Three, I progressed without impediment early on. This means that I never found a problem in leveling up to doing the things that reinforced that writing was a thing I could do, was good at, and that people expected from me. When I showed up to the University of Chicago, pretty much the first thing I did after dropping my stuff in my dorm room was head to the offices of the *Chicago Maroon*, the student newspaper, and announce that I was going to write a column for them. And what did they do with this cheeky twerp who said this? Well, they let me write a column. And then another, and then after that I was a weekly columnist and reviewer of music, books and films.

Later I became an editor and then editor-in-chief, these things in turn opening doors to become an intern at a daily newspaper. That in turn helped me become a freelance writer for newspapers and magazines in Chicago, which (in addition to my degree from Chicago) helped me land my first full-time professional gig as a film critic for the *Fresno Bee* newspaper.

All of this socially reinforced the idea that I was a writer. At Chicago, most people who knew of me knew me first through my column in the newspaper. So, literally, what people knew about me, *before they knew anything else,* was that I was a writer. That column also gave me cachet and status (to a *minor* extent, let's not overegg the pudding) because the students read it, or at least knew it existed. They might have thought it was *terrible* and that I was a jackass, jackassedly spouting jackassed opinions, but they knew who I was nevertheless. Later as the film critic and a columnist at the *Bee*, it was the same dynamic, on a larger scale.

Again: The way most people knew of me, if they knew of me at all, was as a writer.

Four, when I went upward, my reaction was not "now they're going to find me out for sure," it was "look what I just pulled off!" When I got that column gig at the *Maroon*, I was proud of the fact that I was a first-year student writing a weekly column. When I got the gig at the *Fresno Bee*, I was inordinately proud of the fact that, at twenty-two, I was the youngest full-time syndicated film critic in the United States. A couple of years later, when I got a weekly opinion column, not only was I the youngest nationally-syndicated opinion columnist out there, I had achieved my actual life goal—Hey! I'm newspaper columnist! Like Mike Royko or Molly Ivins!—before the age of twenty-five.

The fact that I was objectively *not a very good* newspaper columnist at age twenty-four was immaterial to this feeling (I was just good enough, *barely*, and had a lot of slack cut for me, although unsurprisingly it wasn't until later that I realized that fact). The point was my ego was and always had been turned to "this is good for me!" as opposed to "this is where they find out I'm unqualified."

This can be a dangerous thing—remember that Dunning-Kruger thing? Well, my attitude is pretty much *exactly how that happens*—but I was also fortunate at every step of the way to be surrounded by people (editors, other writers, friends, etc) who helped to rein me in and also pointed out when I was being a jerk, or oblivious to the point of being an ass.

I even listened to them, from time to time. I remember at one point blathering on to my non-fiction agent about something and mentioning my age at the time as a qualifying feature, and he said, offhandedly, "You know, twenty-eight is kind of old to be a prodigy at anything." Which I'm sure he meant as a throwaway point, but which I took very seriously. It meant that I had stop being proud of stepping stone achievements, and start investing more in the quality of the work at hand.

Like I said, offhand comment, but it mattered, and I'm glad that at the time my ego was not so enormous that I couldn't listen.

Speaking of which:

Five, when things hit a wall, I re-invested in being a writer. My ego in my twenties, particularly with regard to being seen as a writer, was huge, in part because it had never been challenged. Turns out it's easy to cruise along in a wafty cloud of clueless self-regard when everything's pretty much gone your way. What's interesting is what happens when it *doesn't*—as happened to me, in 1998, when I was laid off from America Online, where I was then working as a writer and editor.

I've written about this before, but the short version was that being laid off hit me like the proverbial ton of bricks. All my self-regard and ego did not save me from having my job cut out from under me for reasons that didn't have much to do with me (the group I was in was dissolving; I as the in-house writer/editor was a company-wide resource; no one wants to put a company-wide resource on their departmental budget). I was not so special that I was not expendable. Yeah, that hurt.

More importantly, it made me question a lot of things that I had previously just assumed, including centering my image of who I was on my job, and the fact I was a writer. When it was all over, I reordered my self image a bit. I was a writer, yes. It was what I wanted to do with my work life and I was going to find a way to make that happen. But I was also not just my job anymore—or more accurately, the amount of my ego that was invested in "John Scalzi, writer" became less; it got refocused into being a person and husband and (soon-to-be) father. I was comfortable enough about what I did as my job that I didn't have to let it define me to the extent I let it before. I could have the confidence to let it go a bit.

The conscious re-investment in being a writer, *and* re-evaluation of what being a writer meant to me, mattered. I can't speak to anyone else, but for me, as drivelingly cliche as this is to say now, this crisis did become an opportunity, and (this *must* be noted) with the help of my wife particularly, and with the help of friends, I was able to take that advantage of that opportunity.

Much of what my life is now is because of that. This is why I often say now that being laid off turned out to be one of the best things that ever happened to me.

As a result of this:

Six, my view of myself of a writer is now not focused on whether *other* people consider me so. It's not a coincidence that I started writing a blog soon after I was laid off from AOL; it's not a coincidence that the first novel I wrote I decided to post there, rather than try to sell to someone else. To be clear, I like selling work and I like being financially successful as a writer—doing both gives me freedom to make more (and usually better) choices in terms of my career. Nor am I disingenuous enough to suggest that at this point in my career, the awards and contracts and so on aren't useful signifiers.

But ultimately, I've done enough and I know myself well enough that if I never sold another piece of work to anyone, it wouldn't matter in terms of my self-image as a writer. That is what I do. I have millions of words to speak to that point, but more importantly, I have self-awareness of who I am and of what writing has meant to me.

Now, it may be that some other people might then want to deny that I'm a writer, for whatever reason that they would need to do that. But you know what? That's their karma and I wish them joy with that. I'm not obliged to care what they think. I don't need anyone else's approval or approbation to know what I know about myself. I'm a writer.

So there's that.

(And having said *aaaaall* of that, let's note a couple other things. Like: Hey, did you know I'm a straight white male who benefited from a really elite education? That helped—for example, when I forgot to apply for newspaper internships and a friend of mine called his dad, who called his pal the publisher of the *San Diego Tribune,* and a couple of steps later, whoa, look, an internship! Also, I happened to be in my twenties at the same time the first Internet Bubble was puffing up, which was great for finding gigs and building a resume. *Also* also, with respect to novels and fiction, I had been a professional writer for fifteen years before my first novel was published, so I had a decade and a half (not to mention several non-fiction books published prior to *Old Man's War*) to get used to the idea that writing was a thing I could do. Also *also* also, I appear to be generally less neurotic than most writers, or at least, neurotic in somewhat different directions. And so on. It all helped, and helps.)

I think it's important to note something at this point: These are reasons why I believe I've never had Imposter Syndrome. But at the end of the day, the main reason I would say to writers that they shouldn't ever have to feel like they are impostors is that *if you write, you are a writer,* and it really is that simple. Whether you sell a book to a publisher is immaterial to this fact; likewise whether you become a bestseller, or award winner or if you write a book that people are still talking about two hundred years from now.

Here's the question: *Do you write?* If the answer is *yes,* you're a writer. Believe it.

And if anyone gives you shit about it, *including yourself,* come back over here and read this following graph:

Hey, that person? They're wrong. If you write, you're a writer. Done. Now get back out there and write some more.

In Which I Meet
Some Authors

Because it amuses me, allow me to recount my encounters with authors before I was a published author.

• At ten (I know it was this age because it was the age I broke my leg), a moderately famous YA author came to speak at my elementary school, and upon seeing my leg cast, proceeded to sign it, which was nice of him. Later in the day, one of my classmates licked her finger and moved to pretend smudge it out, but then actually connected with the cast and smudged the name. So now I can't remember the name of the author. As a small bit of irony, the kid who smudged the name off my cast would spend the entire fifth grade in a full-torso scoliosis cast. If I were back in elementary school, I would call it justice, but at age forty-two, I recognize that a scoliosis cast just kind of sucks for any kid.

• At twelve I met Ray Bradbury not once but twice, once at a book fair at a local community college, and once when he spoke at the Glendora Public Library, where I was a junior aide. A good friend tells me he was slightly rude to me at the community college event, but I have no memory of that myself; at the library event, which I do remember, he was in fact quite nice to me. I would later write about the Glendora event in the introduction to the Subterranean Press super-deluxe edition of *The Martian Chronicles*.

• In 1991 or '92, when I was at my first job at *The Fresno Bee* newspaper, I pitched a story to my editor about graphic novels being the new hip thing, mostly so I could interview Neil Gaiman on the phone.

And indeed he and I had a nice thirty or forty minute chat, and then I filed the story. I mentioned this to Neil not too long ago; I believe he was amused.

• When I first got on the Internet in the early 90s, I sent Allen Steele my very first piece of fan mail, in e-mail form, and noted to him that he and I both went to Webb Schools, although I went to the one in California and he went to the one in Bell Buckle, Tennessee. His response was polite and friendly and non-committal, which is a skill I have since learned for many of my own fan letters.

• Not too long afterward, I sent an e-mail to Steve Boyett. I had picked up a used copy of *Architect of Sleep*, since it was out of print, and asked him if he'd like to be paid for it anyway. He very politely declined. It took me years to figure out one of the reasons he might have declined, aside from it just not being important to him, is that in the days before PayPal, you'd have to give people a physical address. And maybe it's not a good idea to let random people on the Internet know where you live (it's still not a good idea, incidentally).

• While at AOL in the mid-90s, I once instant messaged AC Crispin out of the blue to ask her a clueless newbie writer question. She was polite with me but annoyed at the random intrusion, as well she should have been. I have since apologized to her for it, although (again quite understandably) when I told her about it she had no memory of it whatsoever.

• Additionally, at AOL in the mid-90s there was a science fiction forum on which Orson Scott Card hung out from time to time, and in it, he posted an early electronic version of his novel *Children of the Mind*, which I downloaded and read with glee, and then sent him an e-mail swearing that I would actually pay for the thing when it came out. He politely thanked me. For the record, I did pay for the thing when it came out. In hardcover, even.

• One of my jobs at America Online was being an editor of a humor area, which gave me a perfect excuse to contact James Lileks, whose newspaper columns (and books thereof) I was a fan of, and ask him if he wanted to write some stuff for me. He did! It's amazing how writers will want to write for you if you offer them money. This same tactic also worked with cartoonist Ted Rall. And one of the writers who submitted work to my humor area was David Lubar, who would also later become a published author, most prominently of the "Weenies" series of spooky stories for kids.

• In 2000, I thought about creating a site where I would interview science fiction authors about their latest books, called "OtherView," and created a beta version of the site so I could show folks who might be interested in funding the site (don't laugh, I created a very successful video game review site called "GameDad" just this way). I interviewed two authors: Orson Scott Card, with whom I had already once chatted, and Paul Levinson, who at the time was the president of the Science Fiction and Fantasy Writers of America. I remember asking him it was like to be the president of that particular organization. Now, of course, I know.

• I sold *Old Man's War* in 2002, so after that I started interacting with rather more authors and they knew of me as a writer, and that my book had been sold (if not yet published), so that changed the dynamic of things a bit. That said, I will recount one final story, which I think is amusing. My very first science fiction convention ever was Torcon 3 in Toronto in 2003; while there, I want to the Tor party, which was (as always) massively packed, so I walked into a side room for a breather and stood next to this older fellow, who either was not wearing a nametag, or was and I didn't look at it. He was quite avuncular and charming and amusing, so he and I chatted for a decent amount of time, after which he excused himself to wander off. When he left, I turned to a guy who was standing nearby and asked him if he knew the name of the fellow I'd just been chatting with. He looked at me like I was an idiot, and said, "yeah, that guy? That was *Robert Silverberg.*"

And there you have it.

It's Okay Not
to Read Me

Jul

2

2012

I noted this briefly on Twitter last night but I think it's worth expanding just a little bit. Last night I read a mostly vaguely negative review of *Redshirts* on a personal blog in which the reviewer basically admitted, in somewhat different words, that they're just not an enthusiast of most of my books. This is of course perfectly fine, because I'm like that too—there are many writers out there for whom I am not the perfect audience, including some for whom it would seem I should be the perfect reader. People are quirky and don't always work the way they're supposed to. Likewise, I have no beef with the (mostly vaguely) negative review; as I've said before, a good (i.e., well thought-out) negative review can be better and more interesting than a positive review, and anyway I'm generally of the opinion that the books I write are good enough to release. So there's that.

What the review made me feel, paradoxically enough, was a bit of sympathy for the reviewer, who (I imagine), once confronted with yet another of my books, sighed heavily and then set themselves down to the mostly unpleasant task of reading an author they have regularly found unsatisfactory. And along with that sympathy, a bit of befuddlement, because, well. They're reading that author (namely: me) *why*, exactly? This particular reviewer was not assigned the book for a gig; they were reading it on their own recognizance. So I suppose that my own thought on the matter is, why would you do that to yourself? Life is often unpleasant enough without choosing to fill your recreational hours pursuing a book from an author with whom ample previous readings have shown you have little rapport.

Here's my thing about my own writing, which I've noted before: I write to make my books to be generally accessible, and generally enjoyable, for just about anyone. I cast a wide net, as it were. But within that general intention for a general audience, there will always be *particular* people who will discover I am not their ideal writer. For whatever reason: Perhaps they don't like how I write dialogue, or plot the stories, or feel like I should be writing the book differently from how I am actually writing, or so on. Yes, it's sad, for both of us; I like to sell books, and I assume these particular readers like to read books. When a writer and a reader find their respective books and tastes don't match, there's always a sad little *moue* of the mind, a wistful wish for what could have been. But then you both go on with your lives. For the writer, there are other readers. For the reader, there are other writers. That's how it works.

As a writer, I'd like readers to give me my work a fair shake—to try what I write to see if we're a good fit. But if they try it and after a couple of fair-minded attempts they decide I'm just not the writer for them, then from my point of view the obvious solution is to acknowledge the fact and thereby avoid the task of grimly tromping through my future books. Because clearly I am not making them happy, and I have to admit that as a writer I don't enjoy the idea of someone joylessly hauling themselves through my prose for whatever reason they determine that they absolutely *must*. I really don't write books to be joyless slogs. Unless it's your job (or, in the highly specialized case of awards like the Hugos and Nebulas, you're reading a slate to determine your voting), there's probably not a good enough reason to do that to yourself.

I mean, if you've determined I'm not the writer for you, it's okay to check in every three or four books and see if I'm still not working for you. Who knows? Maybe I'll have changed my writing and/or something about you will have changed, and then suddenly what I write will work for you. Groovy. But otherwise I really would suggest taking the time you're using to unenthusiastically trudge one of my books and devote it instead either to writers you know you love or (even better!) in the pursuit of newer authors who are looking for their audiences. You could be that audience! It's worth giving *them* a fair shake, rather than looking at one of my books and thinking to yourself, *oh, crap, another Scalzi book. Here we go.*

Don't go. You don't *have* to go. If you don't really enjoy what I write, stop reading it. Read something else, from someone else. If for some reason you need my permission and blessing to do so, here it is. I sincerely hope you find another writer whose work you like better.

A Moment
of Financial
Clarification

Every once in a while someone in the comments here says, usually as an aside to something else, that no one becomes a writer to get rich. So as a point of clarification, and to give everyone else who is slightly exasperated by this sort of comment something to point at:

Hey, I became a writer to get rich. I've always been in the writing business not just to write, and not just to make money, but also to make a lot of money—basically, to get rich at it. Why? Because speaking from experience, being poor sucks, and in the world we live in, things are a whole lot easier if you have a lot of money. The thing I do best in the world in a professional sense is writing, so if I were to become rich, getting rich through writing seemed like the most likely way for me to do it.

Making money—and making a lot of it—has always been part of my professional writing game plan. It's one reason why I have been both shameless and unapologetic about the commercial aspects of my writing, whether it's me working as a writing/editing consultant for business or writing accessible novels. The money I make from writing means less time now I have to devote to sources of income other than writing, and less time later having to find other sources of income when (inevitably) my career slows down from its current happy level. The money I make from writing allows me to do nothing other than writing. So it helps to make a lot of it if at all possible.

Do I write only to make money? No; I write for lots of other reasons as well. Do I only consider money when it comes to choosing writing projects? No; I've written things for the pure enjoyment of writing them as well as for other factors, although once I was done with them I often looked to see how best to profit from them. Does writing with money as a consideration and being rich as a goal mean that waving money at me is the magic key to unlock my participation in something? Not always, because not all money is created equal, and the money I'm looking at is not only what's being waved in front of me now, but what taking the project will make available in the future. I can afford to look long term because making lots of money was always part of my thinking, and because it has been (along with many other factors including staggering good luck) I have the ability to turn down work that doesn't meet the long-term financial goals, and work that just doesn't appeal to me, for whatever reason.

(Nor do I think that everyone has to write with the goal of getting rich or making money. People like to quote/paraphrase Samuel Johnson, who once said "No one but a blockhead ever wrote except for money," but Johnson is as full of shit as any writer on the subject. You can write for all sorts of reasons, money being only one. If you want to be a professional writer, writing for money helps. Otherwise? Optional.

Also, sadly, acknowledging you write for money (or to get rich) will not guarantee success in that endeavor. Yes, that sucks. But there it is.)

At the end of the day, however: This is what I do for money. I don't want to have to do anything else, now and (as far as I can imagine) in the future. As luck would have it, much of what I like to write, and the style I prefer to write it in, appears to lend itself to the acquisition of money. So, yes, I write to become rich. It's always been part of my plan. I suspect that there are at least a few other writers probably write for the same reason. I imagine, like me, it's not their only reason. But it's still a reason.

As a final thought on the point, one of the reasons that "no one writes to get rich" and "no one writes to make money" bug the crap out of me is that this is the sort of thinking, intentional or otherwise, that gives bad people cover to screw writers with regard to money, and gives uncertain writers a reason to shrug off being screwed. If you as a writer buy into the idea you can't/won't make money and that you can't/won't get rich, then you are more than halfway to ensuring that you won't, in fact, make money (much less get rich).

So don't accept it. When someone says it, feel free to contradict them. Some of us do write to make money, and maybe even to get rich. It doesn't lessen what one does as a writer to acknowledge that making money, and maybe even hopefully making a lot of it, is one of the reasons to do it—if in fact it's one of the reasons one does it. It is for me.

A NOTE TO YOU, SHOULD YOU BE THINKING OF ASKING ME TO WRITE FOR YOU FOR FREE

Dec

9

2012

Because apparently it's that time again.

1. No.

2. Seriously, are you *fucking kidding me?*

3. Did you wake up this morning and say to yourself "You know what? A *New York Times* bestselling author who has been working full-time as a writer for two decades, who frequently rails at writers for undervaluing their own work in the market and who is also the president of a writers organization that regularly goes after publishers for not paying writers adequately is *exactly the person* who will be receptive, through lack of other work or personal inclination, to my offer"? And if you did, what other dumb things did you do with your morning?

4. If you didn't know that I was that guy in point three, and just asked me to write for free for you because, I don't know, you heard I was a writer of some sort, although you couldn't say what kind or what I had done, then what you're saying to me is "Hey, you're a warm body with an allegedly working brain stem and no idea of the value of your work—let me exploit you!" I want you to ask yourself what in that estimation of me would entice me to provide you with work, starting with the fact that you didn't do even the most basic research into who I was. Rumor is, it's not hard to find information about me on the Internet! Just type "John Scalzi" into Google and see!

5. If you try to mumble something at me about "exposure," I'm going to laugh my ass off at you. Explain to me, slowly, what exposure you possibly think *you* could give *me* with your Web site or publication. Please factor in that my Web site gets up to 50,000 visitors on a normal day—with spikes into the hundreds of thousands when I write something particularly *clicky*—and that it's regularly ranked one of the top ten book sites and top 100 entertainment sites on the entire Web by Technorati (at this moment, number five and sixty-four, respectively).

6. If you try to mumble something at me about "Huffington Post," I might smack you. Yes, there are some people writing for the Huffington Post for free. They typically are **a)** People in the 1% who aren't working writers who don't already have a well-established way to get their meanderings out there on the Internet; **b)** Writers and/ or other creators promoting a book/album/TV show/whatever. I'm not **a)** and when I am **b)** I have a publicist who handles my media requests; talk to her and be aware I am picky. You're probably not Arianna Huffington in any event. And if you *were* Arianna Huffington and asked me to write for free, I would send you over to points one through three. I *might* let Huffington Post reprint something I had already written here, if it amused me to do so (I've let Gawker's sites do that a couple of times this year), but something new and original? Fuck you, pay me.

7. If you try to mumble something at me about writing for free on *this* site, I might feed you to wild dogs. When I write here, it's me in my free time. When I write somewhere else, it's me on the clock. Here's a handy tip to find out whether I will write for you for free: Are you me? If the answer is "no," then fuck you, pay me.

8. If this is your cue to complain to me how this attitude of mine suggests I am selfish, you're right. I am very selfish with my time. This is all the time I will get in this universe, and I'm going to spend it how I see fit, and this does not generally include writing for free for people who are not me. There are lots of people who will pay me to write, which allows me to eat, shelter my family and otherwise live a tolerable life on this planet. I'm going to write for them instead. This plan has worked pretty well so far.

9. If this is your cue to complain about how this makes me an asshole, ask me if I care. Go on, ask!

10. But now that you mention it, saying "fuck you, pay me," to you does not make me (or anyone else from whom you are hoping to extract actual work from without pay) the asshole in this scenario. It makes me the guy responding to the asshole, in a manner befitting the moment.

THE OFFER ON
OLD MAN'S WAR:
A TEN-YEAR
RETROSPECTIVE

Dec
30
2012

Today is a notable day in my personal history: Ten years ago today, I sold *Old Man's War* to Tor Books.

People who have been following me for any amount of time know how this happened, but might not know the full story, and the newer folks might not know about it at all. So here's how it happened:

In 2001, I began writing a military science fiction book, the conceit of which was that the soldiers were old, but were given new lives in exchange for their service. I finished the book in October of 2001 and then sat on it for more than a year, mostly because the thought of whole tiresome process of submitting the book to agents and publishers filled me with ennui, and I couldn't be bothered.

So instead I serialized it on Whatever in December of 2002. I had some precedent for this: in 1999, I took an earlier novel, *Agent to the Stars* (my "practice novel," i.e., the novel I wrote to see if I *could* write a novel), and posted it on Scalzi.com for people to read, and if they liked, to send me payment for. That had grossed me a couple of thousand bucks up to that time—a not inconsiderable sum in the days when people had to physically mail me a dollar—so I figured I could do it again. My plan was to serialize a chapter a day through December, and also offer the whole novel as a single document, so if someone was impatient, they could just send me $1.50 through that new-fangled PayPal, and read the whole thing at one time. Then after the serialization was done the book would sit on my site, and I would go on doing what I did at the time, which was writing for magazines and newspapers and putting out the occasional non-fiction book.

I finished the serialization on the 28th, and for the 29th, I wrote an essay on the experience of writing the novel, called "Lessons from Heinlein." At the time I was a reader of Electrolite, the blog of Patrick Nielsen Hayden, who was (and is) the senior editor of Tor Books, and I recalled him and his readers having a recent discussion of characters in science fiction. I thought he might find the essay interesting, so I pinged him about it. Here was the e-mail I sent him on the evening of December 28:

> *Hi, there. I'm John Scalzi, who writes the "Whatever" online column.*
>
> *Over the last three weeks, I've serialized a science fiction novel I've written on my site. Having completed it, I've added an afterwards called "Lessons From Heinlein," in which I discuss how RAH's style of writing holds some important lessons for would-be writers, specifically relating to character development (I am an actual published author and science fiction writer, so I don't feel too hinky about dispensing writing advice). The link is here: http://www.scalzi.com/w021229.htm. Some of the afterward necessarily relates to* Old Man's War, *which is the novel I've serialized, but the comments about Heinlein are general enough in the matter of writing to be of interest even to those who have not read the novel.*
>
> *Please note that this isn't a backdoor attempt to get you to read the novel itself; had I wanted you to read it in your official capacity, I would have done the old-fashioned route of printing out the manuscript and shipping it off to your slush pile (being a former editor myself, I do appreciate when people follow submission guidelines). I simply thought the afterward might be in itself of interest to you and the Electrolite readership.*
>
> *Best wishes to you and yours for a happy and prosperous 2003.*

Less than 36 hours later, ten years ago today, I got this as a response (e-mail posted with Patrick's permission):

It's an interesting afterword, but it's an even more interesting novel. I read the whole thing last night; as the blurb cliché goes, I couldn't put it down.

I understand being tired of the schlepping-to-agents-and-publishers thing, but would you be willing to entertain an offer for hard/soft publication of OLD MAN'S WAR? I'm not talking about life-changing amounts of money, but this is exactly the kind of action-oriented-and-yet-not-stupid SF we never see enough of, and I'd like for Tor to publish it.

(If your first response is to point out that this or some other work by you has sat neglected in hardcopy our slushpile for $BIGNUMBER of months or years, I promise not to be surprised.)

Let me know if you're open to this.

And, well. Yes. Yes I was.

I remember where I was when I read this e-mail, which as it happens is almost exactly where I am as I'm writing this: At my desk in my home office in Bradford, looking at a monitor, staring at the words there. It was morning (Patrick sent the e-mail at 8:22 a.m., which is not coincidentally the time I had this entry scheduled to publish on the site), and I was the only one up in the house; my sister and her family were visiting for the holidays and everyone was still crashed out. So there I was with some *really big news*, and no one awake to tell it to. Of course I told them, eventually, after they were all awake.

I date today as the anniversary of the sale of *Old Man's War*, but Patrick has additional details:

I'm certain that I made the actual offer-in-detail on January 2, 2003, because that was the first day Tor's offices were open after the holiday break, and I distinctly remember that the first thing I did on returning was go straight to Tom Doherty to enthuse about this terrific SF novel I'd found. I conveyed the actual offer to you in a phone call. But it makes just as much sense to date it from December 30, since my email of that date pretty clearly says I intend to make you a detailed offer if you confirm that you're up for one.

(January 2, 2003 was, by coincidence, my 44th birthday–and I think most acquiring editors would agree that scoring a book that good makes a heck of a fine birthday present.)

This conforms to my memory of it as well. I held back until January 3, 2003 to tell people about it; Patrick followed up with a post on his own site. At the time, ten years ago, people selling books they originally published on their Web sites was still novel enough that neither Patrick nor I could come up with another example of it happening. When it did happen with me, there was a bit of conversation about it online. These days a blog-to-book conversion is less unusual, although at this point, with all the more direct ways to self-publish online and to get that work into the retail channel, putting a book on one's blog first might seem a little roundabout. It's a reminder that the world of 2002 and the world of 2012 are different places, publishing-wise.

I was asked then and am still asked whether I posted OMW on my site as a way to get around submitting into a slushpile. The answer now is the same as then: No, I posted OMW on my site because I didn't want to deal with submitting the book. I fully expected the novel to live its life as part of my site, and maybe be a calling card to sell another novel somewhere down the line. The skeptical response to this is, yeah, but as soon as the whole thing was up you sent an e-mail to an editor at a science fiction publisher, so who are you trying to fool? My response to this would be, yes, but it was not about the novel itself, and I went out of my way to point out that I wasn't attempting a backdoor submission. To which a further skeptical response would be, then why mention the novel at all?

At which point I will throw up my hands. After ten years I can admit that as I writing the e-mail to Patrick, yes, part of me was hoping that he might be intrigued enough to check out the novel itself, and that when he did and made an offer, one of the first thoughts to come to my head was, *well, that worked out nicely*. But honestly it wasn't the *intent*. Having been an acquiring editor myself, I was well aware of how irritating it was to have someone try to get around the submission process because they think they're special. I assumed Patrick wouldn't look at the novel because if I were in his shoes, getting the same e-mail, I probably wouldn't have. At the time, I knew Patrick hardly at all; I was a reader on his site and had commented there just enough that I felt okay sending him an e-mail. I had no idea at the time how he would respond to it. I know him better now, I will allow.

The original plan, as noted in Patrick's first e-mail, was to have the book out sometime in late 2003, with paperback to follow. In fact the book came out January 1, 2005, so there was a two-year gap between when the book sold and when it hit the stores. At the time, this gap was frustrating; I was a newbie novelist, I wanted to be published now now now *now*. In retrospect, I think it was a very good thing. It gave people in science fiction time to get to know me, so that when *Old Man's War* was published it seemed like I had been around longer than I had been—which worked, because when it was published some folks were surprised it was a debut novel. It also gave me time to grow Whatever; between December 2002 and January 2005, the readership of Whatever tripled, which was useful for a writer with a first novel. And the book benefited from certain intangibles—for example, it seems like in January 2005, just enough people were missing a particular flavor of Heinleinian/Campbellian science fiction that *Old Man's War* offered to help the book take off like a shot.

The idea that waiting to publish to better position your work seems sort of heretical in these "do it now" days, but for me it paid off with benefits. It's something to consider when you as an author (and especially a new/newer/newish author) are weighing the pros and cons of various publishing options and strategies.

Patrick making an offer on *Old Man's War* quite literally changed my life, and almost entirely for the better. The eight novels I have written since are because of that offer and everything that's resulted from it. I have worked on a television series and on a video game because people read and loved *Old Man's War*. The book itself is in the (seemingly endless) process of being made into a movie. If it actually becomes one, it's likely to have interesting knock-on effects. I have sold hundred of thousands of books in eighteen different languages, which have made hundreds of thousands of people happy (and a few unhappy; that's life). Professionally, I have become who I wanted to be when I grew up. It's amazing.

Personally—well. There are so many people who I have met because of *Old Man's War* and everything that's come from it that it's hard to know where to begin with that. I think the best way that I can put it is that just before Patrick made an offer on *Old Man's War*, I remarked to Krissy that I suspected I had by then met every person who would be important to me in my life. The thirty-three year old me was thankfully, laughably wrong. There have been so many people I have met in the last decade who are so much part of my life now that I can't imagine it without them. People I like; people I love; people I wouldn't want to have missed in this world, and gladly, did not have to.

So. Ten years ago today, my life changed. I thought it would be worth making note of the day.

Thank you, Patrick, for making an offer on the book. Thank you, Tor, for publishing it. Thank you all, for reading it.

Just thanks.

Now let's see what happens in the next ten years.

THE OTHER STUFF

Aug

4

2009

Aquestion about the backstage aspects of the writing life, via e-mail:

How much of your time as a writer is spent not writing? As in, all the other things in your professional life that are related to writing and selling your work, but not the actual writing itself.

It's hard to say, either as a flat declaration of time, or as a percentage relative to the amount of time that I do writing. For example, at the moment I'm taking a little bit of a break from major work; I finished my last major project in early July, will be starting the next one on August 17, and between then I've mostly traveled and have written small things, like the AMC column. So in a period like this, obviously "everything else" takes up a significantly larger percentage of the time. But once I start the next project, as a percentage they'll go down. Overall, however, it's a substantial portion of my time, and sometimes, *too much* of my time is devoted to things that aren't writing. And I'm not always happy about that.

I can make a couple of general observations:

• I'm not at the point where I am so famous that I simply *can't* keep up with the outside stuff. I was feeling a bit overwhelmed with it last year and considered getting an assistant, but that was primarily a matter of my tremendously crappy time management skills, which I've since made it a priority to improve. I've gotten a bit better at those skills, which has been helpful, although I think I still have a ways to go in that department. But the fact is learning how to apportion your time gives you more time. It's also cheaper than hiring someone. If I do get to that point where it's no longer practical for me to do everything myself, I would hire someone, but I figure I have some distance before that's genuinely an issue for me.

• That said, I *am* at a point where I get a lot of fan e-mail, personal and business requests, and am asked to do a fair amount of stuff aside from writing. One way of dealing with fan e-mail for me, quite honestly, was by joining Twitter and Facebook, since I know a lot of the folks who would otherwise write fan mail now simply follow me on one or the other of those two (it's also more fun for me to play with). And of course having Whatever here, with its comment capability, also serves that same purpose for fans who want a bit of personal contact (although to be clear it's not Whatever's primary purpose). For the personal and business requests, most of the time it just means I've gotten better at saying "no" to stuff in the last couple of years, and making sure people understand that it's not meant to be a personal slight, I just have to be careful to what I commit to because my time is limited.

• It's also a fact that the further one goes along in the writing business, the more one appreciates working with competent folks. For example, my fiction agent Ethan Ellenberg does a great job dealing with most of the business aspects of selling my work, taking the time I would have to take dealing with it and freeing it up for me to do other things. To be clear I am indeed actively engaged in final business decisions about the work, and it's important for me to be so, but the advantage of having Ethan there is I don't have to be fiddling with the business stuff *before* that point. And that's a huge advantage to have. As another example, I am blessed with having a wife who has a hell of a practical business sense and a desire to handle that end of things, so once again that's more time I can spend on other things, like writing.

• There are still things I'm learning as to how better manage my time when handling this other stuff, however. At one point in my career, I was engaged in a rather long negotiation regarding a major project I hoped to do, and in the end it fell through for various reasons that are none of your business (sorry). I was rather mightily annoyed, for a number of reasons, but most relevant for the purposes of our discussion here because during the negotiations I avoided working on any other potential major projects. The rationale for this was that once the negotiations for this project were through, I would need to start on that project immediately, and I didn't want to leave something else half-finished.

This seemed to make perfect sense at the time, but the fact of the matter was that at the end of this negotiation, all I had to show for it was being generally pissed off, and a three-month smoking crater in my schedule during which I got nothing substantive done, which meant a not-insignificant loss of income and writing time. And as easy and convenient as it would have been simply to blame the other party for that loss of time and money, the simple fact of the matter is they weren't the ones who decided I shouldn't do anything else substantive with that time, it was me. It was a mistake, but the nice thing about being me is that I generally don't have to make a mistake more than once to learn from it. The bad news, of course, is that there are yet other mistakes that I still have to make, in order to learn from them. Such is life.

• At this point, the major time suck away from writing for me is travel, because I find I don't get any writing done at any point when I travel, and travel is not just the time on an airplane and being someplace else, it's all the stuff leading up to it, and it's a day or two coming down from being away when I get back. Going away for a weekend convention ends up being five days out of my schedule. For Worldcon, I've written off nine days. You can see how it adds up.

One way I dealt with it this year as was to notice that my major travel came in "clumps" and to schedule downtime around it. For example, beginning mid-July I ended up having roughly three weeks of travel (meaning the travel and the time preparing for it) interspersed over six weeks. So I worked my writing schedule to have a major project done by July 15th (which it was) and then not start the next one until August 17th. This gave me project deadlines, which I actually prefer having over open-ended time to complete something, and it also let me do all the travel I needed to do during that time, without being stressed about having unfinished work hanging over my head. While my travel schedule this year just happens to lay itself out like this, I think intentionally scheduling my workload this way in the future might make a bit of sense. We'll see how the next couple of years go.

In any event, the point is, yes, as time goes on, "the other stuff" of writing does end up taking a fair amount of your time. It's important to recognize that if unchecked, it'll go ahead and eat up all your time, leaving you very little time to do, you know, writing. So be prepared to deal with it.

THE PATH TO
PUBLICATION

Apr

14

2017

Teresa asks:

From the moment that you wrote the first draft, how long it did it take you to see your first work of fiction published?

Heh. Well, it depends on what one means by my first work of fiction.

If, for example, my first work of fiction is thought to be the very first complete story I ever wrote, which is a story called "Best Friends: Or, another reason not to get sick," then the answer is thirty-three years and counting, since I wrote it in 1984 for Mr. Heyes' freshman English composition class, and aside from a few copies I ran off for friends (mostly the ones on whom the story was based), no one's ever seen it, or is likely to. It was written by fourteen-year-me and while it was good enough for the class—I was the only person in three sections of the class to get an "A"—I suspect it is of very limited interest to anyone else.

(With that said, I think the story's opening graph makes it clear that my general advice of "have good opening lines" is something I knew early on. "Well, if this has taught me anything, it's not to get sick. I get sick for three days, and the world changed" is pretty solid, even if it has a problem with tenses.)

(And yes, I do still have the complete story, along with just about every other story I wrote as a teen. No, I won't show them to you. I'm doing you a favor.)

If one discounts juvenilia, then my next actual complete work of fiction might be considered to be a poem I wrote, "Penelope," which I wrote in 1991. It's written from the point of view of the wife of Odysseus, waiting for her husband to return and delaying having to pick a suitor by weaving and then unraveling a burial shroud. I don't usually consider it to be fiction—my brain generally sections out poetry and prose fiction—but inasmuch as it does have a point of view character, and that point of view character is not meant to be me (spoiler: but it kind of *was*, inasmuch as I was writing it for a girl I pined for and wanted close to me and hey, look, *allegory and metaphor*), it could be called fiction. As it happens, "Penelope" was published in *Miniatures*, my book of very short stories, which was published last year (literally on the last day of the year). So that would be twenty-five years. I'd note I didn't try to publish it prior to *Miniatures*; it was written for a specific person in mind.

If we toss out that poem and stick to prose, the next piece of completed fiction I wrote was *Agent to the Stars*, which I wrote in the summer of 1997 as my "practice novel," i.e., the novel I wrote to see if I *could* write a novel (turns out I could). Inasmuch as it was my practice novel, I didn't write it with the intent to sell it, but when I created my web site at Scalzi.com, I decided to put it up here and let people download it if they liked, and if they wanted, to send me money for it. So it was self-published, and that was in 1999. If you want to count self-publishing on one's Web site as actual publication (back in 1999, I would note, it would generally not have been considered so), then it took two years. If you don't count that as publishing, then you'd have to wait until 2005, when the hardcover version was published by Subterranean Press. In which case: eight years.

But it's important to note that *Agent* got published (by someone else) because that publisher asked to publish it; I didn't shop it. If you're curious about what piece of fiction of mine was the first that I wrote *with the intent* to try to have it published, and which was then in fact actually published by someone else, then that would be "Alien Animal Encounters." I wrote it in 2001 and immediately submitted it to *Strange Horizons* magazine, on the basis that I liked the magazine, and also because it would accept electronic submissions, and I didn't own a printer. For the life of me I can't remember exactly when I wrote it, but I did submit it almost immediately after I wrote it, and it was published pretty quickly after that. That was October 2001, so I suspect I wrote it a couple months before that. Let's say three months to be safe. So: Three months, from writing it to it being published.

(Also, all of these were first drafts, in the sense that I edit as I write, so when I type "The End" I just do a quick copyedit run through. I don't edit less than people who write drafts, I just do it as I go along. Works for me; your mileage my vary.)

So: Depending on how one chooses to define what was my first work of fiction, and what constitutes publishing, the answer to the gap between first draft and the pub date is three months, or two years, or eight years, or twenty-five years, or thirty-three years and counting.

And you know what? I think that's about average, as far as writers are concerned. There are lots of places one could count as the starting point for one's career, and lots of different opinions as to what constitutes being published.

The important thing here is: I *did* start writing. And I *did* start getting published.

Everything progressed from there. And here we are.

REVENUE STREAMS
2010

I n my continuing quest to demystify things related to the business of writing, at least inasmuch as they relate to me, today I am going to talk revenue streams. As many of you know, I am a huge proponent of writers having multiple revenue streams, so that when one of them cuts out on you—and it will cut out on you—you still have money coming in while you look for something to replace the income you've lost. I am also a huge proponent of recognizing that even within an individual stream of income, there can and will be substantial variation from year to year.

To make these points, I'm going to lay out to you my own revenue streams for 2010, and point out what I currently expect from each of these in the coming year. Note that for this exercise I will be discussing only my income from writing and writing-related activities, not my overall household income. I am not noting the specific dollar amount of my income last year (because I've been told not to by the Scalzi Family CFO, i.e., my wife), but you may assume that when Congress and the President chose to extend the Bush era tax cuts on the top income earners in the US for the next two years, one of the people who didn't see his top marginal federal tax rate go up was me.

My income profile has changed significantly over the years; it's only been in the last couple of years that the majority of my income has come from books. Prior to that the largest chunk of my writing income came from corporate consulting work and writing non-fiction and journalism. The change has happened primarily because **a)** I now have a body of work that remains in print and generates royalties and **b)** I now generally get paid more per book.

However, if I am smart what I *won't* do is look at this chart and think, well, *this is the way it's going to be from now on.* It won't be, either in the distribution of income or indeed, in the size of pie in a general sense. To explain why, let me discuss the individual slices of this pie.

Books (new, royalties, foreign sales): This category breaks

down as roughly 40% new sales, 40% royalty payments on existing books, and 20% foreign, both sales and royalties. 2010 was a very good year for me in this area, but there are reasons not to count on this remaining as large a pie slice in 2011. Why?

1. Tor paid me a nice amount for *Fuzzy Nation*, which drove the chunk of income here devoted to new sales. However, the next novel I have with Tor is being slotted in to fulfill an outstanding contract I've had with my publisher for some time; it was originally part of a two-book series I never wrote, for reasons I've mentioned before. That contract's price is substantially below what I'm being paid for *Fuzzy*, and I had already taken receipt of the first installment of that advance several years ago. Basically Tor will be getting my next novel at a discount. I'm fine with this, and I'll almost certainly make it up on the back end, in terms of royalties. But depending on sales and reserves against returns, those royalties will take between 12 and 24 months to get to me. So for 2011, it's almost entirely certain that my "new book" income will go down.

2. My royalty payments have been good over the last few years, but *Fuzzy Nation* is also my first new novel in three years (the last was *Zoe's Tale* in 2008) and while that gap was filled with various editions of *METAtropolis* and *Your Hate Mail Will Be Graded*, there's been a natural decline in backlist sales over time. Now, the announcement of the movie deal for *Old Man's War* has given the backlist a boost, as likely will the release of *Fuzzy*. But thanks to the way royalties move through the system, I'm unlikely to see that benefit for a year or so. Also given the advance for *Fuzzy*, depending on sales it might be a while before it earns out its advance. So for 2011, I'm likely to see my royalty income either stay stable or go down a bit.

3. Foreign sales and royalties have been healthy but again the lack of new novels between 2008 and now has had an impact. The good news is that *Fuzzy* is selling well overseas and that the movie announcement for OMW has spurred interest in markets it's not already in, so that helps. I expect foreign book income in 2011 to remain about the same overall.

So, overall, for 2011, my book income will probably be down from 2010. Where it goes from there depends on a number of factors, including, of course, whether I continue to get out a new novel about once a year, and how well those novels do, both at debut and then as back list. This sort of thing is impossible to predict with any certainty.

Film Option: The film option is in a category I like to think of as "extraordinary income"—that is, income which sort of falls into one's lap and may not ever be repeated again. The option is due to be renewed later this year, at which time one of two things will happen: either it's renewed, in which case I get another nice chunk of income, and the possibility of further income down the line, or it's not renewed, in which case I get nothing (unless we sell the option to someone else). Naturally I hope for the first but would be foolish to assume it's a given. Another wrinkle: the next option step has an 18-month window, which means no film option income in 2012, unless the start of production on this film in that timeframe. So no matter what my film option income will be down, either this year or next.

TV Consulting: This was the money I made being the Creative Consultant on *Stargate: Universe*. The show was canceled, alas; this income stream has gone away, and in the short term, at least, is unlikely to be replicated. So for 2011, the income from this category will be zero.

Film Column: This is the column I first wrote for the AMC.com site and now for the FilmCritic.com site (which is owned by AMC). I enjoy doing it and they seem to enjoy having me do it and as far as I know they're going to keep having me do it. So I expect income in this category to stay the same for 2011.

Corporate Consulting: Primarily for a single client; who it is and what I'm doing I can't divulge due to a non-disclosure agreement. I can say it's been fun and interesting. Because the bulk of my payment so far has been in 2011, I can say income in this category will be going up this year. Where this category goes from there is anyone's guess.

Miscellaneous: This includes income from various small free-lancing gigs, teaching, and other odd bits, like performing at w00tstock. I have no idea what to expect from this category this year; that's one reason why it's called "miscellaneous." Before any of you ask, no, so far I'm not doing any w00tstock 3.0 events. But who knows?

Short Stories: The smallest category of my writing income and likely to stay that way in 2011, seeing as it's already April and I've only written and sold one short story. But I'll probably write at least a couple more between now and the end of the year, which means that I can reasonably expect this category to stay about the same, income-wise.

In all, while I expect 2011 to work out just fine for me—Neither I nor my family will be coming anywhere close to financial instability, for which I am *immensely* grateful—I also expect to make less than I did in 2010, and possibly *much* less, and to have the relative percentages of the categories from which I make money to change, sometimes quite dramatically.

This is the way of the writing life. Year to year, some income categories will go up, some will go down, some will remain static and some will go away completely. And, also, possibly, some new ones might emerge. I might get to do more newspaper or magazine freelancing, for example, or I might get an offer to do a speaking engagement or two, or I might do some editing. Maybe I'll get another consulting gig with a TV or a movie. Maybe I'll have the opportunity to write a comic book—or maybe I'll write a movie script and sell it (ha!). Or maybe *none* of that will happen, my books will fall out of print and no one will be interested in what I'm currently writing. Some of this will be about me, but a lot of it won't be; some of it will be about factors completely out of my control. What you can expect is that I will continue to seek out a variety of writing revenue streams, rather than keep all my financial eggs in a single basket. I will find a way to *work,* one way or another.

What I do expect—and if you are a writer or hope to be, what you should also expect—is that no matter what, year in and year out, writing income will be volatile. It is not a field in which you can expect anything to stay the same for any length of time, nor can you expect your fortunes to be sunny every step of the way. I am thankfully fortunate today. I *hope* to remain fortunate tomorrow. I *work* to allow continued good fortune a place to happen in my life. I *plan* financially with the expectation I will not be so fortunate. This means keeping a sharp eye on expenses, living within (and when possible, below) my means, and saving and investing the majority of what I have come in so that when (not *if*) less fortunate times come we have a margin that allows us to maneuver and prepare and plan for more fortunate times.

One reason I'm airing my revenue pie to you is to make the point that the next time I do it, it will probably look nothing like it does today. That's not unusual. What would be unusual is that if it *did* look the same, year in and year out.

THE SORT OF CRAP
I DON'T GET

Aug

31

2011

(Note: Since this post came out, the amount of crap I get has gone up substantially, much of it in parallel with the Hugo Award fracas with the "Puppies," and the weaponization of Twitter by trolls. However, in the first case, that's largely receded now, and in the latter case I've gotten good at muting nonsense. And even with all of that, I still don't get the level of bullshit other people get.)

Over at Twitter, author Adrienne Martini asks me if I get the sort of jackassed comments and e-mails that Shawna James Ahern, a food blogger, talks about in a recent post (we'll get to the details further down), and wonders if it's a gender-related thing.

The short answer: No I don't get those, and yes, I think it's substantially gender-related.

The longer answer: I do of course get hate mail and obnoxious comments. The hate mail gave me a title for a book, after all, and the obnoxious comments on the site are just part of doing business as a Public Internet Figure™. This is why I have a robust commenting policy and am not afraid to follow up on it. Whenever jackholes pop up, I mallet them down, and that's the way it should be.

What I don't have, however, is the sort of chronic and habitual stream of abuse this blogger describes. There are constantly people annoyed with me (go search "Scalzi" on Twitter today and you'll see some fellows mewling plaintively about me, for example; it's darling), but it doesn't appear anyone makes a *hobby* out of it. It's all situational, in that I'll write something that annoys someone, they'll be annoyed and write about it, and then it all goes away. There are additionally and quite naturally people who seem to have a default dislike of me. So perhaps they are more inclined to be annoyed with me and they'll become so quicker than the average person might, and thus be publicly annoyed with me at a higher frequency.

But again, they don't do it all the time; they're not making it their mission in life to ride me. And to be clear, people are *annoyed* with me, or may mock me, or may even call me names. But these people are not fundamentally (or, generally speaking, not even *slightly*) hateful or hurtful people and it would be wrong to characterize them as such. What I *don't* receive, other than exceptionally rarely, is what I consider to be actual abusive commenting, where the intent is to hurt me, from people who are genuinely hateful.

What follows is my own anecdotal experience, but it's also the anecdotal experience of someone blogging for thirteen years and having been engaged in the online world for almost twenty, i.e., decently knowledgeable. In my experience, talking to women bloggers and writers, they are quite likely to get abusive comments and e-mail, and receive more of it not only than what *I* get personally (which isn't difficult) but more than what men bloggers and writers typically get. I think bloggers who focus on certain subjects (politics, sexuality, etc) will get more abusive responses than ones who write primarily on other topics, but even in those fields, women seem more of a target for abusive people than the men are. And even women writing on non-controversial topics get smacked with this crap. I know knitting bloggers who have some amazingly hateful comments directed at them. They're blogging about *knitting*, for Christ's sake.

Why do women bloggers get more abuse than male bloggers? Oh, I think for all the stereotypical reasons, up to and including the fact that for a certain sort of passive-aggressive internet jackass, it's just psychologically easier to erupt at a woman than a man because even online, there's the cultural subtext that a guy will be confrontational and in your face, while a woman will just take it (and if she doesn't, why, then *she's just a bitch* and deserves even more abuse). Cowards pick what they consider soft targets and use anonymity and/or the distancing effect of the Internet to avoid the actual and humiliating judgment of real live humans that they'd have to receive out in the world.

There's also the fact that culturally speaking, women are burdened with a larger number of things they are made to feel bad about, things that men don't have to bother with. Notes Ms. Ahern, about a recent trip to New Orleans:

> *From those brief 25 hours, I received emails that said, "Don't you know that processed food is killing Americans? How could you have posted a photo with Velveeta cheese?" or "What kind of a mother are you, leaving your child for another trip? Selfish bitch." or "Sausage? Andouille sausage? You don't think you're fat enough already, you have to stuff more sausage in your mouth?" There were complaints about where I ate, how much I ate, how happy I was to be with the people I sat with, that I was bragging by listing the people with whom I had dinner. There were comments about my weight, comments about my parenting, comments about the way I spend money, comments about the farce of gluten-free, comments about my photographic skills, and comments about how often I posted on Twitter (for some, that answer was: too much). Nothing goes undiscussed as being disgusted in my online world.*

I can contrast this with how people approach me on similar topics. When I post photos of processed cheese, I don't get abused about how bad it is and how bad I am for posting about it. People don't abuse me over my weight, even when I talk explicitly about it. I go away from my family for weeks at a time and never get crap about what a bad father that makes me, even though I have always been the stay-at-home parent. Now, it's true in every case that if I did get crap, I would deal with it harshly, either by going after the commenter or by simply malleting their jackassery into oblivion. But the point is I don't *have* to. I'm a man and I largely get a pass on weight, on parenting and (apparently) on exhibition and ingestion of processed cheese products. Or at the very least if someone thinks I'm a bad person for any of these, they keep it to themselves. They do the same for any number of other topics they might feel free to lecture or abuse women over.

It's this sort of thing that reminds me that the Internet is not the same experience for me as it is for some of my women friends, and why I've spent a substantial amount of time drilling into Athena's head that the Internet is full of assholes who like to void themselves all over the women they find. I'm sad this is still the case. But being sad about it isn't going to keep me from trying to build those defenses into her, so that when inevitably she runs up against these people, she can deal with them properly, with a sound that approximates that of a flushing toilet.

That this will outrage them and make them more inclined to rail at her doesn't negate the necessity. It makes it more of a necessity, alas.

Team Scalzi

Not long ago I was having a conversation about some recent business stuff going on in my life, and the person I was having the conversation with noted that I was using "we" instead of "I" a lot when I was talking about decisions. They were curious whether there was more than one person actually involved in my decision-making process, or if I just had a massively inflated ego and was using the royal "we." Well:

1. Yes, I have a massively inflated ego, I mean, *duh*;

2. In this case, however, I regularly rely on other people to help me make business decisions concerning my work, and that's who the "we" refers to. At this point in my life there is, in fact, a "Team Scalzi."

It's not an official team, mind you. We don't have softball jerseys or anything (although, now that I think of it, this could be *done…*), and none of them work *for* me as an employee. Rather, there are people I work *with* on the business side of my life to get things done and/or to help me plan for the future and for future projects.

Nor is this especially unusual; many professional writers (and most pro authors) have a group of people who they listen to, or at least get advice from, in terms of their careers and business and futures. The people in these roles, and the types of role, vary from writer to writer, of course.

So who is my "team"? They are:

Spouse: This would be Kristine Scalzi, who, aside from being my partner in life, has a super-sharp business mind both naturally and by education (she has a business degree). She also handles much of the business end of things here, in terms of tracking and organizing various projects and contracts and such. Also, she handles nearly all the homefront issues, which is important when one travels as much as I do.

Smart authors will often compliment their spouses/spousal equivalents and assure you that they would be nothing without them; in my case this is actually also true. Krissy's organizational and business skills, and willingness to hold down the fort, are nearly entirely responsible for the fact that we are solvent and that I am able to take advantage of as many opportunities as I can. Nothing gets done without her, and everything that does gets done, is made better by her.

Literary Agent: This is Ethan Ellenberg of the Ethan Ellenberg Agency. Aside from a spouse or spousal equivalent, this is probably the most common "team member" for any author. I figure most of you know what an agent does, but for those of you who don't, this is the person responsible for helping me sell my books to publishers, not just here in the US but worldwide. To do this Ethan has his own team, starting with Bibi Lewis, who handles my foreign sales, and also including a large number of subagents from around the world, who help find buyers in foreign territories. Ethan is a very large part of the reason I got a long-term contract with Tor, and why my work is now in two dozen languages worldwide.

Editor: This is Patrick Nielsen Hayden, my editor at Tor (there are others as well, notably Bill Schafer at Subterranean Press and Steve Feldberg at Audible). Aside from editing my novels, a job that's he's done pretty well for a decade now, he and I also strategize about which projects to write and when to put them out, and how to market them to booksellers and readers. In this, Patrick quite obviously has his own team to work with: It's called Tor Books (likewise Bill and Steve at their respective companies). All these teams are pretty good at what they do.

Film/Television Agent: This is Joel Gotler, of Intellectual Property Management. He's the one who shops my work to/fields offers from producers and studios in Los Angeles for possible film/TV projects, and given the number of projects we've had optioned, he's clearly good at it. He also advises me on which projects are mostly likely to get interest at any particular moment, and helps me field non-literary-derived projects as well (not everything I pitch for the screen was originally a book).

Entertainment Lawyer: Hey, did you know contracts are tricky and you might want to have a lawyer look at them and give you advice about them? My entertainment lawyer is Matt Sugarman of Weintraub Tobin. In addition to vetting contracts, I also bend his ear about the entertainment industry landscape as he sees it, and where he thinks it might go from here. I also and independently use a local lawyer, John Marchal, to handle estate planning and other such issues not directly related to entertainment, but which have bearing on my business.

Accountant: This is Julie Boring, of Boring & Associates, who has handled our taxes since we moved to Ohio in 2001 and who has kept up with my (sometimes rather drastically) changing income and tax profile over the last fifteen years. She keeps me up to date on tax issues and concerns and helps me regarding how best to maximize charitable giving.

Financial Planning and Services: Dave Selsor of Fifth Third Securities is helping us here. I'm not a flashy investor and generally I follow the advice I give nearly everyone about investing, i.e., "shove it into an index fund and don't think about it for thirty years." But we have a few other (generally financially conservative) irons in the fire, and a few less-than-usual financial concerns that take a bit of planning.

Note that members of this "team" interact with each other to varying degrees: My agent interacts with my editor and my film/TV agent, for example, but not generally with my accountant or investment planner. The only consistent point of contact here for all of these folks is me. Nevertheless, information is shared one way or another (usually through me).

I will also note that all the members of my "team," save my wife, are part of other peoples' teams as well—my agent (and his agency) has many other clients, as does my lawyer and accountant and so on. It's a little presumptuous to talk about them as *my* team, and I know it. Nevertheless these are people in a privileged position in regards to both knowledge of my career and their ability to assist me with it, and when they're doing that, we're working toward the same goal. Like a team! So there you are.

Additionally—this is *my* particular team, which has been built over the years based on my own career needs. Other folks have some of these people and not others, or others that I don't have. For example, I don't have an assistant, which several authors of my acquaintance have (at least one I know has more than one). I also don't have a manager, which some authors, particularly those who want to work in movies/TV, choose to have. In my case, neither of these make sense. I know other authors who choose not to have agents, a choice I would not be comfortable with personally, but which they seem to be content with. And of course, many writers are single, or might, for varying reasons, prefer not to have their spouses actively involved with the minutiae of their careers.

For what I do and how I do it, this is the team loadout that works for me (literally). In return, most of them get a bit of my income out of it—commissions and fees and such. Which is another thing to think about, incidentally: Whether what you get out of these services will be what you pay for it. In my case it's a yes—I can't even imagine trying to wrangle my taxes at this point, or attempting to sell books in Thailand or Estonia, or wherever. Each of these "team" members either helps me save or make money (in some cases both!) and give me good advice, in their areas of expertise, to make decisions. They are well worth what they charge. Again, your mileage may vary.

Does one, as a writer, *need* people in these particular roles? Well, I always think it's nice to have a spouse, if you can manage it. Other than that a lot will depend on what your career goals are and how much work you want to take on. For example, if you self-publish primarily and don't want or plan to approach publishers, either here or overseas, your need for an agent is lower than mine; likewise if you don't publish books and/or freelance primarily for magazines and Web sites where you can query directly. Also, in many cases, it's not just about you choosing who to work with. They also have to choose you.

In any event, when I say "we" when I talk about my business, one or more of the folks above are the people that are included in the word. They're all good at what they do, and I'm glad that in what they do, they do it with and for me.

Things I Don't Know About My Own Universe

Mar

4

2008

J ust got an e-mail from a reader who had two questions about the Old Man's War universe: How many humans, solider and civilians, have been killed in the wars the Colonial Defense Forces has fought, and how many planets do the humans have under their control.

My responses, respectively: Lots, and depends on the day.

Now, you may be thinking *wow, Scalzi's a jerk,* but the fact is these are the most detailed answers I can give, because when it comes right down to it, I have absolutely no idea how many humans have been killed in the alien wars, and I have only a fuzzy idea of how many planets the Colonial Union has under its control at any one time. Why don't I know these things? Because they haven't ever come up in the course of writing the books in the series. If it doesn't come up in the course of the writing, I tend not to think about it. So, honestly, I *just don't know.*

Conversely, when I do know a specific number of something in the Old Man's War universe, it's because I have a reason for knowing it that comes out of the process of writing itself. For example, in *The Last Colony,* we learn that the Conclave—the big U.N.-ish like entity of alien races—has 412 races in it. Why 412? Because there's a scene in the book where a ship from every race in the Conclave shows up above a planet at the same time. I needed to know how many ships that was, and I needed it to be a fairly impressive number of ships. 412 seemed like a large enough number of ships in one place at one time. So: 412 races in the Conclave. Really, that's why.

Now, I realize this sort of de-romanticizes my world building process: those of you who imagine I have a detailed bible of the entire history and ethnography of the OMW universe will be undoubtedly disappointed to learn that I mostly just make stuff about that universe, as needed, as I go along. But what can I say. We can't all be Tolkien and develop three different languages and five thousand years of history for our worlds before we feel sufficiently comfortable to tell a *story* in the place. Nor, really, would I want to be: That's just too much effort.

For me, when I need to introduce a new element to a universe I've created, here are the two questions I ask: Does it make sense in that universe? And: Does it conflict with anything else I've written about that universe? If the answers are "yes" and "no," respectively, then everything is groovy. I like working this way because it leaves the maximum number of options open for when I write myself into a corner and need to extricate myself from my own foolishness.

Does this mean I make everything up on the fly? Well, no; there are some plot and general universe backstory that I have floating in the back of my head, which have an influence on how I put things together. What I don't have, and am not in a rush to create, are lots of fiddly details that don't have practical application to something specific that I am writing at that very moment.

In this regard, the Old Man's War universe is strongly anthropic: Most of its parts exist in clouds of possibility that only coalesce if and when I need them to. To a large extent, what I know about that universe is what anyone else who reads the books knows—the stuff that's *in* the books. I just happen to know it a lot sooner, and I happen to know it first.

So if you ask me something about the OMW universe or any other universe I work in, and I answer you "I don't know," I'm probably not trying to be a jerk; I'm probably trying to tell you the truth.

THIS MANUSCRIPT
HIRES PEOPLE

Feb

25

2010

Apropos to Charlie Stross' piece today about what goes into making a book and why it's not just as simple as tossing out a bare manuscript to whomever might be willing to buy it, I'd like to point out something that I think gets overlooked as a net benefit to books being made the way they get made in "traditional" publishing, which is:

As an author, my manuscript makes jobs.

For example: When I turn in my manuscript, it's taken up by an editor, who looks at it, gets it into commercial shape, and shepherds the manuscript through the book production process. That editor has a job because of what I wrote.

That manuscript is handed off to a copy-editor, who makes sure that my lack of attention in junior high composition class does not haunt the final book. That copy editor has a job because of what I wrote.

The editor talks to an art designer, who manages the process of giving the book a distinctive look. One thing the art designer does is assign a cover artist, who makes something to catch the potential book buyer's eye from across a crowded bookstore. Then there's the interior/page designer who makes the words on the page look like something other than a Word document. The art designer, cover artist and interior designer have jobs because of what I wrote.

All that done, off my book goes to marketing and publicity, who will do the job of letting other humans know my book is about to exist in the world, and that they should be excited about that fact (and they should!). The marketing person and the publicity person working on my book have jobs because of what I wrote.

And so does the person at the printer who actually prints the book. And so does the person at the warehouse who makes sure the book gets to the bookstore. And so does the person at the bookstore who sells the book to you. They have jobs because of what I wrote.

So, right off the top of my head, ten people who have jobs because I took it into my head to write a story. There are more I'm forgetting about or omitting for the moment, but these ten will do for the point I'm making. How do I feel about the fact they have jobs because of my work? I think it's *pretty damn awesome*, to tell you the truth. Not only does my work feed, clothe and house me (and my family and pets), but it feeds, clothes and houses an exponential number of people as well (and their families and pets).

True, it's not *just* my work that does that for them; they have jobs because of what *other* people wrote, too. But my own work has a direct and material contribution to their employment and well-being. And I like that, a lot. I like the idea of what I do being a cause for many different people, some of whom I will never meet, to have employment and productive lives.

And here's the kicker: Not only do my words give all these people jobs, but under the current system, *I* don't have to pay them anything. In fact, I actually get *paid* to do it! Getting paid for giving other people work—hey, *that* doesn't suck.

Which is one of the other reasons when people declare how great it'll be when there's nothing between authors and readers I give them that cocked-head puppy dog look. What will be so great about *not* giving work to a whole bunch of people, all of whom can do their specific and essential book-creating job better than I could? Sure, I could hire them personally if I felt I needed to, but then I would have to *pay* them. As opposed to someone else paying them, and *also* paying me.

Bear in mind, of course, I'm saying all this as someone who has **a)** self-published, and **b)** has actually hired artists and editors to work on stuff for him, and may do so again in the future when the mood strikes him. I'm not anti-DIY. But I am *pro* creating jobs for other people, and *pro* doing it while getting paid myself. I mean, seriously: Job creation *and* personal profit! How much more rampagingly capitalistic can I get?

So, yes, just one more perspective for folks to consider when they're talking about the future of books.

WHY 2,000 WORDS
WORKS FOR ME

'Ve noted that I'm doing a thing where I don't check into the Internet until I write 2,000 words on my current book project or until noon. People have asked me why the stated quota is 2,000 words. Why not some other number? Why not some specific amount of time? I've answered this question before briefly, but I'm happy to expand on it a little.

1. First, because generally speaking, I'm easily able to write 2,000 words a day. Years of banging out copy, first at a newspaper, later for online sites and magazines (and also here) help with that; the other part is simply that my writing brain seems to have a wide throughput.

2. It's an amount that makes me feel like I'm making real and substantive progress every time I write that amount. At 2,000 words a day, you could have a 100k-word novel in done in 50 days—not a land speed record for a novel, to be sure, but not a horrifying slog with no end in sight ever, either.

Now, the Reality Police compel me to warn you that out in the real world even at a 2k clip, you'll still probably spend more than 50 days writing a novel, because not every word you write will be gold. I threw out about 500 words I wrote the other day, for example, because it turned out I was just faffing about in them. Even so, you're still moving at a nice clip, and for people like me, knowing you're making solid progress on a daily basis helps.

3. 2,000 words is also not so many that the creative part of my brain gets tired. I can and do write more than 2,000 words at a time, often when I'm near the end of a novel and just want to be done, already. But

I do find that, especially after 5,000 words or so of creative writing in a single day, what my brain really wants to do is nothing—which means three to four days of killing zombies. Which is fun, but which isn't finishing the novel, or getting the mortgage paid. Alas.

With 2,000 words, I get enough writing done that I'm happy, and my creative brain doesn't feel pummeled afterward, so it can problem solve regarding where the story needs to go to next. Which means when I sit down to write the next morning, I spend less time figuring out plot, and more time writing up where my brain's figured out the story needs to go next.

4. 2,000 words is enough that even if I can't or don't make the writing quota, I'll probably still have cranked out a decent amount of wordage. The other day, for example, I hit 1,800 words rather than 2,000, and that included those 500 faff-tastic words I mentioned earlier. But even having missed the quota and tossing out 500 words, I still had a net of 1,300 words on the book. That's not my quota, but it also doesn't suck.

5. It's also a large enough sum of words that if I *do* have a day where I do no writing on the book—as I did yesterday, thanks to the daughter's second snow day in a row plus other things that required attention—I don't feel like missing that day means I'm spinning my wheels overall, because overall for the week I've had a decent number of words pile up.

For example, in the two weeks that I've been on the quota train, I've written 15,000 words in the book. That's less than the 20,000 that was the goal, but it also incorporates two snow days and an additional sick day for my kid, who, while I enjoy having her at home, also likes to have attention when she's about, plus those words I threw out. That's good progress for two weeks, or is for me, at least.

6. On the flip side of that, the 2,000 word amount is not gospel if I want to write more; I don't compel myself to stop the instant I cross the 2k line. Today I wrote 2,900 words, because I was in a groove and also because I wanted to get to where would be a natural stopping point in the writing, and also because my wife, who gets to read my stuff first, was saying to me "I want the new chapter. Finish it up OR DIE." But phrased more lovingly, of course.

That said, the nice thing about that 2k mark even when I blow past it is that it means I can relax; I've done what I set out to do for the day and everything I write past that point is gravy. And it's nice to be able to say to one's self, "I'm writing more because I want to, not because I'm in a blind panic on a deadline."

So those are the reasons why 2,000 words is a good daily quote for me. I don't want to suggest it's the right quota for everyone, but for most writers I think it's worth looking at the possibility of incorporating a daily writing quota and seeing if it works for you.

Independently, here's why I have the noon deadline as well:

1. Because I usually have other work I want and/or need to do with my day;

2. Because on the days where it's *just not happening*, it's nice to have a point in time after which you can say to yourself *dude, let it go, we'll pick this up tomorrow.*

The noon deadline does assume I'm up and writing by about nine am at the latest, but since I often take my daughter to school before 8am and the dog whines like a siren if I won't take her outside by 8:30, this really isn't a problem. This may be a reason to consider getting a dog. Or, alternately, if you prefer to write at night, not.

WRITERS AND EGO

Patricia Ruggles asks:

You've confessed before to being at least somewhat egotistical. Do you think it's possible to be a successful writer if you don't have a pretty big ego? Writing is notoriously solitary, and requires long periods of continuous performance without a lot of positive reinforcement. Doesn't take a pretty good opinion of yourself to stay convinced that somebody will want to read your stuff when you are finally finished with it?

Well, I've admitted to having an ego, yes, and can be seen as being egotistical. I think there's a difference between those two things.

Also, no, I don't know that you have to have a big ego in order to be a successful writer.

Part of that is that it depends what you mean when you say "successful writer." What is the definition of success? Material wealth? Excellent writing? Reputation that exceeds one's own mortality? The thing is, none of these in itself requires a large ego, or outsized egotism. Particularly in regard to the latter two, I have in mind Emily Dickinson, who was certainly an excellent writer and whose reputation in death is far greater than it was in her life, in no small part because her first published collection was in 1890, four years after her death. During life, she lived an eccentric and secluded life—not generally the hallmarks of someone with what's generally understood to have a pretty big ego.

Is Dickinson a successful writer? I think absolutely: I strongly suspect her work will be remembered long after mine is forgotten. Did she have a big ego? If I had to guess, I would say no, at least in terms of how I think "big ego" is being referred to here.

Ego can be part of the reason people write. It is for me: I rarely write just for myself, since I already know what I'm thinking and I'm too lazy to write down my own thoughts just for me. I write so I can be read by other people; I like that other people like what I write. But there are also people who only write for themselves, who never have the desire to show others their work—at least, not until well after they are dead. Another historical example: Samuel Pepys, widely considered the English language's greatest diarist, whose diaries, while bound by the author for preservation, were not published until 150 years after his death. Pepys is another successful writer by any account, but save for binding the loose pages of his diary into volumes, where is the evidence of a big ego? I don't know that Pepys ever dreamed his diary (which among other more significant things includes ample evidence of his various adulteries) would ever see wide circulation.

The thing is, people write for a lot of different reasons, not all of them tied to ego. Some people write for other people to read them. Some people write because they want to express themselves. Some people write for just a few people, and to please them, not to please themselves. Some people write simply because they are good at it and people are willing to pay them for it. Sometimes it's a combination of factors. I write for others, but I also write because people pay me for it, and occasionally I'll write something just for one or two people, meant for them alone. And at the end of the day, I write what I would want to read—which is to say that although I write for others I also write for myself. I like reading my own books!

(Also, and independently, as far as writing being solitary: It can be but doesn't have to be. I know writers who band together and take writing retreats with each other—they spent their work day in front of their words but they take breaks to chat with each other about how things are going. Others write in coffeeshops so they can be around people when they work. Writers frequently show works in progress to friends or confidantes—I myself will give my wife chapters to read when I'm done writing them. And writers also splash themselves all over social media and blogs as a way to visit with fans and other writers.)

I think having an ego can be helpful for a certain type of writer, and I'm willing to say that I'm one of those writers. I like writing to an audience and I like interacting with an audience beyond the confines of my books (hello!). My ego helps when it comes time to market books too; I'm usually happy to be interviewed and go do public events and interact with fans and readers. That willingness to be open and accessible, which is in part fueled by my own ego-driven desire for attention and approval, has been beneficial. And finally my ego means that I feel less of the self-doubt and "impostor syndrome" that other writers have been known to have. My attitude about writing as my gig is, *yeah, I got this.* Which is why I could sign that stupid long book contract I did and not freak out about owing a dozen books over a decade.

But that's me, and how I do writing is not the only way, or the best way, or even a *good* way for any other writer who is not me. In my own personal experience I know many writers who I would not characterize as being particularly egotistical or ego-driven; they just like to write and write well enough to sell. Some of them are plagued with self-doubt and the belief that no one really wants to read what they write, and sometimes their work basically has to be dragged out of their hands by an exasperated editor or agent. At least a couple of these authors sell at least as well as I do, as far as I can tell. They just do their thing differently than I do. Which is great! There is no one true path to being a successful writer, in no small part because, again, there's no one definition of what "successful" means, when it comes to being a writer.

So, a pretty ego can be useful when it comes to being a writer. But I think you can be a writer—a good writer, a successful writer—without one. All you really have to do to be a writer is write.

WRITING

(Note: This was written as part of a "Thanksgiving Advent" series, in which each day in November 2011, until Thanksgiving, I wrote about something I was thankful for.)

Over the course of this Thanksgiving Advent adventure, I've talked about a number of things associated with writing, and how they've affected my life. I haven't talked about writing itself, however. So I'd like to focus on that for today, independent of all the trappings, benefits and side effects. Because the fact of the matter is that even if I never became a professional writer, or became a financially successful writer, or even had more people than my immediate circle of friends ever read anything I wrote, I would still write. I would still be a writer.

I would still be a writer for the simple reason that I find the act of writing extremely pleasurable. There is something lovely about sitting down to a blank screen (or blank page, if you want to get old school) and filling it with words. There is likewise a fantastic feeling that comes from taking what are unformed and chaotic thoughts in one's head and giving them form and structure with words. People often note that ideas and thoughts which seem deep and meaningful inside their head seem banal or pointless when they're written out, but allow me to suggest the problem is not that that these ideas were *reduced* when they were translated into words; instead, they were *revealed*. Your brain lies to you about the awesomeness of your thoughts. Words are the friend that says "Dude. Stop hitting the bong." On the other hand, if you have a fantastic idea in your head, and it's still fantastic when you put it into words, you know what? It may in fact be fantastic.

This organizing and structuring that comes through writing comes in handy for me, because it means that I have an outlet to express thoughts I have that run deeper than "I have to take out the trash." My wife understands this perfectly well; on more than one occasion, after I've completely fumbled expressing something to her, she's said to me "you need to go write that out." And I do and then I actually have a way to express that idea, so that the next time I try to verbalize it, I have a framework and a method that doesn't involve increasingly wild hand gestures and the use of the phrase "you know?" every five or six words. Writing makes me a better verbal communicator, funny as that sounds. For which I suspect my wife, who has to live with me, is grateful.

Another reason writing is pleasurable is that I am good at it, and it feels good to do things you are good at. When I was young, I was a good writer—"good" being highly conditional on context, mind you, and I could have benefited from my own list of tips for teenage writers—and especially when you're young, doing something you know you can do well (and possibly better than almost anyone else you know) means a lot to you and your concept of yourself as a person. You may be goofy or short or socially awkward or pocked with strategically embarrassing zits or *whatever*—but you can make words do things, things other people can't, and that's a hell of a thing when you're fourteen and you're trying to find a place in the world and to have it all make some sort of sense.

As I got older another aspect of the joy of writing came to the fore: the enjoyment of the craftsmanship of it, of the appreciation of a turn of phrase, or the right word, or the presentation of a concept *just so*, that could make an idea pop or turn a sentence from a merely functional string of words conveying meaning into something that stuck into a reader's brain like a piton driven into a cliff wall. It's the meta-awareness of a thing you're doing and how you're doing it and how it's working, and the realization of your own competence with it, brought on by a combination of talent, practice and the occasional out of the blue taser jolt of inspiration.

And through all of this is the pleasure of the flow of words that comes when you are caught up in the act of writing, when everything you know about writing and everything you think about it and everything it might have earned you (or that you want it to earn for you) slip off to the side and it's just you laying out the words, one after the other, into an inevitable sequence. It's the same thing a musician gets in the middle of an epic jam session, or a painter when the image emerges out of the paint or the actor who has subsumed himself in the moment, no longer thinking about his character because the character is *there*.

This state of being has been described from a psychological point of view, but conceptualizing it and feeling it are of course two entirely different things. It feels like a gift from the universe to you. And maybe it is. I'm not of the opinion that you have to be good at what you're doing in order to experience this sort of flow, although it may help. What's important is that you're so far into the thing you're doing that in that moment, everything else doesn't matter. I've gotten this feeling from other things, but where I get it the most is when I'm writing.

It's a relationship with words, essentially. I have one and it manifests itself through my fingers, usually onto a computer screen but occasionally with pen and paper. It's a relationship in which I feel defined, in no small part because in the act of writing I have been able to define myself, to myself and to others.

Independent of anything else writing has done for me—and it's done a lot—this aspect of it has been extraordinarily important to me, and I'm thankful for it, and the pleasure it's given me. And ultimately it's why I write, why I keep writing, and why, if everything else that writing ever did for me went away (and it might), I would still do it.

How, and If, I Will
Be Remembered

| Mar |
| 22 |
| 2016 |

Steve asks:

Have you ever wondered how you will be remembered by the "science fiction community"? How future critics will use you in comparison to future authors......about the legacy you have left behind you when you have gone...... if you will be lost among the hundreds of authors, as many from the 50's have been.....? No offense......but even great authors have no books reprinted.... etc etc.....

Well, one, after I'm dead I don't think I'll be worried about how I'm remembered, by the science fiction community or anyone else, because I'll be dead, which I suspect means I'll be beyond caring about anything. This is a strangely comforting thought: *So long, universe! It's your problem now!* So there's that.

Prior to my incipient oblivion, which is to say for the next 40 to 50 years, I don't worry too much about *not* being remembered. One, presumably I will continue to produce work for the next 25 or 30 years at least—writing is a career where one can have some longevity—so I'm likely to continue to be in the stream of commerce and notability in my field. Two, I have enough status in the field thanks to existing work, sales and awards that my inevitable decline into irrelevance might be managed as a gentle descending glidepath rather than a precipitous cliff fall.

Three, you know what, if until I die I have friends and family and people I care about and who care about me, even if I *were* forgotten by the science fiction public while I were alive, I would probably be fine. I had a nice run in there, and there are worse things than to be forgotten.

In any event, the question is not *whether* I or my work will be forgotten, but *when*. Why? Because nearly every writer is forgotten, as is their work, given enough time. A couple get cosmically lucky in terms of their cultural legacies—Shakespeare is the go-to example in English—But between 1616 (Shakespeare's death) and today, 400 years later, hundreds of thousands of published authors in English alone (if not millions) have slipped out of history. Their work may *exist*, in libraries or rare volumes or in archives like Project Gutenberg, but no one reads them, save the occasional academic desperate for a serviceable thesis. When you know that the vast majority of those who write, and the vast majority of what is written, tumble down history's hole, you have a pretty good idea of what your eventual fate will be.

You don't even have to be dead for it to happen. The large majority of my published work prior to 2005 is "out of print"—either officially out of print in terms of publication, or accessible only through specialized archives, digital or otherwise. I have a publishing history that goes back to 1991 (or 1987 if you want to throw in my college newspaper), which includes thousands of film and music reviews, hundreds of columns, dozens of newspaper and magazine features and several books, all published before 2005. Unless you *already* have a physical copy of any of these, you are unlikely to see any of them, ever. For that matter, the first four years of this blog—1998 through 2002—are not on the current iteration of the site; they're accessible through the Internet Archive, but there's no real indication anyone visits that. Other things I've written on other sites on the Internet are likewise inaccessible, though closed sites, reorganized sites, link rot and other such things.

Again: The majority of everything I've ever written—things that had audiences of hundreds of thousands of people when they were printed—has already effectively vanished from history, when I'm 46 years old and still actively writing.

DON'T LIVE FOR YOUR OBITUARY

Is this a horrifying tragedy? Well, no, not really. I mean, if you *really* want to find my *Fresno Bee* review of, say, the long-forgotten 1993 Wesley Snipes thriller *Boiling Point*, then knock yourself out. But I guarantee you that if you do find it, you will not marvel at its genius. The review doesn't necessarily deserve to be forgotten, but it doesn't make a very good argument to be remembered, either. A lot of my "lost" writing is like that.

But in time even my good writing is likely to slip out of the public consciousness, even in specialized fields like science fiction. Look, new science fiction readers have *heard* of Asimov and Clarke and Heinlein— the chances they've *read* them, or at least read anything more than their one or two "greatest hits," is increasingly slim, and will get slimmer the more time passes. This may outrage some folks who think you can't truly appreciate the genre unless you take a survey class in it, but the average reader doesn't care about that. They're not going to go all the way back to Jules Verne or even Larry Niven just to have sufficient historical perspective in the genre to read the latest book by James S.A. Corey, or Ann Leckie or by me. 40 years from now, new readers aren't going to read *our* stuff as a prerequisite to read whatever is new and exciting in the genre then.

And that's fine. I've frequently said that I'm not interested in writing for the ages, since I won't be there and the ages will take care of themselves in any event. I'm writing for people *now*, who will enjoy the work *now*, and also and not entirely coincidentally, pay me for my work *now*, so I don't have to do anything else for a living. Will it last? You got me. I suspect I'll still be remembered fifty years now because people who are reading me now will still be alive then. A hundred years from now I may be remembered for one book. If I'm remembered two hundred years from now, I'd be impressed as hell with myself, if I weren't already dead for probably 150 years.

(Incidentally, the book of mine that already exists that I suspect I'd be best remembered for in 100 years? *Redshirts*. It's not my "obituary book," the book that'll show up in the opening graph of stories about my death; that will be *Old Man's War*. But I suspect it's the one that will age the best, in part because it's specifically about its time and therefore resistant to going "out of date" in terms of technology and prediction (particularly of social mores) the way science fiction can do; in part because it functions as both story and metastory, commentary and metacommentary, which means it'll be interesting to teach, and being taught is important for the longevity of a work; and in part because it's funny and easy to read. Will I be right? Well, on the slim chance anyone's reading this in 2116: You tell me. Or tell my corpse; again, I'm probably long dead.)

None of this isn't to say I wouldn't be happy, in an existential sense, to have my work, and therefore *me*, remembered 100 or 200 years (or more!) into the future. I'm not going to live forever and any personal immortality I will earn will be through what I write. I think it might be nice for any future descendants of mine to brag to their friends that the book they've been assigned in class is from their great-great-great-grandfather (or granduncle, or whatever). I think it'd be fun to have people argue about whether I still have relevant things to say or should be considered "of my time." It'd be nice to be remembered for being a writer, hopefully positively, when I'm gone.

I'm just not staying up nights worrying if it will happen. If it does, great. If not, I'm having a hell of a lot of fun now, and enjoying the small serving of notability I get today, for doing what I do. It won't last; it never does. On this side of the grave or the other, I'll likely to be forgotten, and no matter what the sun will eat the earth five billion years from now anyway and eventually the entire universe will proton decay out of existence, so, you know. Be ready for that.

In the meantime, I'm going to enjoy what I have today, with the people I have with me now. Seems the best thing to do.

ACKNOWLEDGEMENTS

First, thanks to Bill Schafer of Subterranean Press for going ahead with this book, and Yanni Kuznia for poking and prodding me to get it finished (it's finished now, Yanni!).

Also thanks to Geralyn Lance, Nate Taylor, and Gail Cross for helping to make the book read well and look good. And to everyone at Subterranean Press, because it's a pretty awesome place to be published.

Many of the pieces in this collection were originally taken from "Reader Request Week" entries on my site, where I was answering specific questions posed to me by readers. Thanks to each of them who posed a question. Indeed, thanks to all my "Whatever" readers over the years. We're coming up on 20 years of me writing on that blog now. I mean, *damn*.

Finally and as always thanks to Kristine Scalzi and Athena Scalzi, because my life would suck without my family.